£1·80

My Servants the Prophets

OTHER BOOKS BY THE AUTHOR:

THE PROPHECY OF DANIEL

AN INTRODUCTION TO THE OLD TESTAMENT

ISAIAH 53: A DEVOTIONAL AND EXPOSITORY STUDY

THE MESSIANIC PROPHECIES OF DANIEL

ARABIC FOR BEGINNERS

My Servants the Prophets

by

EDWARD J. YOUNG

Professor of Old Testament,
Westminster Theological Seminary,
Philadelphia, Pennsylvania.

WM. B. EERDMANS PUBLISHING CO.
Grand Rapids   Michigan

PHOTOLITHOPRINTED BY GRAND RAPIDS BOOK MANUFACTURERS, INC.
GRAND RAPIDS, MICHIGAN, UNITED STATES OF AMERICA

1971

To My Wife

*"Since the day that your fathers came
forth out of the land of Egypt unto this day
I have even sent unto you all my servants
the prophets, daily rising up early and
sending them"* JEREMIAH 7:25.

Preface

In ancient Israel there appeared a body of men, extending over the course of several centuries, who claimed to have received messages from God and to be the deliverers of those messages. The present work seeks in a modest way to defend the claim which the prophets made for themselves. It therefore flies in the face of the widely prevalent view that a correct understanding of the prophets can be secured only after we have ascertained, in as far as that is possible, the actual historical situation in which or because of which each prophetical utterance arose.

In order to accomplish its purpose the present investigation begins with a consideration of what the Old Testament itself has to say about the origin of prophecy and the prophetic institution. It then proceeds to deal with questions such as the position of the prophet in the Divine economy, the relation between false and true prophets and the relation of the prophets to the ancient Near Eastern world in which they lived.

Acknowledgment is gratefully made to the Princeton University Press for permission to use brief sections of the Egyptian translation of Dr. John A. Wilson which are found in the volume *Ancient Near Eastern Texts Relating to The Old Testament,* edited by James A. Pritchard.

My sincere thanks is due to Miss Margaret Robinson and Miss Ruth Stahl for the careful manner in which they have prepared the typescript of the work.

— *Edward J. Young*

Philadelphia,
June, 1952

Contents

My Servants the Prophets

CHAPTER I

The Divine Origin of the Prophetic Institution

AN examination into the origin and nature of the prophetic movement must, of course, pay due heed to the testimony which the Old Testament itself has to offer. There is one passage in the Old Testament which speaks with some detail about the origin of the prophetic institution, namely, the remarkable prophecy given in Deuteronomy 18:9-22. As it stands, this passage first warns the Israelites, who are about to enter the promised land, against learning the abominable practices of the heathen nations. God's people, it teaches, will have no need to resort to such devices for God will Himself raise up for them a Prophet who will act as a mediator between themselves and God, and who will also speak unto them all the words which God will place in his mouth.

Thus, according to this passage, the prophetic institution is of Divine origin. The prophets, so Deuteronomy teaches, were men raised up of God, in whose mouth God's word had been placed, and who uttered that word. They were to stand as a counterpart to the soothsaying and divination of Canaan, and to them Israel was to hearken. Such is the plain meaning of the prophecy found in Deuteronomy.

Criticism of Deuteronomy

Is the plain meaning of the prophecy, however, acceptable today? Are we justified in holding that in this passage we have the words which God spoke to Moses beyond the Jordan in Moab? Literary criticism has been busily engaged in the study of Deuteronomy, and many literary critics, although they may disagree among themselves as to the precise nature of the book of Deuteronomy, nevertheless are at one in their conviction

13

that Moses did not write it, and therefore, that the prophecy now before us cannot be accepted at face value. For this reason it will be necessary to consider briefly the course of critical study and opinion with respect to the book of Deuteronomy.

It appears to have been a universal belief in the early Church that Moses was the author of Deuteronomy. Sometimes, it is true, appeal has been made to Jerome, as though he were an exception, but in reality he also accepted the commonly held view. He did mention Deuteronomy as the book which had been found in the Temple during the reign of Josiah,[1] and he also in one passage, spoke of the Pentateuch in such a manner that some have gathered from his words that he did not wish to commit himself upon the question of its authorship.[2]

The attack upon the Mosaic authorship of Deuteronomy may be said to have begun with the doctoral dissertation of DeWette, in 1805-1806, who contended that Deuteronomy was the law book of Josiah.[3] DeWette held that the greater part of the book was the work of J, and that as we have it, it was the latest book of the Pentateuch to be written. DeWette's view gained rather wide acceptance, although as early as 1829 Gramberg contended for a post-exilic date.[4]

With the ascendancy of the school of Graf, Kuenen and Wellhausen, DeWette's view seemed to be firmly established. Indeed, Wellhausen himself could write: "About the origin of Deuteronomy there is still less dispute; in all circles where appreciation of scientific results can be looked for at all, it is recognized that it is composed in the same age as that in which it was discovered, and that it was made the rule of Josiah's reformation, which took place about a generation before the destruction of Jerusalem by the Chaldeans."[5]

Although the book was thus alleged to have been produced before the time of Josiah's reformation, nevertheless, there was difference of opinion as to its extent. Wellhausen, for example, at first thought that the paranetic framework, namely chapters 5-11 and 28-30, was a later addition.[6] Although opinions might have differed as to Deuteronomy's extent, it was nevertheless

---

1. Notes will be found at the end of this volume.

rather generally held that the book must have been written previous to the year in which the reformation occurred.

This assumption raised certain problems. If the book of Deuteronomy was written just before the reformation, who was its author? Wellhausen assumed that Deuteronomy was the first public legislation in Israel, and that it rested upon a prophetic foundation. This position found able advocacy at the hands of Emil Kautzsch, who sought to show that it must have come from outside the priestly circle.[7] If, however, the authors were prophets, certain difficulties immediately present themselves.

If an unknown prophet or group of prophets composed Deuteronomy, it is strange that they should have labored so hard to make it appear that the book was the work of Moses. Such a procedure is without analogy in the Scripture. The prophets always came forth openly and spoke in the name of the Lord. They did not engage in subterfuge, but evidenced a holy boldness. They believed that God had spoken to them, and consequently, they delivered His words fearlessly. Whatever else may be said about the prophets of Israel, they were men of conviction and they boldly expressed their convictions. There is a psychological difficulty involved in the assumption that prophets of Jehovah would secretly produce a work such as Deuteronomy and rely upon the name of Moses to carry their message.

Suppose, however, after all, that such men were the authors. There is one conclusion that cannot be evaded or escaped. It is that they were dishonest men. They sought to give the impression that Deuteronomy was the work of Moses, whereas in reality it was nothing of the kind. They, therefore, were not good men. This conclusion cannot be avoided. How different is this crafty stratagem of these unknown "prophets" from the open honesty of the known prophets of the Old Testament! We are forced to assert that the authors of Deuteronomy, whatever their motives may have been, were engaging in deceit when they sought to give the impression that the writing which they produced was the work of someone else.

If the unknown authors of Deuteronomy had really engaged in such a stratagem, how is it that they were able to produce the noble book which forms the conclusion of our Pentateuch? The teaching of this work is so exalted that our Lord, when tempted of the devil, turned to it for weapons with which to refute the deceit of the adversary. If Deuteronomy itself were the product of deceit, it is difficult to believe that it would have been of much help in fighting against deceit. A problem thus remains. Sweet waters do not come from bitter fountains, and a book such as Deuteronomy cannot be written by evil men.

Abraham Kuenen realized the difficulties involved in the assumption that Deuteronomy came from prophetical circles, and he therefore maintained that it was written by priests.[8] But there are grave difficulties entailed even in this view. For one thing, if Deuteronomy was actually written by priests, how explain the high honor which it attributes to the prophets? It teaches that the nation is to hearken unto the prophets just as to Moses. Such honor, however, is somewhat difficult to account for, if there really was the tension between prophet and priest which, according to the Wellhausen school, was supposed to exist.

It should be noted also that all the available evidence shows that the priests of Josiah's day and before were not the kind of men to be interested in a reformation. They were, rather, men of corruption. Thus Jeremiah speaks of them, and of the prophets also, for that matter, "As the thief is ashamed when he is found, so is the house of Israel ashamed; they, their kings, their princes, and their priests and their prophets." "The prophets prophesy falsely, and the priests bear rule by their means; and my people love to have it so: and what will ye do in the end thereof?" "For from the least of them even unto the greatest of them every one is given to covetousness; and from the prophet even unto the priest every one dealeth falsely." "For both prophet and priest are profane; yea, in my house have I found their wickedness, saith the Lord."[9]

These words, in which the boldness of a true prophet is exemplified, make it clear that the priests of that time were not interested in a reformation. And if priests of such a character were the authors of Deuteronomy, we are at a loss to explain a passage like Deuteronomy 18:6-8, which gives portions and priestly rights even to priests in the country.[10] Such a generous law is difficult to understand at the hands of priests "who bear rule by their means."

The difficulty of identifying the author of Deuteronomy has at times been recognized, and Pfeiffer presents a view which seeks to take account of some of the difficulties. He believes that the author was a man with prophetic ideals who, at the same time, was keenly aware of the people's failure to grasp these high ideals and who realized that the nation was merely following the cult. This man sought to effect a compromise between the current trend in Judaism and the high religion of the prophets. He was a priest in Jerusalem who had been deeply impressed by the prophetic teaching. However, to accomplish his reconciliation of priests and prophets, he saw the necessity of mutual concessions. Such was the man who became the author of the Deuteronomic Code.[11]

This unknown priest, however, we are constrained to point out, did not become sufficiently imbued with prophetic ideals, for in his one great act of religious service he proceeded in a dishonest way. His one legacy to posterity was an act of deception. Hence, even though Pfeiffer has succeeded in removing some of the difficulties of authorship, he has not removed the greatest of them. A man, zealous for prophetic ideals, would have acted with the same boldness as the prophets. He would not have resorted to subterfuge.

Inherent, therefore, in the view that Deuteronomy is a product of the seventh century B. C. is the tremendous difficulty connected with the question of its authorship. There are other very weighty arguments which also tell against this date for Deuteronomy, but our present purpose is merely to lay stress upon this particular consideration.[12]

The question of the extent of Deuteronomy as well as that of its authorship, also engaged the attention of scholars. Steuernagel in particular made a thorough study of the alternation in use of the singular and plural pronouns of the second person in an endeavor to discover what he thought to be the original writing. It was his conviction that an original Deuteronomy (Urdeuteronomium) had been published in several later editions, and that these had been combined.[13] According to some, the original Deuteronomy was the book that was discovered during the days of Josiah. The problem of ascertaining precisely what this original Deuteronomy was, however, was by no means an easy one. The alternation between second person singular and plural was soon shown to be an illigitimate criterion.[14] Bertholet believed that the true criterion was to be found in the passages of Deuteronomy which agreed with the supposed picture of centralization given in Second Kings 22.[15]

A different method of approach was adopted by Johannes Hempel.[16] According to Hempel, the book found in Josiah's days was not an original creation. Rather, its author, who had introduced the idea of centralization of the cult, had worked over an old Temple rule of service, and had incorporated into it his ideas of centralization and certain social directions. It was this work which was found at the time of Josiah. Later, other editions appeared, and finally, about the time of the exile, Deuteronomy, as we now have it, was completed.

Not all scholars, however, were agreed that there was a relation between the Deuteronomic law and the reform of Josiah.[17] Gustav Hölscher, for example, made a definite attempt to show that no such relationship had ever existed.[18] Rather, the Deuteronomic law, according to Hölscher, was a good hundred years after Josiah's day. Hölscher made a minute examination of the first thirty chapters of Deuteronomy in order to determine the limits of the supposed original. This he compared with the literature of the fifth and sixth centuries B. C. in order to arrive at a more precise date for the time of composition.

According to Hölscher, the original Deuteronomy appeared in chapters 6-28 where the singular was used.[19] This corresponded essentially with the passages which Steuernagel and Hempel had assigned to their original. In addition, Hölscher included the speeches of warning in chapters 6-11 and the blessings and curses of chapter twenty-eight. Since this material, according to Hölscher, bears an idealistic character, it must have arisen after the fall of Jerusalem. Thus, he concluded,

Deuteronomy was composed to regulate the conditions of the post-exilic Jewish community.

Very different was the solution proposed by Theodor Oestreicher.[20] He pointed out, what had long before been observed by conservative scholars, that Josiah's reform concentrated not upon centralization of worship but upon purity. He even claimed that Josiah did not wish to attain any permanent limitation or restriction of worship at Jerusalem, and that the book of Law which was discovered, while it did comprise Deuteronomy, also included the provisions of the Law of Holiness.

Well known to English readers is the work of Welch who goes so far as to maintain that Deuteronomy 12:1-7 is the only passage in which there is a regulation confining worship to one place.[21] Furthermore, Welch believes that the Code of Deuteronomy arose, not in Jerusalem, but in northern Israel as a warning against worship at the shrines of Baal and Astarte. Likewise, Edward Robertson has argued that Deuteronomy was composed at the time of the foundation of the monarchy.[22] Gerhard Von Rad has also contended for an origin of Deuteronomy among the national prophets outside of Jerusalem. He believes that it arose during the times of the later kings.[23]

These various challenges to DeWette's work do not, of course, prove that the time honored conception of Mosaic authorship is correct. They do, however, lend encouragement to the defender of that view. It is one thing to point to difficulties in a certain position. It is another thing to establish an alternate position that is less free from difficulty. For a time — a long time, indeed — it seemed that De Wette had established a view of the authorship of Deuteronomy that was more free from difficulty than the view presented by the book itself. At last, however, the inherent weaknesses of the view began to manifest themselves to sober scholars, and the challenges became more and more frequent. It would require a prophet to tell what the future course of Deuteronomic studies will be, but it does look as though De Wette's view of the book will have to fight for its existence as never before.

For our part, we believe that Moses is the author of Deuteronomy. For one thing, the book claims over and over again, that the addresses which it contains were delivered by Moses. This is a witness which, in our opinion, is not lightly to be discarded. Furthermore, we do not believe that the contents of the book are inconsistent with Mosaic authorship, and we do not believe that critical scholarship has shown them to be such. Hence, we propose to examine Deuteronomy 18 with the belief that it was spoken by Moses to Israel and that it is in every sense a bona fide prophecy.[24]

Exposition of Deuteronomy 18:9-22

Our examination will begin with verse nine, and we note first the opening words. Moses addresses the nation as an individual, using the second person singular. The setting shows that Israel has not yet entered the land which the Lord is about to give her. Before she enters she must be warned of certain teachers who will instruct her in the abominations of the new land, and she must further be told what the Lord will do for her to enable her to avoid these abominations.

There is a connection between this prophecy and the verses which have immediately preceded. These preceding verses deal with the functions of the Levites, who were the appointed guardians and promoters of the Law. It was their task to instruct the people in the Law and also to promote, as far as possible, a living fellowship and relationship with the Lord by means of the sacrifices at the altar.

The Mosaic institutions would not, however, in themselves, prove to be sufficient for the needs of the people in the altered circumstances of the new land. The law of Moses was of course the foundation upon which the theocratic kingdom was to be built, and embraced the general principles upon which the life of the nation and the individual was to be founded. In itself, of course, the revelation at Sinai was amply sufficient to make known the will of God. Man, however, because of the sinfulness of his heart and because of his tendency to go astray, following after false gods, after the entrance into Canaan would need more detailed instruction as to the way in which the Lord would have him walk.

In the promised land there were to be new circumstances of life and new conditions in which the nation would have need of further revelation from God. It was to be a time of transition from the extraordinary circumstances of the wilderness wanderings to the more settled conditions of Palestine, and in this more settled existence Israel needed once more to hear the voice of the living God. The work of the Levites was not sufficient for that time and so God is to give to Israel His prophets, who would declare His will to the nation.

The necessity for this gift of the prophetic institution is to be seen, however, not only in the need of the nation for more detailed instruction from God than was found in the Mosaic institutions. It is to be seen also in the dark background of superstition which characterized those nations in whose midst Israel was to dwell. When those nations desired detailed knowledge concerning the future they had sources of information readily available. Such sources of information, however, were declared by the Lord to be abominations.

The first thing that is told to Israel, therefore, is that when she is come into the land which the Lord her God is about to give her, she is not to learn to do according to the abominations of those nations. It is thus made very plain that Israel's whole course of life is in the hands of the Lord. She had been His people, whom He had brought forth from the land of Egypt. Now, He is ready to give her the promised land. It is not a land which she will be able to take in her own strength, but one which is to be given to her as a gift. Therefore, since it is her God Who gives this land, He also has the right to state what is to be her conduct therein.

Nine superstitions are enumerated, practices which for one reason or another the Canaanites employed. At the head of the list stands februation, or the custom of passing one's son and daughter through the fire. The purpose of this rite was either to obtain an oracle or else to help in averting a calamity. In the eyes of the writer of Deuteronomy it is the most heinous of the practices of the Canaanites. For that reason, evidently, it is placed at the head of the list, and also for that reason it is singled out for mention in chapter 12:31 where the writer says:

"Thou shalt not do so unto the Lord thy God: for every abomination to the Lord, which he hateth, have they done unto their gods; for even their sons and their daughters have they burnt in the fire to their gods."

After the first abomination there follow three terms which describe various methods of divination. We may perhaps translate the first phrase as "the diviner of divinations" or "the one that obtaineth oracles." Basically, the word seems to have the idea of obtaining an oracle by means of drawing lots. It is used generally in the Old Testament as a common designation of divination. The second word may be rendered "soothsayer," and the third "an observer of omens."

The precise significance of these words may not be known, but there is a passage in the Old Testament which throws considerable light upon their general usage, namely, Numbers 23:23. In this passage the word *qesem* appears, and also the substantive *nahash* (which is cognate to *menahash*). There are two principal interpretations of this verse, depending upon whether the preposition *be* is to be translated as "against" or "in." If the preposition is to be translated "against" we then have the following rendering: "For there is no omen against Jacob, and no divination against Israel: at the time it is wont to be said to Jacob and to Israel what God doeth." If, however, the preposition be taken in the sense "in," we may translate as follows: "For there is no omen in Jacob, and no divination in Israel: at the time it is wont to be said to Jacob and to Israel what God doeth." If the first of these renderings be correct, it teaches that there is no enchantment or soothsaying which has any power against Israel, for Israel receives her information by means of revelation. Israel is the people of God, to whom He speaks, and therefore, enchantment cannot prevail against her. There are however, considerations which weigh against this view. For one thing, nowhere in the Scriptures is it held that enchantment can prevail against anyone. This interpretation appears to give to heathen enchantments a power which the Scripture nowhere else recognizes.

It is far more natural to understand the passage as expressing a distinction in the methods of obtaining information. In

Jacob and Israel, the passage would then teach, there is no omen and divination, for there is no need of these things. At the appropriate time in Jacob and Israel God gives revelation. The chosen nation is characterized by the fact that she possesses the Word of God.

This Word of God is of course found in the prophets. The verb which is employed includes the idea of frequency or repetition, and we may perhaps bring out this force by translating, "it is wont to be said." Whenever the necessary time arises, then God speaks to His people. And the means by which He speaks is the prophetical institution.

To return, however, to the text in Deuteronomy. With the last phrase of verse eleven, Moses brings us into the realm of sorcery. The sorcerer and the charmer, he teaches, are also to be condemned. Then, finally, Israel is not to seek after the dead. The words "ghost" and "familiar spirit" are used side by side elsewhere in the Scriptures. Thus, in speaking of the iniquities introduced and practised by Manasseh, the book of Kings says that he instituted the ghost and familiar spirits (2 Kings 21:6). What the text means, of course, is that he brought in those who dealt with these things and permitted them to practice. He allowed spiritualism to flourish in his land.

Although these two words, "ghost" and "familiar spirit" are used side by side, there was nevertheless a distinction between them. The person who was possessed of an *ob* (ghost) was evidently a ventriloquist. Like the witch of Endor he might call up the *ob* and describe what he saw. Those about him would probably hear only a muttering or twittering which seemed to come from the ground. The "familiar spirit" however, was evidently a spirit that was at the beck and call of a particular person.

Lastly, a general term is given for spiritualism. He that "seeketh unto the dead," we are told, is to be condemned. The practice of "seeking unto the dead" is therefore also an abomination. This is evidently a comprehensive term which includes all forms of spiritualism and superstition.

The list is indeed impressive. These superstitious practices which were so much in vogue among the Canaanites of ancient time are the reason why the Lord will dispossess these people of their land. Moses then advances a step. Not only are these practices in themselves abominations, he says, but also every one that doeth them is an abomination in the sight of the Lord. It is for this reason that God will drive out the Canaanites from their land.[25] It is well that we should grasp this fact, for it has sometimes been maintained that the God of the Old Testament was an arbitrary despot, who drove out the Canaanites and brought Israel into Palestine, and this, it has been said, was a cruel, arbitrary act. Such a judgment, however, is unjust, and out of accord with the facts. God, in dispossessing the Canaanites, was doing a gracious and merciful thing to the remainder of the world. The Canaanites, through their abominations, had themselves become abominations. If there was to be any salvation for the world, Canaan must go. The cup of their iniquity had filled, and they could no longer be permitted to exist as heretofore. Let no one, then, charge God with lack of justice in His treatment of Canaan.

Israel, God's chosen nation, was not to be as the Canaanites. She, rather, was to be perfect in her dealings with the Lord. When Moses stresses the word *perfect,* he of course is raising a high standard. The word *tamim,* as here used, seems to connote freedom from moral blemish. Before the Lord, then, Israel was to be unlike the nations that worked abomination. She was to be perfect. It is a high standard and one which has never been relaxed.

Verses nine through thirteen have throughout been couched in the singular. Israel has been addressed as though she were an individual. Thus tenderly has God, through Moses, warned and admonished His nation. The temptation to learn of heathen nations has been forcefully yet gracefully stated, and has formed the dark and dismal background against which the bright promise of the gift of prophecy is to be placed. Surely, if anything is clear from this passage, it is that prophecy, the gift of God, and the superstitions of Canaan, have nothing to do one with another.[26]

Attempts have sometimes been made, however, to obliterate or at least to obscure the sharp distinction between soothsaying and prophecy. Thus, Pedersen says that originally there cannot have been much difference between the two.[27] He appeals to Proverbs 16:10 "Divination is upon the lips of the king; in judgment his mouth will not be faithless." He further says that ". . . a typical man of God like Balaam" is called a soothsayer, and asserts that soothsaying is sometimes the task of prophets (Micah 3:11).[28]

In soothsaying, he tells us, the most important thing was the decision, and this decision could be obtained by means of various practices. In prophecy, on the other hand, that which was distinguishing was the prophet's psychic experience, and that which made the phenomenon distinctively Israelitish was that this experience was in the name of Yahweh. Herein, according to Pedersen, lay the distinction between soothsaying and prophecy. Under the term *qesem,* both prophecy and soothsaying were probably originally included, and both were originally Canaanitish. Prophecy, however, could separate itself from the Canaanitish elements, whereas exorcism could not. Thus, the latter in time incurred reproach.[29]

At this point we shall merely consider the passages to which Pedersen makes appeal. Later in our discussion we shall have more to say about the theory that prophecy was of Canaanitish origin.[30] A mere glance at Micah 3:11 however, should make it perfectly clear that this passage does not teach that soothsaying is sometimes the task of prophets. Micah is reproaching the sins of his nation, and he denounces the false practices of her priests and prophets and the false security in which they rest. In the midst of his moving words appears the verse: "Her (i. e., the nation's) heads judge for reward; and her priests teach for a price: and her prophets divine for silver; and upon the Lord they lean, saying, Is not the Lord in our midst? there will not come upon us evil." In other words, Micah is condemning the prophets, because they divine for money. He is not saying that this is their legitimate task. Rather, he is denouncing them most severely, because what they are doing is not their legitimate task. They should be declaring the word

of the Lord. Instead, they have sunk to the level of the soothsayer, and are divining for money.

Again, we do not understand how Pedersen can call Balaam
a typical man of God. Without enlarging further upon the
thought we may say that Balaam is represented in Scripture as
a heathen soothsayer, upon whom the Spirit of God came to
compel him to perform a specific task. For a time he possessed
the prophetic gift, but not the prophetic office. Surely legitimate
appeal cannot be made to Balaam of Beth-peor to show that
prophecy and soothsaying were originally one.

With respect to Proverbs 16:10 the context requires us to
understand the word in a good sense. In judgment, we are told,
the mouth of the king will not be treacherous or faithless. In
other words, when the king pronounces judgment, he will
pronounce a just judgment. Parallel to this is the first member
of the verse, namely: *"qesem* is upon the lips of the king." In
such a context *qesem* must be rendered by some such word as
oracle. As far as the present writer is aware, this is the only
such usage of the word in the Old Testament. However, even
this one usage may be sufficient to establish the fact that sometimes the *qesem* was not superstition but a pronouncement. The
word doubtless had different connotations, and apparently could
have the sense of declaration or judgment. In such a context
it is divorced from superstition entirely. Hence, it cannot serve
in proving Pedersen's point. *Qesem,* in the Old Testament, is
ranked among the superstitions and is condemned. That false
prophets may often have engaged in the practice of *qesem,* is of
course amply shown by the Old Testament.[31] But the practice
in itself had nothing to do with prophecy.

Before proceding to announce the establishment of the prophetic institution, Moses declares that these nations which Israel
is about to possess make a practice of harkening unto the diviners and enchanters. The verb which we have translated
"hearken" has a frequentative force. It expresses that which is
the custom of the nations of Canaan. These nations had regular
sources of information to which they would go to learn concerning the future and present needs. Israel, however, was not to
use such sources of information. "Thou,"—and Moses stresses

the word by giving it the emphatic position in the sentence; "thou—not so has the Lord thy God given to thee."

Thus, there is seen to be a distinction between the people of God and the world. The world has its sources of information, but the people of God are not to use them. When the Church, discarding the Word of God turns to the wisdom of men, she does a heinous thing. The world, by its wisdom knew not God. The Canaanites, by their wisdom, became an abomination.

If, however, the people of Israel were not permitted to use the sources of information which the Canaanites regularly consulted, where would Israel learn that which was necessary for her life in Palestine? Moses is now ready with the answer.[32] "A prophet from thy midst, from thy brethren, like me will the Lord thy God raise up to thee; unto him thou shalt hearken" (Deut. 18:15). In the stead of the superstitions of Canaan, we thus learn, God will raise up a prophet. The people of Canaan hearken unto the diviners and the enchanters; Israel however, is to hearken unto the prophet. There is thus a vast difference between Israel and Canaan; a difference which is to characterize their daily life. One nation hearkens to the word of man; the other is to give ear only to the Word of God.

The prophet whom the Lord will raise up is said to be "from thy midst" and "from thy brethren." In other words he is to be an Israelite. One who does not meet these requirements cannot be a prophet and it is this fact which excludes a man such as Balaam, who was not an Israelite, and so did not occupy the prophetic office.

Furthermore it is stated that the prophet is to be like Moses. The nature of this similarity is set forth in verses sixteen through eighteen where it is shown that Moses was the mediator between God and the people. At Sinai the nation had cried out at the sight of the accompaniments of the Theophany, "let me no longer hear the voice of the Lord my God, and as for this great fire, let me no longer see it, that I die not." This cry revealed a conviction of sin and unworthiness upon the part of the nation which the Lord commended, "They have done well in that which they have spoken." Henceforth, it is announced, the Lord will speak to them through Moses, the go-between or

mediator. It was in this sense, then, that the prophet is to be
like him. As Moses was a mediator, representing God before
the people, so the prophet is to be also.[33]

It does not necessarily follow from this that the prophet will
be the representative of God in the same degree as was Moses.
The Lord declared that He would place His words in the
prophet's mouth, but his declaration does not raise the prophet
to the same position as that which is elsewhere ascribed to
Moses.[84] It is not the degree of representation that is in view
here but the fact. Moses was indeed a representative of God in
a higher degree than were the prophets, but that is not the
thought of this present verse. The thought of this present
verse, rather, is that both are representatives of God. It is in
the capacity of representative that the prophet is to be like
Moses.

Nor is it strictly accurate to say that Moses is named a
prophet in this particular passage. He is not here actually called
a prophet. Rather, the prophet is compared with Moses, who
is the standard of comparison. He is not here put upon an
equal plane with the prophets, but is rather adduced as a standard or measure with which the prophets may be compared.
They are said to be like him, for just as he was a mediator
between God and the nation, so also they are to be.

One further point may be noted. In ancient Israel there were
two kinds of mediators. On the one hand there was the priest,
who represented the people before God. On the other hand
there were the prophets, whose primary task was not to come
before God on behalf of the nation, nor to present before Him
the needs and hopes of the people, but rather, to be His spokesmen unto the people, and to represent God before the nation.

This is clearly stressed in the declaration "And I shall place
My words in his mouth, and he shall speak unto them all that
which I command him." According to this passage the message
which the prophet delivered was not his own, but had been
received by him from God. And it was precisely this message,
no more and no less, which the prophet was to declare. Thus,
in the sense that he represented God before the people, the

prophet was to be like Moses. Unto the prophet, therefore, as the representative of God, the people were to hearken.

The Identity of the Prophet

The reader must have been struck by the use of the singular noun in that Moses speaks of a prophet rather than of prophets. It was this phenomenon which led some of the older Jewish expositors to seek to identify the prophet with some individual figure of Israel's history, such as Joshua or Jeremiah.[35] A little reflection, however, will show that such an interpretation is not satisfactory, for it is against the background of continuous superstitious practice that God will give to Israel the prophet. The use of the singular, then, whatever else its force may be, does not permit us to understand that only one individual is in view.

In fact, such an interpretation is definitely excluded by verses twenty-one and two which present criteria by which the Israelite might distinguish between true and false prophets. Elsewhere also in Deuteronomy, namely, in chapter thirteen, further criteria are given to enable a distinction to be made between the true and the false prophet. Consequently, we must very decisively reject the interpretation which would understand the singular use of the noun as permitting the existence of only one individual who might be called a prophet.

Perhaps more erroneous, however, would be the view which sees in the word "prophet" a reference only to a group of prophets, or to the prophetic institution as such.[36] For this interpretation pays no attention whatever to the use of the singular. If we are to arrive at a correct understanding of this remarkable passage, therefore, it will be necessary to give full heed to the context. We must note for one thing that the word "prophet" is employed over against the background of continuous superstition and we must also pay full attention to the fact that the word "prophet" is employed in the singular.

It seems rather clear then, in the first place, that the promise does have some reference to the establishment of the prophetic institution as such. In addition to the considerations which have already been adduced, there are also further factors which demand notice. After the enumeration of superstitious practices which he condemns, Moses says, "Not so has the Lord thy God given to thee" (Deuteronomy 18:14b). It is of importance to note that the verb employed is in the past. The implication is that God has not permitted Israel to practice these abominations, but He has given to her the obligation of doing something else, namely, hearkening unto the prophets. It would seem, therefore, that this passage presupposes that there were already prophets in existence, and since this was so, the nation could go to them instead of to the abominations. Perhaps too much stress should not be placed upon this use of the past tense, but it does at least suggest the idea of a gift of God which had already taken its beginning, even now, at the time when the promise was being uttered.

It is also of importance to note the wider context of the book of Deuteronomy. Deuteronomy prepares for the time after the death of Moses, when the nation shall have come into the promised land. It speaks of civil magistrates and also of priests not so much as individuals but as institutions. The presumption is then, that in mentioning the prophet, it would again have reference to an institution. This presumption becomes the stronger, when we consider that the passage concerning the prophet appears in the same section of the book which treats of the other institutions.

There are two further considerations which also have their place. That the prophetic institution did bear a prominent status in the life of ancient Israel is a fact that cannot successfully be called into question. Since, however, the institution did occupy so prominent a position, we naturally look for some word of Divine authorization for it. In the Old Testament there is no such word, unless it be the present passage. In other words, if Deuteronomy eighteen does not give Divine warrant for the existence of the prophets, no passage of the Old Testament does. The character of the entire Mosaic legislation leads one to believe that so prominent an institution as prophecy might be expected to have Divine authorization and that such authorization would be recorded in the Law.

The second consideration which supports the idea that the present passage has reference to the establishment of the institution of prophecy is the reflection upon it in Luke 11:50, 51; "That the blood of all the prophets, which was shed from the foundation of the world, may be required of this generation; From the blood of Abel unto the blood of Zacharias, which perished between the altar and the temple: verily, I say unto you, It shall be required of this generation." That this passage has reference to Deuteronomy 18:19 is shown to be the case by the repetition of the verb "be required." In these words from the Gospel of Luke we have a Divine commentary upon the prophecy under consideration.

Hence it appears justifiable to regard the promise uttered by Moses as having a reference to the prophetic line. However, when this is said, the promise is by no means exhausted. The prophecy has reference to a line of prophets, an institution, but it has reference to more than that. The singular noun, "prophet" stands out. Why did not Moses say "prophets"? Why, if the reference is only to a group, this strange use of the singular? Coupled with this occurrence of the singular is the contrast with a single individual, even Moses. We have seen from the context that the similarity between the prophet and Moses lay in the realm of mediator. At the same time, if justice be done to the words, the prophet to be raised up must be a mediator in the full sense that Moses was. And none of the prophets were mediators in this high sense. In Deuteronomy 34:10, it is said: "There arose not a prophet since in Israel like unto Moses, whom the Lord knew face to face." Again, in Numbers 12:1-8 the true prophets are contrasted with Moses in such a way as to show that he is far superior to them. The whole group of prophets, then, cannot be the "prophet like unto me." Moses stood out as one who had performed the mighty task of founding the theocracy. The task to be accomplished in the future, the bringing of salvation to the Gentiles, would need to be the work of one who was like Moses, yea, who was greater than Moses. If this great work of future salvation be kept in mind, and it must be kept in mind, if the Pentateuch, as it stands, be taken seriously, then the phrase "a

prophet like unto me" must have a higher reference than to
the historic prophetic institution.

Also in favor of the individualistic interpretation is the evidence of tradition. At the time of the New Testament there
seem to have been two prevalent interpretations of the Deuteronomy passage. One of these regarded the prophecy as
Messianic. Thus, after the feeding of the five thousand, the
people say: "That this is truly the prophet, who is to come
into the world" (John 6:14). So also the woman of Samaria:
"I know that the Messiah cometh, who is called Christ; when
that one comes he will tell us all things" (John 4:25). The
other interpretation was to the effect that some great prophet,
not the Messiah, would appear. Thus, in John 1:20, 21 a distinction is made between Christ and "that prophet." In these
verses John the Baptist denies that he is the Christ or Elijah
or "that prophet." This same distinction appears also in John
7:40, 41. In these verses the people are divided in their
opinion of our Lord. Some say that He is the great prophet.
Others say: "No, he is not the great prophet; He is the Christ."
Thus, it is seen, in the days of our Lord there were two opinions, both of them regarding the prophet as an individual. According to one, this individual was the Christ; according to the
other, he was not the Christ, but some great prophet.

It is the direct evidence of the New Testament, however,
which proves the correctness of the Messianic interpretation,
and to this evidence we must turn. Objections to such a use of
the New Testament are constantly being made, but we do not
believe that they are valid. The New Testament, we are sometimes told, is only an interpretation, and it may be very different from that which was in the mind of the Old Testament
writer.

In answer to this line of reasoning there are certain things
that need to be said. It is of course true that the writer of
Deuteronomy, whom we believe to have been Moses, may not
have understood the full depth and content of the words which
he penned. What the extent of the writer's own understanding
may have been is a very difficult thing for us to learn. In this
particular instance it would seem that he understood that God

would raise up a body of prophets which was to find its supreme expression in one great prophet, who would stand in peculiar relationship to himself. A careful study of Moses' words, such as we have been endeavoring to engage in, makes it clear that at least that much must have been the understanding of the Old Testament writer.

It must also be remembered, however, that the writer wrote under the inspiration of the Spirit of God and that the words which he wrote were a revelation from God to man. Ultimately, they are not the words of Moses, but the words of God. Hence, no mere finite creature, not even Moses, could ever completely fathom their profundity. Since they are the words of God, any interpretation which God Himself places upon them must be taken into consideration in attempting to understand them, and the New Testament, we believe, is such a Divine interpretation. This is not the place to state the arguments for believing that the Bible is the revelation of God to sinful man, since those arguments have been presented time and time again. Suffice it to say that we are deeply impressed with the validity of such arguments. We believe that the words of Moses in Deuteronomy eighteen are a revelation of grace from the one living and true God to His people just before they entered the promised land. We believe also that the New Testament is a revelation of that same living and true God, a revelation which is the completion and fulfillment of the Old Testament. Therefore, if we are properly to understand the Old Testament, we must also take into consideration what the New says concerning it, for it is in the New that the Old is fully explained. We are of course perfectly willing to seek to interpret the Old Testament by itself. We would not read into it what is not really to be found there. By all means one should seek to find out just what Deuteronomy eighteen, taken by itself, means. Deuteronomy eighteen is a revelation from God, and the earnest student should seek with all diligence to understand the Divine words as they appear in this chapter. But God has revealed to us more than Deuteronomy eighteen. He has also revealed its interpretation. In order that we may know all that He has said upon the subject we should study all that He has revealed.

We need not be ashamed then to turn to the New Testament in order to learn what further revelation God has given concerning the proper interpretation of Deuteronomy eighteen. There will be little need of doing more than quoting the relevant passages since they speak for themselves. In John 5:45-47 our Lord said: "Think not that I will condemn you before the Father; there is one who condemns you, even Moses, in whom you have trusted. For if you had believed Moses, you would have believed in me, for he wrote concerning me." John 5:43: "I am come in My Father's name, and ye receive Me not." Compare this with Deuteronomy 18:19, "Whosoever will not hearken unto my words, which he shall speak in My name, I will require it of him." John 12:48, 49: "He that rejecteth me, and receiveth not my words, hath one that judgeth him: the word that I have spoken, the same shall judge him in the last day. For I have not spoken of myself, but the Father which sent me, he gave me a commandment, what I should say, and what I should speak." Matthew 17:5: "While he yet spake, behold a bright cloud overshadowed them: and behold a voice out of the cloud, which said, This is my beloved Son, in whom I am well pleased; hear ye him." Acts 3:23 admits of no doubt, "For Moses truly said unto the fathers, A prophet shall the Lord your God raise up unto you of your brethren, like unto me; him shall ye hear in all things whatsoever he shall say unto you. And it shall come to pass, that every soul which will not hear that prophet, shall be destroyed from among the people." These words are quoted by Peter with direct reference to Jesus Christ. From the New Testament, therefore, we learn that Jesus Christ did regard Himself as the subject of the great prophecy in Deuteronomy.

At this point it may be well to pause and summarize the results of the study thus far. Deuteronomy eighteen, we have learned, seems to contain a double reference.

1. There was to be a body of prophets, an institution, which would declare the words that God commanded.

2. There was to be one great prophet, who alone would be like Moses and might be compared with him, namely, the Messiah.

The question now arises as to the relationship between these two emphases. Some have held that we are to understand a collection or group of prophets to which Christ would also belong, as the perfect realization of the prophetic body. This however, is not a legitimate thought to derive from the words. It is far better, because more faithful to the text, to regard the prophet as an ideal person in whom are comprehended all true prophets. The prophetical order is thus an ideal unity, which is to find its focus point in the historic Christ. For the Spirit of Christ was in all the true prophets. When finally Christ appeared upon earth, the promise was fulfilled in its highest and fullest sense. It is, therefore, a Messianic promise.[37]

A Gift of God

It must be obvious to every reader of the Bible that the picture of the origin of prophecy given in Deuteronomy attributes that origin to God Himself. Jehovah speaks to Moses directly and announces that He will raise up the prophets. This explanation has ever been accepted by the Church of Christ. In these remarkable words the heart of faith has found delight and hope and encouragement. To many, however, this reverence and acceptance of the Christian heart is something foreign. There are many to whom the noble words of Moses have little meaning. It is therefore most necessary that we consider certain implications of the statement of Deuteronomy.

For one thing, the eighteenth chapter clearly presupposes the objective existence of Jehovah, an existence independent of Israel. He is a God who can speak to His people and address them as "Thou." He can hear the cry of His people and pass judgment upon it (cf. vs. 17). He is, therefore, a God who possesses an objective, metaphysical existence. Furthermore, Jehovah controls the destinies of His people. He can warn them of the abominations which are practiced in Canaan. He was with them at Sinai where He caused them to see "this great fire" and to hear His "voice." To protect His people from the sins of Canaan He will raise up for them the prophets. He will place His words in the mouths of the prophets, and He will continue to do this in the future. He will command these prophets, and they shall speak all the words which He will command them. In other words, Jehovah is able to reveal His will. Finally, it should be stressed that He will bring His people into Palestine. It is He who gives them this land, and who dispossesses the Canaanites of it. He controls the destinies, not only of His own, but also of the inhabitants of Canaan. The Canaanites had continuously done things which were abominable to Jehovah, and so, for that reason, He intends to deprive them of their land. It is clear enough, therefore, that the Jehovah who spoke to Moses was no local, tribal deity, but the Lord of heaven and earth. And it may with all confidence be said that anyone who held the conception of God given in the eighteenth chapter of Deuteronomy was a monotheist in the fullest sense of the term.

The institution of prophecy, therefore, is to be regarded as a gift of God. It is He who raised up the prophets and gave them their messages. They were not merely men of religious genius, nor did they appear because Israel was a particularly religious nation. In fact, according to the picture which they themselves give, Israel was a corrupt and backslidden nation, a people of evil doers and hard of heart. The more one considers the character of the Israelites, as that character is presented by the prophets, the more one wonders how so sublime an institution could have risen in the midst of such great corruption. The answer which the Bible gives, and the answer which we shall endeavor to defend in these pages is that this sublime institution was none other than a gracious gift of God.

It follows then, that, whatever else may be said about the beginnings of prophecy, the institution in no sense found its origin in Canaan. Moses makes the sharpest possible distinction between what the Canaanites do and what God will do for Israel. What the Canaanites do is an abomination. What God will do is to raise up men to whom Israel is to hearken. If, then, we are to take the Bible with any seriousness, we must make clear at the outset that the origin of the prophetic movement is not to be found in Canaan. It is perfectly true that there are some superficial resemblances between the actions and practices of the prophets and those of heathen soothsayers. But it is very necessary to make a distinction that is often overlooked. There is a distinction, and indeed, a profound difference, between essential resemblances and those which are merely superficial or accidental. If we fail to make this distinction, we shall also fail to arrive at the truth.

It will be most necessary to study carefully the superficial or accidental resemblances which exist between the prophetic movement in Israel and alleged similarities elsewhere. But since prophecy is of Divine origin, and the practices of the heathen are not of Divine origin, we may be sure that there are no essential resemblances. Rather, despite whatever accidental similarities there may be, there in reality exists a great difference. Between the two a vast gulf is fixed, and no man can pass over. Hence, any attempts which seek to derive the prophetic movement from Canaan are bound to fail at the outset. And, despite the attempts which have been made thus to explain prophecy, we must pronounce them failures. The New Testament is right in its interpretation: "For the prophecy came not in old time by the will of man: but holy men of God spake as they were moved by the Holy Ghost" (2 Peter 1:21).

CHAPTER II

Moses and the Prophets

THE Mosaic law and institutions, as we have seen, were not sufficient to enable the nation to meet the new conditions which would appear when it was settled in Canaan. Consequently, the Lord announced His purpose of raising up the prophets in order that the nation might hearken to them, and might thus be guided by the Word of God rather than by superstitious abominations. It is necessary, however, that we study more carefully the relationship which existed between the prophets and the Mosaic law. Were the prophets superior to the Law? Could they advance beyond Moses in giving revelation, or were they under Moses, and must their messages be in agreement with the foundational Law of the people?

There is a passage in the Old Testament which answers these questions with great clarity, and to this passage, namely, Numbers 12:1-8, we must now somewhat briefly devote our attention. The occasion for the revelation given in these verses is a complaint against Moses on the part of Miriam and Aaron. This complaint is heard by the Lord who rebukes Miriam and Aaron and then announces the distinction between true prophets and Moses. As a result Miriam is punished by leprosy for seven days.

The account as it stands is a compact unity. This unity, however, is denied by some scholars. Thus, Baentsch concludes that from the two-fold motivation in complaint, the narrative cannot be regarded as a unit.[1] Originally, he thinks, there was only the complaint of Miriam against the marriage of a Cushite woman. It was a family quarrel. This original account, as Baentsch seeks to show by an appeal to linguistic phenomena, belonged to the so-called E document, and to this source he would attribute verses 1, 2b, 3, 9-16. A later author, he thinks, has worked over this original material into a "prophetical study," in which it may be seen that he had behind him the prophetical development of the eighth century. This second account should be given to an author whom Baentsch calls E², and to it he attributes verses 2a, 2-8.

Somewhat similar is the position of Dillmann.² According to him the narrative belongs originally to E (Dillmann calls it B). At the same time there are linguistic phenomena which are thought to remind one of J (Dillmann's C). Hence, we should probably conclude that a redactor has taken two very similar accounts, one of E and one of J, and worked them together. Perhaps, thinks Dillmann, in the original account of E Aaron did not take a strong part, and so he is not punished by leprosy as is Miriam.

For our part, we cannot agree with this process of splitting up the text. Language is the property of no one person, and to attribute passages to different authors upon the basis of linguistic criteria is a very subjective and perilous process. Furthermore, if there really were two original accounts, why did the "redactor" for the sake of uniformity, not include Aaron in the punishment?

The "critical" analysis rests upon a profound misunderstanding of the nature of the passage. It should be noted that the instigator in the complaint is obviously Miriam. She is mentioned first, and the verb which is used is feminine. This is probably the reason why she alone is punished with leprosy. Aaron was not a man of strong character. It seems that he could easily have been led into sin. He follows Miriam here just as he was easily persuaded in the episode of the golden calf. Miriam's entreaties are two much for him, and he unites with her in her complaint against Moses.

The Complaint of Miriam and Aaron

Actually there are not two complaints. The real grievance which Miriam and Aaron had was that they were not being recognized as was Moses. "Has not the Lord spoken also with us?" they ask. It was a case of jealousy. The question concerning the Cushite woman is only a pretext for complaint. The workings of jealous minds are well known. They find flaws wherever they can. The real concern of Miriam was not the marriage to a Cushite woman. The real concern was that Miriam thought she was not being recognized as much as Moses. Hence, her jealousy gets the better of her, and she finds an occasion for complaint.

Miriam and Aaron spake against Moses for the purpose of arousing resentment against him. In this manner, by calling attention to his marriage, they thought that they could turn the nation against him. Thus they could accomplish their end, and yet conceal the real grievance. It is true that verse two begins with the words, "And they said." However, it does not necessarily follow that they had spoken this complaint before the people, for such a complaint would have brought rebuke upon their own heads. Verse two serves the purpose of showing what was the real cause of their discontent. Evidently it was to one another that they had spoken, and not to the people at large.

The complaint which they enunciate was that Moses had married a Cushite woman, and to show that this complaint is founded in fact, Moses adds, "for he had married a Cushite woman." What, however, was to be condemned in such a marriage? Why should there be objection to it? It should be noted that the Israelites were not prohibited from second marriages, save with the Canaanites.[8] This woman, however, was not a Canaanite. Hence, no legitimate objection can be found in the fact that Moses had married a second time, if such actually was the case.

Apparently, there had been a second marriage. The reference cannot be to Zipporah, for she was not a Cushite, and even if Miriam in disdain had thus referred to her, the text would not have confirmed this by the statement that Moses had married a Cushite woman. Also, it would surely be strange to bring in a complaint at this particular time against the marriage to Zipporah. Moses had married Zipporah many years earlier while he was a fugitive from Egypt. The time for complaint against any such marriage had long since passed.

It is difficult to tell precisely what is intended by the word "Cushite." Jewish tradition offers some interesting interpretations. According to one view it is thought that the word is merely a euphemism for beautiful. To say that Moses' wife was a Cushite, according to this view, would be the equivalent of saying that she was as beautiful as the Ethiopian is black. Another Jewish tradition asserts that the numerical value of the word Cushite and the numerical value of the phrase "beautiful of appearance" is the same, namely 730. These views, however, we may dismiss as mere exegetical curiosities.

In the Bible the word Cush is a synonym for Ethiopia. It is also possible that it may have reference to a place in northern Arabia. Probably we should adopt one of these interpretations. Moses had married a woman who either had come from northern Arabia or else who actually was an Ethiopian. The phrase is not merely an expression of contempt upon the part of Miriam, but also is designed to indicate the racial descent of the woman.

The reason then why Miriam complains is that Moses had married a foreign woman. Evidently this woman was a sojourner who had left Egypt with the Israelites. In Miriam's eyes, Moses should have married a native Israelite instead of a foreigner. This position was criticized by Wellhausen who declared that enmity against foreigners and strong national feeling began to make their appearance only at a much later time. Against this, however, Dillmann has pointed out that if the account were late, there would have been no reason for the writers to identify the woman as a Cushite.[4] Why also would they have permitted Miriam's objection to be reproved of God? If the account were late and were really an evidence of nationalistic antipathy, the writer would have supported Miriam and rejected the Cushite.

We may conclude, then, that Moses in marrying a foreign woman had offended Miriam, whose narrow nationalism stands in marked contrast to Moses' own act. The real reason for the complaint however, was something quite different. The real complaint which Miriam and Aaron discussed between themselves had to do with the relationship of their position in Israel with respect to that of Moses. They did not wish to be the recipients of revelation which was subordinate to that received by Moses but rather of that which was equal to that given to him. There is truth, of course, in their statement. God had indeed spoken to them. Aaron had the exalted privilege, which was not even vouchsafed to Moses, of using the Urim and Thumim in bringing the people's rights before God (Exodus 28: 30). Miriam was called a prophetess (Exodus 15:20), and occupied an honored position among the women of Israel. Furthermore, the importance of the work of Aaron and Miriam is stressed in Micah 6:4, when they are mentioned in the same connection with Moses as gifts to the people. Their complaint did indeed have truth in it. God did not speak only with Moses; He spoke also with them.

Although God did speak with them, and although each of them had a work to do which Moses himself could not do, they were dissatisfied. Evidently, in their minds it was not sufficient that God should merely speak with them; He must speak with them as He did with Moses. Thus, in their very complaint, they tacitly acknowledge the fact that Moses is superior to themselves in his relationship to God.

There is something else also that they acknowledge. They acknowledge, although unaware that they are doing it, that they themselves are not worthy to receive these high gifts from God. For Miriam and Aaron, instead of rejoicing that God had so highly honored them as to entrust them with these gifts, in reality were honoring the gifts themselves rather than the One who gave them. They were boasting in the fact that they had been the recipients of revelation, when as a matter of fact, they should have been overcome with awe and gratitude that God had so signally honored them. The Scripture states that the Lord heard, and by these words we are prepared for the announcement of judgment to follow.

The Meekness of Moses

Moses, however, apparently did not hear. At least he took no notice, and we are told: "Now the man Moses was meeker than any man upon the face of the earth." At this point objections begin to arise. How, it may be asked, could a humble servant of God speak thus of himself? Is not this boasting? Even some who are eager to defend the trustworthiness of the Bible feel that they cannot regard Moses as the author of these words, and so conclude that this verse must be an interpolation.[5]

The problem, however, cannot thus simply be solved, for the verse bears none of the marks of an interpolation. For one thing, it appears in all the ancient versions of the Old Testament. It also bears an obvious relation both to what precedes and to what follows. We shall presently seek to determine more precisely what this relation is, but that there is a relation seems to be apparent from a mere reading of the text. We cannot simply dismiss this verse as an interpolation because we happen to think that Moses would not thus have spoken of himself.

Dillmann, who does not believe in the Mosaic authorship of the passage, asserts that the verse is not an interpolation. For him Moses is not the author, and he feels that there is no difficulty unless one posit Mosaic authorship. We who do believe in the Mosaic authorship must face the text however, and seek to explain its difficulties, but in doing this there is one caution which must be held before us. We cannot deny the verse to Moses on the mere grounds that since we should not thus have spoken concerning ourselves, we may therefore legitimately conclude that Moses would not so have spoken.

There are two ways in which this verse may be connected with what precedes. One is to take it as an explanation of the phrase "and the Lord heard." The force of the passage would then be: "Miriam and Aaron complained saying, 'Has God spoken only with Moses, has He not also spoken with us?' And the Lord heard their complaint, and He heard it righteously, to condemn it, for as a matter of fact, Moses was the meekest of men, and Moses would not answer such a complaint." It seems better however, not to consider verse three as an answer to the complaint, but to regard it as an explanation of the reason why the Lord heard it. The force of this view may then be brought out somewhat as follows: "The Lord heard the complaint and took note of it. This Moses would not do, for, being the meekest of all men, he would not bring disrepute to his office by answering a personal attack against himself." The cogency of this will become clearer as we proceed.

Verse three may be described in terms of Hebrew grammar as a circumstantial clause; that is, a clause in which there is no finite verb and which describes a condition existing at a particular time. In this instance it expresses the conditions which were in existence at the time when the Lord spoke. We may thus paraphrase: "The Lord spoke, and the conditions under which He spoke were that Moses was the meekest of men." At the same time a contrast is introduced between God and "the man." God—heard; now, as to the man Moses—he was very meek. We are reminded of the very similar contrast presented in Exodus 11:3.

This contrast, which the grammatical construction of the verses makes apparent, shows that Moses did not cry to God for vengeance, but rested his case in God's hands. This he did for he was meek. Luther unfortunately translated this word by the German, "geplagter"; i. e., *plagued, harassed,* but such a translation is not accurate. The true meaning was seen long ago by the translator of Codex B of the Septuagint, who rendered *praus;* i. e., meek.[6]

Is it possible, however, that Moses would write of himself this way? Would he assert that he was the meekest of all men? Is not this rather an example of proud self-praise? If we consider carefully what Moses is saying, we shall see that he is not praising himself in any self-righteous manner. The first thing that strikes us is the use of the third person. There is a certain objectivity about this. If Moses had said; "I am the meekest of men" we might indeed have questions as to its propriety. Moses did not do this; he speaks of himself in the third person. He thus objectifies himself, just as he had done in Exodus 11:3, and in thus objectifying himself, shows that his statement is not motivated by self-pride. He further discloses that he is seeking to draw attention not to himself but to his position, and to the reason why he could not enter into a defense of himself.

Moses was the meekest of all men, because Moses had been exalted in position by God as had no other man. He occupied a place in the Old Testament dispensation which was utterly unique. For this reason, he abstains from all self-defense, and also does not call out to God for vengeance, but leaves the entire matter in the hands of God. There is, indeed, a Pharisaical type of piety, as Hengstenberg long ago pointed out, which refrains from taking vengeance upon an enemy, but prays rather, in the hope that God Himself will exact such vengeance.[7] This type of piety really entertains a spirit of revenge and also insults the purity of God. It was not thus that Moses acted. He was truly meek. He kept silence, not in the hope that God would take vengeance, but out of a deep consciousness of the highly exalted office which God had given to him. This verse, therefore, stands as a tacit condemnation upon revenge in its most subtle and refined form; it is a clear refutation of the false notion that the Old Testament enjoins revenge.

Well and good, it may be said, but we today would not speak of ourselves in such a way. To which the reply should be made that we must measure Moses, not by our standard, but by his. He was in a position quite different from us today. No man has ever occupied the high status which was his. And, while he praises himself here, if it really be praise, so elsewhere he humbly condemns himself. How many can relate their own defects and mistakes as humbly as Moses has done? We read of his tragic errors with sadness of heart, yet never with the feeling that there is mock humility in what is related. Think only of the narrative of the slaying of the Egyptian, how objectively it is told, and how the sad consequences of that act come upon Moses. Such an account was not written by a man of false humility, but by one who was deeply conscious of the wrong. There is a certain impartiality and objectivity about it which causes us to behold more the evil of the sin than the attitude of the sinner. In fact, the entire life of Moses is characterized by just this objective meekness of which the present verse speaks. These are the words of a man who has utterly and completely sacrificed his own life to the office unto which God has called him. And these words of Moses later formed the basis of another declaration of self-commendation, a declaration spoken by One Who was far greater than Moses: "Take my yoke upon you and learn of me, for I am meek and lowly in heart: and ye shall find rest unto your souls."[8]

We are now prepared for the declaration of verse four, "And the Lord spake suddenly." Some of the older Jewish expositors took this to mean that the Lord spake without Miriam and Aaron expecting it. More likely, however, by the word "suddenly" we are to understand that while Aaron and Miriam were yet uttering their complaint, the Lord spoke. Moses, then, because of the unique position in which he stood, would not defend himself. For this very reason the Lord seeks immediately to defend the honor of His servant.

Moses and the Prophets

He calls the three to the Tent of Meeting. In this address there is a tacit rebuke to Aaron and Miriam, for the order in which God addresses them is Moses, Aaron, Miriam. Moses is given the place of priority; and Aaron is placed ahead of Miriam. This is as it should be. Miriam had transgressed in leading her brother. She should have hearkened to him, rather than he to her. It is a great mistake, then, to follow the Septuagint, and to reverse the order of the names, merely to bring them into conformity with the order given in verse one.[9]

In obedience to God's call, the three go out to the Tent of Meeting. Here the Lord comes down in a pillar of cloud and addresses Aaron and Miriam. He calls them by name, mentioning Aaron first. In response to His call, Aaron and Miriam go out and Moses evidently remains inside.[10] The Lord then speaks to the two.

There next follows a profound declaration upon the part of the Lord in which the position of the prophets is stated in contrast to the position of Moses. This declaration is prefaced by the command: "hear, I pray you, My words." It is well to note that the doctrine to be announced is placed in an ethical setting. Out of the jealous action of Miriam and Aaron arises some of the most profound doctrinal teaching in all the Old Testament, and this conjunction of doctrine and ethics is characteristic of the entire Old Testament.

The words which the Lord speaks, however, are difficult to understand, and in order that the difficulty may be clearly seen, we shall offer a literal translation:

6b If there shall be your prophet Jehovah;
    in a vision unto him will I make myself known,
    in a dream will I speak with him.

7. Not so My servant Moses, in all My house He is faithful.

8. Mouth unto mouth will I speak with him, and plainly,
    and not in enigmatic sayings, and the form of Jehovah
    he will see;
    so why have ye not feared to speak against My servant,
    against Moses?

The principal difficulty is occasioned by the fact that the prophet, in verse six, is equated with Jehovah. The ancient versions as might be expected, sought to smooth out the difficulty. The Septuagint, for example, read "If your prophet should belong to the Lord"; the Vulgate, "If anyone among you should be a prophet of the Lord" (si quis fuerit inter vos propheta Domini). Without doubt these renderings bring out the true sense or at least part of the true sense. They cannot however, be accepted without question. And above all, in our evaluation of the Septuagint, we must not fall into the error of supposing that because it differs from the Hebrew, it therefore is to be preferred as preserving a more original reading. Without doubt, the Septuagint is endeavoring to present the sense of the Hebrew smoothly, and that explains its present divergences.

The most weighty objection to the translation offered in the Septuagint, however, is that it is grammatically impossible.[11] For this reason, a number of scholars have apparently adopted the position that since they cannot follow the Septuagint, and since they cannot understand the Hebrew, the Hebrew text must be corrupt. Ewald, for example, wanted to read "a prophet from you," and to move the word "Jehovah" to a position immediately after the first verb. The sentence would then read: "And the Lord said, Hear My words, if there be a prophet from you, etc."[12] Baentsch would read "a prophet among you," and would omit the word "Jehovah," regarding it either as a simple gloss or a variant of "he will be." Dillmann likewise seeks to follow a similar procedure, adopting either the reading "from you" or "among you," and considers "Jehovah" to be a gloss, which either belonged originally after the verb "and he said" or else had been purposely inserted in order to guard against false prophets.

Essentially this position is adopted by most commentators today. It is accepted by the Revised Version, although the word "Lord" is retained. Thus: "If there be a prophet among you, I the Lord, etc." As Rowley has pointed out, however, this involves a tacit emendation of the text.[13] Furthermore, the word "Lord" is too far removed from the verb to allow of the rendering "I the Lord, etc."

There are at least three remaining expedients. We may read, "If thy prophet be from the Lord, etc." and then we shall need no change of the text. At the same time, the singular "thy" is out of place, since God is addressing both Aaron and Miriam. Hence, we may read, "If your prophet be from Jehovah, etc." This reading involves the addition of only one letter to the text, and has much to commend it.

There remains, however, another expedient. We may leave the text just as it is and translate literally: "if your prophet be the Lord." This would be a strong way of expressing the thought that the prophet was truly of the Lord, a Jehovah prophet. Such a translation is grammatical, and is in every sense legitimate. Thus, for example, in Psalm 45:7 we read "Thy throne, O God, (is) everlastingness and eternity." This is a vivid way of asserting the eternity of God's throne. In English we should say, "Thy throne is eternal." Yet, how much more vivid and graphic is the Hebrew method of expression! Again in Psalm 109:4 we read, "And I am prayer." The meaning is "I am prayerful."

It is perfectly possible to allow the text to remain as it stands. If we do we note that it makes very clear the fact that the prophets to be discussed are true prophets. They are from Jehovah in the fullest sense. It is as strong as possible a method of stating the genuineness of these prophets. We need not dismiss the text as corrupt. Either we should translate it as it stands or we may adopt the other alternative and read "if your prophet be from the Lord." In either case, the meaning is clear; it is a true prophet concerning whom the Lord wishes to speak, someone who like Aaron and Miriam, was the recipient of true revelation from God. At the same time, the genuineness of the prophet is indicated by the possessive "your"; the prophet indeed belongs to the people, he takes his rise from among them.

To such true prophets it is announced that God will communicate by means of vision and dream. We may perhaps understand the force of the verb if we compare Genesis 45:1 where the same stem is also used. In this passage Joseph commanded that all men should be removed from him and that no man should stand with him "while Joseph made himself known unto his brethren." It is obvious that the basic thought is that of self-disclosure. By means of visions God will disclose Himself unto the true prophet.

As employed in this passage the word "vision" means simply "that which is seen." We may understand its force by noting its use in such a passage as Genesis 46:2. Jacob had journeyed to Beersheba, and at Beersheba he had offered sacrifices to the God of Isaac his father. "And God spake to Israel in visions of the night, and He said, Jacob, Jacob; and he said, Here am I." The meaning seems to be clear. During the night Jacob saw a vision and in the vision God spoke to him. It is with this force also that the word is employed in Numbers. Since it is used in connection with "dream," we are probably to understand the "vision" in a restricted sense, and not as a broad, comprehensive word for revelation. The other method by which God would communicate with true prophets was the dream. The vision and dream, then, stand out as the two media by which God will reveal Himself to true prophets.[14]

Very different, however, was the case with Moses. He is placed in a unique category. When Baentsch asserts that the writer is making a distinction between two kinds of prophets, those who receive revelation through vision and those to whom Jehovah speaks directly, whose ideal type is Moses, he has completely missed the point of the passage.[15] There is not a comparison here between two types of prophets, but a comparison between true prophets on the one hand and Moses on the other. Indeed, Moses is not called a prophet in this passage. He is not regarded even as the first and greatest of the prophets. All true prophets, according to this passage, belong in one group; Moses belongs in an entirely different category. That is the point that must be kept in mind if we are to do justice to the text.

The introductory "not so" of verse seven is very forceful. At one stroke it separates Moses from the prophets. Visions and dreams may characterize the revelation granted to the prophets, but they do not characterize that given to Moses. And the reason why they do not characterize the revelation given to Moses is that he is faithful in all God's house. It is high honor to Moses when he is thus characterized by the Lord as "My Servant."

The term of course is taken from human relationships and is a designation of affection and trust.[16] It was applied to each of the patriarchs, Abraham, Isaac and Jacob, and also to the prophets and to the whole nation Israel. Its highest use is as a designation of the Messiah, and in this sense it is employed in the latter part of the prophecy of Isaiah. The prophets were servants of the Lord in that they were entrusted with individual tasks or duties. Moses' commission, however, comprised the entire house of God, so that he might be regarded as an over-servant.[17]

By the phrase "My house" we are not to conceive a dwelling place of God such as the tabernacle. If this were the case it is difficult to understand the use of the adjective "all." Furthermore there would not be much meaning in such a statement. The words rather have reference to all God's dealings with His people in olden times, in other words, to the Old Testament dispensation. In the economy or management of God's people, — the covenant kingdom regarded as a nation — Moses was faithful.

It is somewhat difficult to translate the word *ne'eman* in such a manner as to bring out its full force. It surely is wrong to translate it "entrusted," as though the thought were merely that Moses had been entrusted with the management of the Divine economy. Such a rendering does not begin to do justice to the word.[18]

The word comprises the ideas of being firm and constant, of verifying or attesting, and also of proving true or trustworthy. The present form of the word — it is a passive participle — means faithful or proved, and is well translated by the Septuagint *pistos*. Of course, if a man is faithful to God, it follows also that he is trusted by God. Hence while we have rendered the word "faithful," we are ready to admit also its connotation "trusted." Moses was faithful before God in the discharge of his duties, and he was also trusted by God. It may be, therefore, that Ibn Ezra and some of the older Jewish expositors were right when they interpreted the word to signify that Moses could approach God at any time and need not wait for a dream or vision. At any rate, the word does serve to set apart or to distinguish Moses from the true prophets. It shows that his relationship to God and the prophets' relationship to God were in a different category. Moses, in other words, occupied a unique position in the Divine economy, and stood in an unparalleled relationship to God.

Moses My Servant

To Moses therefore, God will reveal Himself in a unique manner. Four phrases are used, and they all go to emphasize the fact that God's speaking to Moses will be plain and clear in distinction from the more obscure methods used in communicating with the true prophets. In the first place it is said that God will speak to Moses "mouth unto mouth." The phrase appears only in this present passage, and signifies that God will speak directly and immediately, without reserve, as friends converse together. So we read in Exodus 33:11a: "And the Lord spake unto Moses face to face, as a man speaketh unto his friend." In free personal intercourse, without any mediation, and with the same clarity and certainty that the spoken word carries, God would make known to Moses His will and ways. And in this connection it is of interest to observe the characterization that was made of Moses after his death: "And there arose not a prophet since in Israel like unto Moses, whom the Lord knew face to face" (Deuteronomy 34:10).

This first expression is strengthened by the others that follow. The second statement should be taken as an adverbial accusative, and may be rendered "as to view" or "sight," i. e., plainly. Thirdly, it is said that God will not speak to Moses in dark, enigmatic sayings. An example of such riddles or obscure sayings is given in the prophecy of Ezekiel 17:2ff. which is explicitly labeled a "riddle" (*hidhah*). It may be noted that since God will not thus speak to Moses, the assumption is that He will speak thus to the prophets. Lastly, of Moses it is remarked that he will see the form of the Lord. This remarkable statement does not mean that Moses will see the essence of God, for according to the consistent representation of the Bible God is a spirit. No mortal man can behold the unveiled glory of the holy God. On the other hand, the statement does not have reference to the appearances of God as the "Angel of Jehovah." Moses was not the only one to see the Angel of Jehovah; this was a privilege and blessing which was also granted to others. Nor is the "form of God" to be identified with appearances of God in human form which occurred in dreams or visions. Isaiah, in vision, saw an appearance of God seated upon a throne, high and lifted up. Ezekiel, in vision, saw the likeness as the appearance of a man above the likeness of a throne. Daniel, in the majestically conceived vision of his seventh chapter, saw the likeness of a son of man. What these prophets saw was indeed objective to themselves and not merely the product of their own minds. It was far more than a "psychological" experience; it was a

Divine, objective revelation. At the same time, it was not this that is here promised to Moses. What was promised to Moses, as Keil has so well stated it, ". . . stood in the same relation to these two forms of revelation, so far as directness and clearness were concerned, as the sight of a person in a dream to that of the actual figure of the person himself."[19]

When we consider those instances in which God spake with Moses, we are struck with the fact that, although Moses was permitted to see the form of God, nevertheless, even in this permission there was some restriction. For one thing, according to Exodus 33:17-23 Moses could not see the face of God. "And I will take away mine hand, and thou shalt see my back parts : but my face shall not be seen" (Exodus 33:23). God also permitted His goodness to pass before Moses, and in Exodus 34:5 we read: "And the Lord descended in the cloud, and stood with him there, and proclaimed the name of the Lord." In the strange statements of Exodus 24:10 we are told that Moses and the elders saw at least "the feet" of God. Nowhere, however, in the Old Testament is there a clear example of Moses beholding the "form" of the Lord. That God did thus appear to Moses because of the present prophecy, we need not doubt. At the same time, we are compelled to take notice of the restrictions which the Old Testament itself places upon the recorded appearances. How glorious and unique these were, however, may be seen from the fact that, when Moses came down from the mount, the skin of his face shone (Exodus 34:29, 30).

Even this unique blessing which caused the skin on Moses' face to shine cannot be compared with the glory of the New Testament dispensation. Thus Paul says: "But if the ministration of death, written and engraven in stones, was glorious, so that the children of Israel could not stedfastly behold the face of Moses for the glory of his countenance; which glory was to be done away: how shall not the ministration of the Spirit be rather glorious?" (2 Corinthians 3:7, 8). Paul's words substantiate the teaching of Numbers. The ministration of Moses is the Old Testament dispensation. We may note that Paul speaks of the ministration of Moses and not of that of the prophets. The prophets are not upon an equal plane with Moses; they are under him. It is Moses' ministration, and this ministration, in Paul's mind, is to be compared with the ministration of the Holy Spirit.

From our interpretation of the passage it surely has become clear that in the Divine economy or dispensation of the Old Covenant Moses occupied a unique and unparalleled place. As Keil remarks: "God talked with Moses without figure, in the clear distinctness of a spiritual communication, whereas to the prophets He only revealed Himself through the medium of ecstasy or dream."[20] From this it follows that Moses was not merely one of the prophets, not even the first among equals. Rather, all the prophets are under Moses, who is the human founder and the mediator of the Old Covenant. The prophets belonged to this covenant; they built upon the foundation which Moses had laid.

It is necessary also to note that the revelations granted to the prophets had somewhat of the obscure about them. They are characterized as dreams and visions, and probably, enigmatic sayings. Moses, however, because of the unique position which he occupied in the theocracy, received revelations from God without this element of obscurity. It might be remarked in passing that when we seek to interpret the words of the prophets, we should always keep in mind the manner in which revelations were made to them. Unless we first recognize precisely the subordinate position which the prophets occupied in the Mosaic economy, we shall never properly understand their messages.[21]

Since Moses occupied so unique a position, Miriam and Aaron sinned grievously in complaining against him. Important as was the revelation granted to Miriam and Aaron, they were in a subordinate position. They were under Moses, and for them to seek to compare the revelation granted to themselves with that given to Moses was sinful indeed. It is for this reason that Miriam is punished so severely. "Why did ye not fear to speak against My servant, against Moses?"

From what has been said thus far, it will be apparent that Moses, although he was a trusted servant in God's house, was nevertheless only a Servant and not a Master over the dispensation. He was serving in a dispensation of preparation, as may be seen from the fact that in the revelation of the "form" of God, there was a certain restriction. It is necessary to understand that the Mosaic age or economy was a type and preparation for a future age. This fact is revealed in the Epistle to the Hebrews, in a brief passage in which a comparison is instituted between Moses and Christ.[22] In this comparison Moses is greatly honored, in that his name is introduced in such close connection with the Name of Christ. At the same time the comparison results in a great contrast. Moses, as a servant, it is said, was faithful in all his house, but Christ as a Son is over His house. The contrast is between the servant in the house, even Moses, and the Son over the house, Christ. Christ is shown to be the founder of the house whereas Moses is but a creature in the house. The Mosaic dispensation is expressly said to be a witness or testimony of those things to be spoken of. It was the age of preparation, of incompleteness, of type, and it pointed forward to the salvation later to be revealed.

Very wondrous then was God's dealing with His chosen nation in ancient times. From the house of bondage He had delivered them with a strong right arm. He had brought them to Sinai and established them into a nation. He had given to them a foundational law, and a great mediator to be the human founder of the theocracy. And when this mediator should pass from the scene, He would raise up others, who were to build upon the foundation of the great mediator and to speak His word to the people. All that they would say was to be in accord with the work of Moses. So the Mosaic economy would continue until the time of preparation was to come to an end. Then in the fulness of time there would appear One like unto Moses, Who would declare God's word and will to His people, and of Whom it would be said, "This is My beloved Son; hear ye Him."

CHAPTER III

The Terminology of Prophetism

IN the promise uttered by Moses in Deuteronomy 18:15, the prophet is designated with the word *nabhi*. The blessing which God promised to His people as a counteractive to the abominations of the Canaanites was to consist in the raising up of a *nabhi* who would declare His will. What, precisely, is the meaning of this Hebrew word? The answer to this question is by no means easy to give. Much has been written upon the subject, and many attempts have been made to discover the etymological significance. It will not be our purpose to review the entire literature of the discussion, but merely to sum up some of the views that have been presented.

In his masterful *Thesaurus*, Gesenius had suggested that the Hebrew root *nb'* was connected with the Hebrew *nb'*, and that the ' had been softened (*emollito in*) to '.[1] The root *nb'* means "to bubble forth." According to Guillaume, this identification was made because the root *nb'* does imply more than the proclamation of a message.[2] But this means of showing that the prophet was one who was excited by inspiration must surely be rejected, since the two roots are not thus to be connected.

Meek derives the Hebrew *nabhi* from the root *nabu*, which does not appear in Hebrew but is of frequent occurrence in Accadian.[3] *Nabu* means "to speak," and Meek therefore interprets *nabhi* as a speaker or spokesman of God. In this he has been followed by R. B. Y. Scott.[4] Others have attempted to derive the word from the Arabic, *naba'a,* "to announce."[5]

Theodore Robinson has asserted that the name indicates ecstatic behaviour,[6] and Pedersen declares that it is perhaps derived from the "ecstatic incoherent cries."[7] Recently, Albright has called attention to the use of the word upon the Code of Hammurabi, where in the epilogue the phrase *na-bu-u pale-ia* appears, which may be translated "who will declare my reign" or "declared, called of my reign."[8] Albright regards this form as a verbal adjective, and translates it "called." He also appeals to the word *nibitu* which has a passive sense, and to the fact that the verb *nabu* means "to call." Hence he concludes that the correct etymological explanation is "one who is called (by God), and who has a vocation (from God)."

On the other hand, Eduard König takes the word in an active sense and translates it "speaker."[9] He adduces four reasons for this translation. First of all, he correctly points out that the form *qatil* need not necessarily have a passive connotation. Secondly, he endeavors to show that *nabhi* itself is not passive. Thirdly, in a number of passages, *nabhi* is practically a synonym for "mouth." Lastly, König thinks that there is no force in the argument that the Hebrew verb *nb'* is derived from the noun *nabhi*. He appeals to other Hebrew nouns, whose roots appear in Arabic or Babylonian but not in Hebrew.

In all of this learned discussion, however, there is too much uncertainty. To the present writer, it does not seem possible to ascertain the precise significance of the word *nabhi* upon philological grounds alone. The root *nb'* which appears in the Hebrew Bible is almost certainly derived itself from the noun *nabhi*.[10] It is apparently denominative, and the root from which the noun *nabhi* itself is derived does not appear in the Bible. To seek to derive the word from either a Babylonian or an Arabic root, therefore, is very difficult, and attempts along this line do not seem to have been successful.[11]

A Spokesman for God

If we are to arrive at a proper conception of the function of the *nabhi*, we must look elsewhere than to philology. We must examine the actual usage of the word in the Old Testament, and from such usage seek to determine what it meant. In Deuteronomy 18:18b the essential nature of the prophetic function is clearly set forth: ". . . and I shall place My words in his mouth, and he will speak unto them all which I command him." Here the function of the prophet is that of declaring the word which God has given. It may be noted also that in this context even the false prophets acted as did the true. Even the false prophets spoke forth a message, and the writer of Deuteronomy presents criteria by means of which the words of false prophets may be distinguished from those of the true. In any case, according to this passage, the man who bears the designation *nabhi* is a man who speaks forth a message.

Precisely this same thought appears also in the classic text, Exodus 7:1 "And the LORD said unto Moses, See! I have set thee (as) God to Pharaoh, and Aaron thy brother will be thy prophet. Thou shalt speak all that which I command thee, and Aaron thy brother shall speak unto Pharaoh, etc." In this passage Aaron clearly appears as the mediator between Moses and Pharaoh. Moses stands in relation to Pharaoh as God to the people, and the message of Moses is given to Pharaoh by means of Aaron. Here again the function of the prophet is that of speaking forth a message which has been received from a superior.

This passage is particularly reinforced by some verses in the fourth chapter of Exodus.[12] Moses has complained about his lack of ability to speak. The Lord then declares that Aaron his brother is coming, and says, "I know that he surely can speak." The entire emphasis, let it be noted, is upon the function of speaking. Then God says: "And thou shalt speak unto him, and thou shalt place the words in his mouth, and I shall be with thy mouth, and with his mouth, and I shall teach you that which ye shall do. And he will speak for thee unto the people; and it shall be that he will become thy mouth (lit., he will be to thee for a mouth), and thou shalt become his God (lit., be to him for a God)" Exodus 4:15, 16. Again Aaron appears as a Mediator between Moses and the people. The words of Moses come to the people by means of Aaron. The *nabhi,* according to this passage, is clearly one who speaks a message for a superior, who in this case, was Moses.

In this connection it will be very instructive to consider the call of Jeremiah. In this call the Lord says: "And thou, thou shalt gird thy loins, and thou shalt arise and thou shalt speak unto them all that which I shall command thee" (Jeremiah 1:17a). The similarity of this language with that of Deuteronomy 18:18 is striking. The function which Jeremiah is to discharge is that of speaking the words which God gives him. It is thus also that the prophet himself understood the call. In verse five, God had declared that even before his birth, Jeremiah had been sanctified and had been set apart to be a *nabhi*. Immediately upon hearing this announcement, Jeremiah cries that he does not know how to speak. Evidently Jeremiah, as soon as he hears that he is to be a *nabhi* thinks of speaking, and complains that he is unable to fulfill the function of a *nabhi*, namely, speaking. To his mind, the word *nabhi* called up immediately the connotation of speaking. Jeremiah was to be a *nabhi*, therefore he would have to engage in speaking, and it was the thought that he would be required to speak that caused him to complain. In his understanding of the function that would be required of him as verse seventeen clearly shows Jeremiah was perfectly correct. In 15:19 this connotation appears again, when the Lord tells Jeremiah that if he does certain things he will be as God's mouth.

In Isaiah 30:2 those who go down to Egypt are condemned, because they have not asked of God's mouth. This striking phrase means simply that God has not been consulted. The mouth of God is of course an anthropomorphic term to express the place where God speaks, and in ancient Israel God spake through the prophets. In other words, to consult the mouth of God is equivalent to consulting the prophets of God. The same thought appears in 1 Kings 8:15 where Solomon blesses the Lord "which spake with his mouth unto David my father." The reference appears to be to the remarkable promise given to David through Nathan the prophet and recorded in 2 Samuel 7. For God to speak with His mouth and to speak through His prophets is the same thing.

The brief survey which we have just given makes it clear that the function of a *nabhi* was to speak a message on behalf of a superior. In the case of Aaron, this superior was Moses, although ultimately, of course, it was God. As far as the prophets were concerned the superior was God Himself. He it was with whom the word to be spoken originated. He placed that word in the mouth of the prophets, and they in turn declared it unto the people. At the two termini we have God and the people. God would speak to the people, and this He did by means of His mouth, the prophets. We conclude, then, that upon the basis of the Old Testament usage, the *nabhi* was a speaker who declared the word that God had given him.

There is one passage in the Old Testament which, at first sight, seems to militate against the connotation of the word *nabhi* which we have adopted. In reality however it does not do so. In Genesis 20:7 Abraham is called a *nabhi* who is to pray for Abimelech, in order that Abimelech may live. Hence, a superficial reading of the verse may give the impression that a *nabhi* is here conceived as one who intercedes for others, but not as one who declares the message of God to others. The superficial reading, however, will give way as soon as one considers the passage more carefully. Abimelech is told to restore Sarah to Abraham who is a *nabhi* and who will pray for Abimelech that he may live. When Abraham is designated a *nabhi,* we are to understand that he is one who may intercede successfully on behalf of others. Being a *nabhi* he stands in a peculiarly close relationship to God. The passage really says nothing one way or another with respect to the function of the *nabhi.* It does not teach that his function is exclusively that of intercession. Indeed, it does not even teach that his function is that of intercession. It merely points out that a *nabhi* is one who can make prevailing intercession with God. It stresses, in other words, the close and intimate relationship which existed between the *nabhi* and God. Its emphasis is not upon the office of prophet, but upon his confidential relation with God. Consequently, legitimate appeal cannot be made to this particular passage as in any sense modifying the force of the word *nabhi* as elsewhere employed.

The Seer

Another word by which the prophets are sometimes designated is the participial form *ro'eh*, which is principally employed as a designation of Samuel. It will be best first of all to consider the contexts in which it is used, and then to discuss its etymology. The most instructive passage is 1 Samuel 9, wherein, according to Hölscher, Samuel is pictured as a seer or man of God who for a reward can give information on all kinds of subjects, even the whereabouts of lost asses.[13] With this evaluation we cannot agree, for in the passage the Seer is first characterized as a man of God. Saul and his servant had set forth in search of the lost asses of Saul's father. In this they had been unsuccessful, and at Saul's suggestion, were about to abandon the search. The servant however pointed out that in the city (evidently a city south west of Bethlehem, the name of which cannot be determined) there was a man of God. The servant does not assert that the man of God lived in the city, but merely that he was then present in the city. Of this man of God the servant had heard, for he went on to say that he was an honorable man. More than that, he looked upon Samuel as a prophet, for he immediately stresses the principal function of Samuel, ". . . all that which he speaketh will surely come to pass." The language is obviously reminiscent of Deuteronomy 18:22. It is, in other words, the prophetic function of Samuel which stands uppermost in the servant's mind. It is not the manner in which Samuel receives his messages, and it is certainly not clairvoyancy which looms first in the servant's words, but, it is the fact that Samuel is one who successfully performs the tasks of a prophet. What the servant is describing is simply the function of a *nabhi*.

Upon hearing this news Saul is hesitant, for he has nothing to give the man of God. It is wrong to conclude from this statement that, unless a present were given, the man would not reveal the will of God.[14] The present was probably a token, although it may be that Samuel did in part depend upon such presents for his livelihood. The servant announces that he has the fourth part of a shekel, a small coin containing about sixty particles of silver. Saul and the servant then set off toward the city, and are told that Samuel will bless the sacrifice at the high place. When Saul meets Samuel, he is invited to Samuel's house to eat with him. On the next day, as Samuel prepared to send Saul away, he accompanied him to the end of the city, and there, alone, commanded Saul to stand still that he might cause him to hear the word of the Lord.

In this entire passage, the function of Samuel is that of a *nabhi*. That which Samuel does is to declare the word of God, and this is in perfect harmony with the fact that earlier Samuel had been called a *nabhi*. In verse nine there is a parenthetical remark of the utmost importance. The verse reads: "Before in Israel a man would speak thus when he went to seek God, Come, let us go unto the *ro'eh* (Seer), for the *nabhi* (Prophet) of today was formerly called the *ro'eh* (Seer)." The general sense of this explanatory note seems to be that at the time when the book of Samuel was written the man of God was called a prophet, but in former times, namely, at the time of Saul, the prophet was called a seer. Hence, when a man wished to enquire of God in those days, he would say, "Come, and let us go unto the Seer."[15]

In the Septuagint, a different reading appears. "And formerly in Israel, thus spake each man when he went to enquire of God, Come, let us go to the Seer, because the people formerly called the prophet 'The Seer.'" The reading of the Septuagint may easily be explained. It has substituted "the people" for "today." It is not to be preferred above the Hebrew text, and therefore, we shall base our discussion upon the Hebrew rather than the Septuagint.

According to Johnson the note in Samuel, when isolated from the context, is thought to be ambiguous.[16] The reason for this is said to be that it does not make clear that the respective terms indicated two types of individual, whereas, according to the context this was actually the case. There were, thinks Johnson, two types of individual in ancient Israel, the *ro'eh* and the *nabhi*. The distinction between the two was not that the *nabhi* was a mere 'ecstatic,' deriving his knowledge through a temporary stimulus of his mental powers so as to produce a 'vision,' whereas the *ro'eh*, on the other hand, was an interpreter of signs and portents.[17] The *nabhi* in early times at least could be consulted for the sake of oracular guidance. He was a man who was 'seized by the Spirit' and so engaged in frenzied behaviour. This condition was for the most part brought on by artificial stimulation.[18] The early *nabhi* then, belonged to a group. When consulted for information he would obtain Divine guidance by entering an abnormal condition which for the most part he himself would bring on. The *ro'eh* also might be consulted; for he was a man whose information came to him through visual and auditory experiences.

Thus, Johnson makes a distinction between the early *nabhi* and the *ro'eh*. The passage in Samuel, he thinks, does not imply that the *ro'eh*, as a type, had disappeared at the time when the passage was written; it merely shows that Samuel is no longer a *ro'eh* but a *nabhi*.[19]

For our part we are unable to see that the passage in I Samuel 9, although it employs the two words, yet makes a distinction between two types of men of God. Certainly it would be wrong to say that the expression *nabhi* was taken up into the Hebrew language only after this time. For it should be noted that, in this very context (I Samuel 10:5) Samuel himself uses the word. Further, the expression occurs in the Pentateuch in passages which are earlier than the present one. The key to the difficulty has been pointed out by König, although it is not necessary to follow him in his preference of the Septuagint over the Hebrew.[20] It is that *ro'eh* was the prevailing popular designation of a man of God. When Saul, an ordinary country lad, met the maidens coming to draw water, he enquired of them as to the presence of the *ro'eh*. In Saul's days people used such a designation to indicate the prophet. The technical name of the man of God was *nabhi,* but the people commonly spoke of him as *ro'eh*. Hence, all this passage teaches is that the man of God, the *nabhi,* was popularly designated as the *ro'eh.* At any rate, and what is of importance for our present purpose, the function of the *ro'eh* is the same as that of a *nabhi.* He is a man who declares the word of God.

There is one other passage in the Old Testament which casts some light upon the work of the *ro'eh.* In Isaiah 30:9, 10 we read:

For, it is a people of rebellion, deceitful sons,
Sons who are not willing to hear the Law of the LORD;
Who say to the Seers, 'Ye shall not see,'
And to the Beholders, 'Ye shall not observe for us right things:
Speak for us smooth things,
Behold deceitful things.'

In these verses the *ro'eh* and the *hozeh* are addressed by the deceitful people as those who declare messages. The seers are commanded not to see, that is, not to see as they had been doing, and as a consequent of their having seen, to speak their messages. The function of the seer, according to this passage is to speak the message which has already been received through seeing. As far as function was concerned, it may confidently be asserted, there was no difference between the *ro'eh* and the *nabhi.* Both were spokesmen of God. Both declared the message which had been given to them by a superior, namely, God.

Was there, however, no difference whatsoever? Are the two words to be regarded as precise synonyms? As far as function was concerned there was no difference. Both were men who stood in intimate relation to God, who received their messages from Him, and who declared that message. At the same time, there was a difference, and this difference is merely one of emphasis. The primary connotation of *nabhi,* as far as the context shows, was that of speaking the word of God. On the other hand, the etymology of *ro'eh* is clear, and that etymology casts light upon the word. The expression *ro'eh* is a participial form of the root *ra'ah,* which means simply *to see.* Hence the *ro'eh* was one who saw the revelation which God

granted to him. Whether this act of seeing consisted of supernatural insight or understanding and thus a metaphorical use
of the word is involved or whether it lay in a particular mode
of "seeing" the revelation of God, is not our immediate concern. What is important for us now is to stress the fact that
the word has primary reference to the prophet's relation to
God. Herein lies the difference. The word *nabhi* stresses the
active work of the prophet, in speaking forth the message from
God. The word *ro'eh*, on the other hand, brings to the fore
the experience by means of which the prophet was made to
"see" that message. One word lays emphasis upon the prophet's relation to the people; the other upon his relation to God.
Both however, may refer to the same individual, and the function of that individual, whether he be designated by one word
or by the other, was to declare the message which God had
given to him.

The prophet was also upon occasion designated by the word
hozeh. As may be seen from Isaiah 30:9, 10 the *ro'eh* and the
hozeh performed similar functions, and the two words were
practically synonyms. Like the *ro'eh*, the *hozeh* also was to
declare the message of God. Amos is called a *hozeh,* and this
in a context where he has been declaring the word of God.
Like *ro'eh,* however, this term stresses the reception rather
then the declaration of the prophetic message.

A learned attempt has been made by König to show that
these two terms were not synonyms.[22] König believed that
the root *hazah* was applied only to the false prophets, whereas
ra'ah was restricted to true prophets. Isaiah 30:9, 10 stands
in opposition to this view. Here the two are addressed as men
who have been declaring right things. It is very difficult indeed to see any practical distinction. We must conclude that
the two words were synonyms.[23]

At this point it may be well to sum up the argument of the
chapter. This may be done as follows:

1. The principal word used to designate the prophets was
nabhi. Its precise etymology cannot be ascertained with certainty, but its usage shows that its primary meaning was one
who declared the message which God had given to him.

2. Two other words are also used, namely *ro'eh* and *hozeh,* which are practical synonyms. Both stress the method of receiving revelation, namely, seeing. At the same time, the function of those who are designated by these terms is that of declaring the word of God. The three words, therefore, are used to designate the same individual, namely, the prophet.

What Is "To prophesy"

We have adopted the position that the verb "to prophesy" which occurs in the Old Testament is a denominative; that is, it is derived from the noun "prophet." Before we can conclude our survey of the terms which are employed to designate the prophet, we must pay some attention to this verb.

It will be well to begin with a consideration of the well known passage in Amos. "And Amaziah said unto Amos, Seer! Go, flee thee unto the land of Judah, and eat bread there, and there do thou prophesy (*tinnabhe*). But at Bethel, do not thou any-more prophesy (*lᵉhinnabhe*), for it is the sanctuary of the king and it is the house of the kingdom. And Amos answered and said unto Amaziah, I was not a prophet, nor was I the son of a prophet, but a herdman and a dresser of sycamore trees. And the Lord took me from following after the flock, and the Lord said unto me, Go! prophesy unto My people Israel."[24]

The translation just given, which is essentially the same as that found in the Revised Version, has been rejected by many modern scholars. They believe that it is incorrect to translate the reply of Amos by the past tense, and instead would render, "I am not a prophet (*nabhi*) nor am I the son of a prophet." There is a reason for this preference of the present over the past. According to many scholars, Amos at this point is refusing to be classed among those who can be called *nabhi.* Heschel may be taken as a representative of this position.[25] According to him the *nabhi* was a man who through the influence of a higher power was enabled to speak in tongues and to utter meaningless expressions. The later prophets, such as Amos, are to be sharply differentiated from him, and hence Amos is strongly repudiat-ing the idea that he belongs to such a group. Others have given slightly different reasons for Amos' repudiation, but whatever the reason given, considerable unanimity does appear in claiming that Amos is denying that he is a *nabhi*.

Upon the basis of grammar and syntax alone, it is impossible to decide whether the present or the past is to be preferred in translation. Each is permissible. The question must be decided upon the basis of other grounds, namely, the context.

The modern interpretation may be paraphrased as follows: "I am not a prophet, nor am I the son of a prophet. I am something else. The Lord however took me away from my former occupation and commanded me to act as a prophet. Hence, although I am not a prophet (*nabhi*) I am acting as a prophet (*leⁿhinnabhe*)." Rowley's remarks are perfectly in order: "It would certainly be surprising if one should protest that he was not a poet, but only a writer of poetry."[26] Amos was acting so much like a *nabhi* that Amaziah actually thought he was one. And Amos himself in describing his call, uses the same root. He is conscious that he has been called to act like a *nabhi*. We must therefore, if we are properly to understand the reply of Amos, adopt the past in preference to the present.

If we do adopt the past, we find ourselves in the presence of a passage that is rich with meaning. The initiative had been taken by the priest Amaziah who had complained to Jeroboam that the land could not bear all the words of Amos. This is interesting, for according to this complaint, Amos had not been acting as an ecstatic, but had been preaching. He had been performing the very task and function of the *nabhi;* he had been speaking forth words on behalf of a superior. Amaziah even quotes some of Amos' message. It does not sound like the message of a man in frenzied condition, but rather is a sober warning of judgment to come.

Amaziah identifies Amos as a seer (*hozeh*), and then insinuates that Amos is prophesying in order to support himself. "Amos has been uttering words of doom," declares Amaziah in effect. "He must stop doing this. Amos! go to Judah and earn your living there. Prophesy there, but do not prophesy here." Now it is obvious that what Amaziah understood by the word "prophesy" (*tinnabhe'*), was the very act of proclaiming the message of doom. It was in uttering his prophecy of the impending exile that Amos, in the eyes of Amaziah, had acted as a *nabhi*.

Amos is in perfect agreement with this understanding of the term. In his rejection of the fact that he was not always a prophet and that he was not of prophetical descent, there may possibly be implied a criticism of some of the prophets of the time. At any rate, whether this criticism is implied or not, Amos is determined to make it clear that he was not always a prophet. He was following some other occupation when the Lord took him and commanded him to go and to prophesy. Since this was the case, Amaziah was to listen while Amos declared the word of the Lord. The very context reveals Amos as a speaker for God, engaged in the act of prophesying. From this brief survey therefore, we conclude that the denominative verb, based upon the root *nb'* has, as its basic meaning, *to act as a prophet*.

That this is the case may be seen from an examination of many passages in which the verb occurs. Thus, for example, in Ezekiel 37:4 the Lord says to Ezekiel: "Prophesy (*hinnabhe'*) unto these bones, and thou shalt say unto them, oh! ye dry bones, hear the word of the Lord." Here it may be clearly seen that prophesying and declaring the word of the Lord are one and the same thing. In verse seven Ezekiel continues, "And, I prophesied even as I was commanded," and this language is reminiscent of Deuteronomy 18:18b.

There are some places, however, where this primary connotation does not appear, and to these we must now pay brief attention. The first passage which calls for comment is Numbers 11:24-26. Moses had gathered the seventy elders about the Tent: "And the Lord came down in the cloud, and He spake unto him, and He set apart of the Spirit that was upon him, and He set it upon the seventy elders, and it came to pass that, as the Spirit rested upon them, that they prophesied and they did not add." Two of the men, Eldad and Medad, remained in the camp and they also prophesied (*wayyithnabb'u*).

When this was told to Moses, he cried: "Would that all the Lord's people were prophets, and that He would put His Spirit upon them."

From the context it is clear that in this case, whatever the exact nature of "prophesying" was, it was not proclaiming the message of a superior. For, in reporting the affair to Moses, the young man employed a participial form (*mithnabb'im*), which implies continuous action. "Eldad and Medad," we may paraphrase, "are now engaged in prophesying in the camp." For some reason these two, although they had been conscripted, remained behind in the camp, and there prophesied. It is very difficult to see how their actions can be equated with preaching.

What then, was the nature of the prophesying? To answer this question we must consider carefully all that the text says. For one thing Moses is here presented in distinction from the others as a man who possesses the Spirit. God withdrew or set apart of His Spirit which rested upon Moses, and set His Spirit upon the seventy elders. This was not for the purpose of rebuking Moses, nor does the action in any sense signify a diminution of the Spirit as possessed by Moses. It was rather, as Dillmann has observed, an impartation of the Spirit in the best sense of the word. In order that the seventy might work with Moses in one spirit and purpose, they were equipped with the same Spirit which had filled him.

When the Spirit thus rested upon them they began to prophesy. The act of prophesying, then, is the direct result of the impartation of the Spirit. According to Heinisch this was a state of ecstatic rapture.[27] Such rapture, however, must have assumed some outward expression, and possibly we are to understand that the seventy spake in an elevated state of mind, perhaps giving utterance in tongues, as was the case at Pentecost, when the Spirit of God came upon men. The seventy did not add; that is they did not repeat the prophesying further.

Upon Eldad and Medad who had remained in the camp, the Spirit also rested, and they prophesied in the camp. When Joshua heard of this he was jealous of Moses' prerogatives and objected. Moses, however, rebuked such jealousy and rejoiced in the manifestation of the Spirit's presence, for he saw in it a token to all the nation that God has given them His Spirit to be his helpers. In this fact Moses delights, and he wishes that all the people of the Lord were prophets (*nebhi'im*). Moses, then, denominates prophets those who are acting as are the seventy. From this we learn that in certain cases, the word *nabhi* might have a wider connotation than that of declaring a message for God. At least in this passage it (and its denominative verb) may indicate those who are engaged in abnormal behaviour.

Very instructive for our present purpose is the tenth chapter of First Samuel. Samuel tells Saul that when he comes to the garrison of the Philistines, he will meet a company of prophets, and they will prophesy (verse five). At the place where the conquerors of the land, the Philistines, had set up their military posts, the Spirit of God would come upon Saul to endue him for his office. Saul would meet a band of prophets, preceded by musicians playing upon various instruments. As they were coming down, the prophets would be prophesying (*mithnabb'im*). The act of prophesying, in other words, would be engaged in as the prophets were coming down from the high place. Surely one cannot conceive of "prophesying" in this context, as an act of preaching. It is difficult to perceive the relationship between the instruments of music and the act of prophesying. It may be that the presence of the musical instruments and the playing upon them brought upon the prophets the ability to prophesy. More likely, however, the actual act of prophesying took some form of singing or ecstatic utterance.

It was announced to Saul that the Spirit of the Lord would rush upon him and he would prophesy with the band. The meaning is perfectly clear. Saul's prophesying would not be the result of mere enthusiastic contagion; rather, God's Spirit would rush upon Saul as He had upon the band of prophets. Saul, therefore, would prophesy as did these others. Further, he would be changed to another man, so that, while he prophesied, he would be as one whose whole heart was filled with devotion to God. A temporary change would be effected, and during this change Saul would prophesy. The change and the resultant actions would be so marked that they could be designated by the phrase "these signs." The phrase reminds one of the signs which Moses employed when he went to speak with Pharaoh (Exodus 4:8). The phrase further casts some light upon the nature or manifestation of the change which would take place within Saul. It would not be merely a proclaiming of a message in which Saul would be engaged; rather, it would be behaviour which might justly be called abnormal. Saul would act in such a way, whether through ecstatic utterances, cries, songs or even bodily behaviour, that those who saw him would regard him as a prophet.

The prophecy (and we may notice that Samuel was engaged in speaking forth the word of God) of Samuel came to pass, for we read: "And it came to pass that when he turned his shoulder to go from the presence of Samuel, that God changed to him another heart; and all these signs came to pass on that day" (I Samuel 10:9). Saul did, as a matter of fact, meet a band of prophets, and the Spirit of God (not 'Lord,' as in verse six) rushed upon him, and he prophesied in their midst. Those who knew him saw that with the prophets he also prophesied (*nibba'*); and so there arose the proverb, "Is Saul also among the prophets?"

It is not our purpose at this present juncture to discuss further the interpretation of the passage. Suffice it to say that the very existence of the proverb concerning Saul points to the fact that Saul had been doing something more than preaching. Hence, even this brief survey has been sufficient to make it clear that when Saul prophesied in the midst of the prophets, he was engaging in some form of abnormal behaviour. For our present purpose, that is sufficient to know.

Some attention must also be given to I Samuel 18:10. We may translate as follows: "And it came to pass on the morrow that an evil spirit of God rushed upon Saul, and he prophesied in the midst of the house, and David was playing with his hand, as day by day, and the spear was in the hand of Saul."

In the first place it may be noted that not the Spirit of God but an evil spirit came upon Saul. This was a higher evil power, to be distinguished from the Spirit of God. It was indeed from God, sent upon Saul as a punishment, to induce in the mind of Saul feelings of jealousy and despondency, so that Saul's actions became those of a raving madman.

This evil spirit, then, was from God, and in God's strange providence, was permitted to rush upon Saul. The resulting madness of the king proceeded from the righteous vengeance of God and was a punishment of the king's sins. When this evil spirit came upon him Saul prophesied and cast the javelin at David. What is meant, however, by the statement that Saul prophesied? The meaning must be that Saul acted as a *nabhi;* that is, he acted as one upon whom a higher power had come, and who was, in word and action, under the control of that higher power. Saul was not, of course, truly acting as a *nabhi;* he was merely in an outward sense appearing to do so. Certain symptoms which characterized the "prophet" appeared also in the actions or behaviour of a madman, but it would be most unjust to appeal to a passage such as this to show that a *nabhi* always behaved as did a madman.

At the same time the passage does teach that one who acted as a *nabhi* might engage in strange, even frantic, behaviour. Saul became a raving man who seemed to lose control of himself. In his case the frenzy had an evil turn for he cast his javelin at David in an effort to kill. In the case of true prophets, such evil action would of course not follow, even though they too might at times act as mad men. From all this we learn that the verb "to prophesy" might be applied to one who acted in a raving manner.

A further passage in I Samuel relates that when Saul sent messengers to take David, they saw a band of prophets engaged in prophesying (*nibbe'im*), and Samuel was standing at their head. The Spirit of God then came upon Saul's messengers and they also prophesied. Whereupon Saul sent other messengers, and they too prophesied. A third time Saul sent messengers, and they did likewise. From this we see that when the Spirit of God came upon a man He controled that man. The Spirit came upon these messengers in order to prevent them from carrying out their task of taking David. While the Spirit was upon them they were compelled to prophesy, and could not go about their normal business.

Saul, therefore, set out himself to find Samuel and David. He went toward Naioth in Ramah, and the Spirit of God came also upon him as He had upon the other prophets, and Saul continued on his way, prophesying as he journeyed. Saul then took off his garments and prophesied before Samuel, falling down naked all that day and night. Hence this episode was used as a basis for the proverb, "Is Saul also among the prophets?" (1 Samuel 19:24).[28]

In this account we may note that Saul's lying naked was probably an act of his alone and not of the messengers and prophets. The words "he also" are not repeated in the description of the act. Saul is distinguished from the others by lying in an ecstatic condition. He had most bitterly opposed David and had throughout his reign been disobedient. Now he is singled out, and the Spirit of God comes upon him in mighty power. The messengers had been halted in their attempt to seize David, and they were turned into men who prophesied. Upon Saul, however, the Spirit comes in peculiarly compelling force. It is an opportunity given to the rebellious king to repent and turn to God. The overpowering influence of the Spirit of God left Saul without excuse. Saul had been the enemy of the theocracy, even though he was king. He had been disobedient. The grace of God was manifested to him in order that he might repent. This however he would not do.

Like the other passages which we have been considering, this one also makes it clear that the verb "to prophesy" may be used to characterize strange behaviour. In this instance attention is directed particularly to Saul, who stripped off his garments and fell down naked. Whatever the nature of the state which was thus brought upon Saul, it was an abnormal one, and this condition of abnormality was at times a charac-

teristic of those who were called "prophets" and who "prophesied."

That the term "to prophesy" had a wide extension of usage
may be seen from the fact that it was applied to the frenzied
action of the prophets of Baal upon Mt. Carmel. After describing how these prophets were cutting themselves "after
their manner" until they drew blood, the sacred writer continues, "And it came to pass when the noon had passed, that
they prophesied until the offering of the *minhah*" (I Kings
18:29a). Here it would seem as though the act of prophesying
and that of cutting themselves was identical. At any rate there
seems to be no doubt that the prophesying here mentioned
involved frenzied action. And it is of interest to note that in
this instance the word is applied, not to prophets of Jehovah,
but to those of Baal.

It is difficult to tell the precise significance of the term
"prophesy" as applied to those who prophesied before the two
kings in I Kings 22:10. The participial form is used, which
would indicate continuous action. At the same time Zedekiah
delivers a message to the kings in the name of the Lord. And
in verse twelve we read: "And all the prophets were prophesying (*nibbe'im*), thus saying." Perhaps there is nothing of
the abnormal in their actions, and the main emphasis is rather
to be placed upon the fact that they spake messages to the kings.

The term *nibbe'im* is also used to describe those who played
upon musical instruments in the worship of God. David is
said to have separated those who prophesied with various
musical instruments, and certain ones are mentioned who thus
prophesied. It is difficult to give to the term in this instance
its precise significance. Does it indicate that the musicians
were overpowered by the Divine Spirit and so under His
compulsion played for God's glory and praise? Or, is the
thought rather that in "prophesying" with musical instruments, the players were telling forth the praises of God? In
all probability the first alternative is correct but it is not clear
that the latter should be excluded entirely. At any rate, the
term is not employed in a technical sense, and the passage is

illuminating in that it permits one to see how widely the concept might be held.

In this connection one more passage calls for mention. In Jeremiah 29:26 we read, "for every man that is mad and that acts as a prophet" (*mithnabbe'*). What is here of interest is the fact that the acting as a prophet and the being mad are practically equated. And it should be noted that Jeremiah is mentioned as one that acts as a prophet. Abnormal behaviour, or at least, what men called abnormal behaviour, did at times characterize the prophets, not only the early bands, but also a man like Jeremiah.

We may bring this chapter to its conclusion with a brief summary of the results attained. We have confined our investigation so far to a consideration of the principal technical terms which are employed in the Old Testament as a designation of the prophets. From these terms we learn that a prophet was a man into whose mouth God placed His message and who in turn delivered that message. He was, in other words an accredited speaker for God. Sometimes he was called a Seer, and while this term in itself stressed the manner of reception of the prophetic message, it nevertheless designated one whose function was to proclaim the message of God.

From a consideration of the denominative verb "to prophesy" we learn that behaviour, which to us seems abnormal, was at times characteristic of the prophets. This was the case particularly in the time of Samuel and in connection with the bands of prophets. It applied also, however, to Jeremiah. All in all, it was a secondary connotation. Primarily, the prophet was one who spoke in the Name of the Lord. It was an institution of such men that God in grace established to convey His message to Israel.

CHAPTER IV

Prophecy and the Theocracy

IF what we have been saying in the previous pages is correct, the prophetic institution was raised up of God to serve as a protective against the abominations of Canaan. The prophets were under Moses, and their function consisted in declaring the Word which God had given unto them. It is necessary, however, to enquire more precisely into the position which prophetism occupied in the history of revelation. Were prophets to be found throughout the entire course of Israel's history, or did the institution as such represent a particular stage or period in the history of God's revelation?

Attempts have been made, of course, to regard prophecy as simply a more or less natural development, the product of various circumstances. Meek, for example, would attribute the rise of prophecy to times of stress and strain.[1] At the time of the Philistine conquest, he thinks, when Israel was under the yoke of a foreign master, a definite prophetic movement of the *nabhi'* type arose, and not only its origin, but also its later development were largely determined by the conditions which gave it birth. This type of explanation, however, is too facile.[2] There is too much which demands explanation to permit one to rest satisfied with a theory of such character.

In the Scriptures the prophetic movement is as we have seen, regarded as a gift of God. In rebuking the people of his day, Amos relates the goodness of God as it had been manifested to the Israelites. God, he tells the nation, had destroyed the Amorite from before them; He had brought them up out of the land of Egypt and caused them to wander for forty years in the wilderness. He had also raised up the prophets from their sons, and the Nazirites from their young men.[3] The meaning of the passage is very clear. Israel was now in possession of the land. She had not always possessed the land, however. Before she entered it, there were present the Amorites who stood in the way of her possession. By her own strength she could not have taken the land, but God destroyed the Amorites before her. He, in other words, removed the obstacle which stood in the way of Israel's occupation of Canaan. More than that, He had been with the nation during her forty years of wandering in the wilderness. She had been in His care, and He had nourished and protected her, that she perish not in a waste and wilderness. From the condition of bondage in which she had once been in Egypt, God had set her free. The deliverance, then, from its inception to its completion, was the work of God. Not by might nor by power did Israel leave Egypt and come into possession of Canaan. Her history was a history of grace. God had ever been with her.

In addition to the deliverance and the possession, God had done something else. He had given to Israel the gift of prophecy and of the Nazirites. What is of importance for our present purpose is to notice the relationship in which, according to Amos, prophecy stands to deliverance. The first great gift of God was redemption from the bondage of Egypt and establishment in the promised land. The next great gift is that of prophecy and the Nazirites. The two latter follow upon the first. The gift of prophecy therefore, is regarded as a gift which came after the deliverance from Egypt.

It will be well to understand the grammatical relationship of these verses. A general statement concerning the destruction of the Amorites is first made (verse nine). We are then introduced to a sequence of events, the order of which may perhaps be brought out somewhat as follows. "And I — I brought you up — and then I caused you to go in the desert — and then I raised up from your sons to be prophets." First comes the deliverance from Egypt and the forty years' march in the desert, and subsequent to this the raising up of the prophetic institution. Prophetism was a gift of God which followed upon the heels of the deliverance from Egypt.

It is important that we keep this relationship clearly in mind. The exodus formed the foundation for a number of events and for their accompanying explanatory revelation. It set the stage for the establishment of the theocracy and the necessary revelation which would explain the nature of that theocracy. Saving events, while themselves revelatory and accompanied by special revelation, at the same time are thus followed by new waves of revelation. And the great influx of new revelation which followed the exodus was prophetism. Thus, Mosaism, the religion of redemption, gives way to Prophetism, the religion of redemption's outworking in the life of the nation.

In saying that saving events give rise to new waves of revelation, we do not mean that saving events are not in themselves also revelatory. It is perfectly true that God's mighty miracles in Egypt, for example, were wondrous displays of His power and majesty which left all who beheld them without excuse in not acknowledging Him to be the true God. At the same time, it is necessary to insist, particularly in the light of present day emphases, that God's saving acts were also accompanied by special revelation. Eichrodt, for example, lays stress upon the character of revelation as consisting in acts.[4] Well and good; but when he goes on to contrast this with God's self disclosure as conceived speculatively or offered in the form of dogma, we have our questions. Acts in themselves, although they must be to a certain extent revelatory, do not give a very full revelation unless accompanied by explanation. Hence, we cannot for a moment regard God's self-disclosure as limited to His saving acts. God did communicate to man certain information concerning His being and ways, and this objective body of communicated knowledge formed the basis or material for thought and for doctrinal formulation.

We are living in a day when the word "revelation," like other good words, has had its meaning lifted from it. There was a time when the word had very definite connotations. Revelation meant the communication of information from God to man, such as man by his own unaided efforts could not attain or discover. Now, however, the word has lost this high meaning, and it seems to be employed merely to signify an enrichment of man's knowledge, which has somehow come to man in the course of natural development. Man may attain unto this new knowledge it would seem, merely by way of reaction to certain circumstances which have caused him to view things in a new and different light. Very little is said today however about revelation as the actual communication of information to the mind of man by God in a special, direct way.

If we are at all to do justice to the representations of the Old Testament we cannot be satisfied with the modern view of the word "revelation." Indeed, one of the greatest services that anyone can render the modern Church is to rescue the vocabulary of revealed religion from the eviscerating process to which such terminology has been subject for a good many years. One of the crying needs of the Church is for a rehabilitation of her glorious terminology.

With respect to the word "revelation," then, we would do more than pay lip service. We wish to give to that word all the high honor and wealth of meaning which it has enjoyed during the long centuries of the Church's existence. We regard the prophetic movement, therefore, as an explanatory revelation (or explanation) which God gave to Israel, both to follow the exodus and to accompany the theocracy.

If this conception of prophetism be correct, we may note that it does not necessarily exclude the existence of prophets before the time of the theocracy. Abraham was a prophet, and Miriam and Deborah were prophetesses. At the same time the institution as such is to be looked upon as an accompaniment of the theocracy. It is thus that Peter apparently regards it, when he says: "Yea, and all the prophets from Samuel and those that follow after, as many as have spoken, have likewise foretold of these days" (Acts 3:24).

The Theocracy

In order therefore to understand more clearly the position of prophetism, it will be necessary to give brief consideration to the nature and purpose of the theocracy. At the time of the deliverance from Egypt it was announced to Israel that she was to become a kingdom of priests. In the book of Deuteronomy the king himself had been promised.[5] These promises, however, were not to find their realization until the nation was settled in its land.

Under the leadership of Joshua, the nation engaged in aggression in an effort to obtain possession of Canaan. The period of the Judges found the people in the land, but sorely divided. This was a time of confusion, when every man did that which was right in his own eyes. Geographical barriers separated the people, and the religion of the Canaanites offered a serious rival to the claims of the pure worship of Jehovah. Thus, longings and aspirations after a king would be awakened.

At the time of Samuel the people asked for a king, and Samuel regarded their request as tantamount to a rejection of the Lord. It has sometimes been thought that this action is inexplicable in the light of the clear promise of the king in Deuteronomy. Hence, the conclusion has been drawn that if Deuteronomy had actually been in existence at the time of Samuel, he would not have acted as he did. This, however, by no means follows. It is not to be expected that the people, in asking for a king, would make an appeal to the written law. For one thing, peoples in their daily lives, apparently settled their disputes and difficulties without reference to any written law. Furthermore, this particular people had no desire to be obedient to any law. They wished merely for a king, that they might be like the nations round about them. It is quite probable that such people would be without knowledge of the provisions of their law.

What, however, shall we say about Samuel? Why did not he act in accordance with the promise in Deuteronomy? The answer, we think, is that he disapproved of the untheocratic spirit in which the nation made request for its king. Even if he were completely aware of the prophecy of Deuteronomy he might very well have thought that, in the light of the manner in which the demand was made, the proper time had not yet come for the people to have a king. Surely, there is nothing in the attitude or actions of Samuel which will support the view that the book of Deuteronomy had not yet been written. It might even be added that, assuming Samuel to have acted in complete ignorance of the provisions of Deuteronomy, it does not at all follow that the book was not in existence at that time. One might as well argue that, in the light of the almost total absence of any teaching of the doctrine of justification by faith alone during the Middle Ages, the New Testament, which so clearly expounds that doctrine, was not then in existence, but was only written at the time of the Reformation.

At any rate, a king was given. By means of a Divine revelation Samuel was commanded to hearken unto the people's voice, yet at the same time to show to them the kind of ruler that they would have. For a time an evil king reigned. Saul was a man whose heart was ever far from the Lord. There is no evidence in the Bible that he was a regenerate man. His beginning seemed to be propitious, but he soon showed how little concern he had for the true welfare of a theocracy. By his life the people were taught what the king should not be, and were ready for the reception of a ruler after God's own heart. The preparation was therefore two-fold in nature. First was a period without a king, and so the necessity for centralized authority was inculcated in the nation's mind. Secondly, by the presence of the wrong kind of leader, the nation came to realize the need for a man after the heart of Jehovah.

In asking for a king, the nation desired merely to be like the peoples round about. In their question there is revealed a profound misunderstanding of the very nature of the theocracy, for Israel, above all else, was to be different from the nations round about. In the nations of antiquity the rulers were despots, who ruled very largely for their own advantage and glory. The man on the throne of Israel, however, was to be a type of the greater king to come. He was to be a man who would execute justice and righteousness in the Name of the Lord of hosts. He would call attention, not to himself, but to God. In the true theocracy, mercy and justice would meet each other, and righteousness and peace would kiss one another. The power of human might would not be depended upon, for the Lord Himself was the true king.

The prophetic institution as such may be regarded as the guardian of this theocracy. The prophets were to build upon the foundation of the Mosaic Law, and to expound that law unto the nation. They would thus be the preservers and defenders of the principles upon which the theocracy had been founded by God. Their work in one sense was to supplement that of the king and the priests. It would be difficult to conceive of a more profound misunderstanding of the nature of the prophetic institution than that of Wellhausen, William Robertson Smith and others of their school, who sought to make a cleavage between the priests and the prophets. The theocractic kingdom, and all that it involved, was dear to the hearts of the prophets.

It is for this reason that the prophets so often appear in the presence of the rulers. It would sometimes seem as though they were primarily sent to kings. For through the king they might the best influence the welfare of the nation. Hence, also, their closeness to the priest.

It would be a grave mistake, however, to assume that, because of the great interest of the prophets in the monarchy, they were themselves primarily politicians. Their political activity is always subservient to a religious end. They did serve as the counsellors, but they did so in order that the theocratic kingdom might prosper.

Thus, God very graciously granted to His people a continuous, accompanying revelation, which would endure side by side with the theocracy. In all its many vicissitudes the theocratic people might hear the Word of the Lord through the prophets, and when finally the theocracy of the Old Testament disappeared, never again to be restored, and the period of the Old Testament passed into the inter-testamental days, the gift of prophecy ceased, and the voice of heaven was silenced, until in the fulness of time God spoke to the world in His Son.

CHAPTER V

The Schools of the Prophets

A FTER Samuel had anointed Saul, he announced to him that when Saul came to the hill of God where the garrison of the Philistines was, he would meet a company of prophets coming down from the high place. In several passages in both the books of Samuel and Kings we read of bands of prophets or sons of the prophets. What is the meaning of these terms?

For a proper understanding of the question it is necessary to recall that even in the time of Moses the seventy elders received of the Spirit which was upon him. The nation had complained, and Moses gave utterance to the thought that the office which had been placed upon his shoulders was too heavy for one man to bear (Numbers 11:14). In response to this utterance upon the part of His servant, the Lord commanded seventy elders to be chosen in order that Moses might be assisted in his task. He then withdrew (a part) of the Spirit which was upon Moses, and He set (of the Spirit) upon the elders (Numbers 11:25). This does not mean that Moses was somehow singled out for disgrace or condemnation, nor does it mean that the portion of the Spirit which had been upon Moses was diminished. Rather, as Theodoret so accurately expresses it, "Just as a person who kindles a thousand flames from one, does not lessen the first, whilst he communicates light to the others, so God did not diminish the grace imparted to Moses by the fact that He communicated of it to the seventy."[1]

At the same time, although this statement accurately sets forth the essential idea, nevertheless, there is a danger in the use of such illustrations. The Spirit of God is not a flame of fire. The Spirit of God is the Spirit who gives life, and even in the Old Testament is conceived as a Person. There is, therefore, in the usage of the expression, "God imparted of His Spirit," an element of mystery. We cannot comprehend how God did this. At the same time we are to understand, if we would be faithful to the meaning of the text, that the Spirit of God rested upon Moses, just as He had done before, and that, in lesser degree, He also rested upon the seventy. The Spirit who rested upon the seventy had previously rested upon Moses alone.

There was no increase of the Spirit upon Moses, for that was not necessary. The Spirit still abode or rested upon him sufficiently that he might carry out his tasks, and what was needed was not an increase of this Spirit upon Moses, but rather the assistance of men upon whom the Spirit likewise rested. When the Spirit came upon the elders, they prophesied, and the whole scene would convince Moses and the nation that these men were now suitably endued for the accomplishment of the tasks which lay before them.

When the period of the Judges had come to its close, or at least was entering the shadows of night, Samuel stood forth almost alone. He was a true prophet of the Lord (I Samuel 3:19-21) and served in the crucial period between the close of the Judges and the first beginnings of the monarchy. It may well be expected that there would be others, perhaps of lesser stature than Samuel upon whom the Spirit of the Lord would also come.

It is thus that we are to understand the groups who are sometimes designated bands of prophets or "sons of the prophets." Concerning these groups much has been written, and all too often insufficient care has been given to that which is actually stated in the Scripture. Thus, when Meek would compare the early Hebrew prophets with oracles of the shamanistic type,[2] or when Pedersen describes the prophets whom Saul met as raving ecstatically,[3] we believe that they have not given sufficient heed to the text. In our study of the question we shall seek to make a careful examination of the Scripture.

Only so can we hope to arrive at a proper understanding of the question.

Saul and the Prophets

It was told to Saul that when he came to the hill of God he would encounter (*paga'*) a band of prophets. We may note that the word *nabhi* is here employed, and there is no reason for assuming that the word as it stands here has a different connotation from that which it bears elsewhere. The prophets are together, and hence are designated as a band (*hebhel*). The word is an interesting one. It usually signifies a cord or line, but in the present passage may be suitably rendered as "company" or "band." As far as the word itself is concerned, we learn nothing as to the nature of this band. Whether there was a formal organization or merely a loosely-knit group, the word does not permit us to know. Perhaps we shall not be far wrong if we simply take the passage as teaching that Saul was to meet a company of prophets. If we are to learn anything about the nature of that company, we must do so from considerations other than that of the designation itself.

The prophets are described as descending from the high place. We are not told why they were descending, and there is certainly no point in concluding that there was at the high place the seat of a school of the prophets. Possibly they had been to Gibeah upon pilgrimage. They were accompanied by musical instruments, and this may have been indicative of a festal procession. However, we cannot be sure. We do not know why they had been upon the high place, nor why they were at this particular time descending.

Before the prophets there were musical instruments, and the prophets were "playing the part of a *nabhi*." According to some scholars, we have here a case of ecstasy, and this ecstasy was induced by the accompanying music. Hölscher, for example, thinks that this is the account of an ecstatic dance or procession, and the accompanying music is said by him to have characterized such processions or dances.[4] Pedersen believes that in these groups there was a definite aim of obtaining the experience of ecstasy, and the prophesying here described is thought by him to have reference to ecstatic raving.[5]

It should be very carefully noted, however, that there is not a hint in the text to suggest that the prophesying was brought on by the music, as though the music were a stimulant. The musical instruments were carried *before* the prophets, and the implication given is that they were employed merely by way of accompaniment. Hence, the prophesying in which these men engaged was not a meaningless raving, but rather a devout praising of God to the accompaniment of music.

If we employ the word "ecstasy" to describe the prophets, we must use the word with care. That they were under the compelling influence of the Spirit of God, there can be no doubt, for it is said to Saul that when he meets the prophets, the Spirit of Jehovah will rush upon him and he will prophesy with them. The fulfillment of this prediction is related as follows: "And the Spirit of God rushed upon him, and he prophesied in their midst" (I Samuel 10:10b). From this it appears that the act of prophesying in this particular instance was a result of the rushing upon of the Spirit. God's Spirit came upon the prophet, and the result was that he prophesied. The source of the "ecstatic" condition, therefore, is not to be found in the presence of music, nor of voluntary association, nor in contagion, nor for that matter in any self-imposed or induced stimuli, but only in the "rushing upon" of the Spirit of God.

It is without a doubt true that when the Spirit of God thus came upon a man, that man was in an abnormal condition. There was resting upon him a Divinely imposed compulsion so that he could not but speak forth and sing the wondrous works of God. To this extent we may agree the prophet was in a state of ecstasy.

To Saul it was also announced that he would be turned into another man (weneh-pak-ta le'ish 'aher). This phenomenon is further described by the statement that God gave to Saul another heart (I Samuel 10:9). It would be a grave mistake to equate this remarkable change with that work of God's Spirit known as regeneration. Regeneration is certainly a work of the Spirit of God, but it involves a whole-souled change. In the work of regeneration the soul that once was dead in trespasses and sins is made alive in Jesus Christ. It was however not this blessing that was here promised to Saul. The change remained, we may say, upon natural ground. There was to be no passing away of old things. The heart, with its sinful, rebellious nature, would remain, and, alas did remain with Saul until his death.

The new heart given to Saul was we believe quite different from the new birth that is given to the sinner by the Holy Spirit. At the same time there was to be an actual change. Saul was to become a different man. It would, however, be a change of degree rather than of kind. Saul was to become a different man, in that he would now have the ability to act as a king should act. He would have a wider vision of the duties that were required of a king, and he would receive the capacity to carry out those duties. He was to be a greater man than before. Narrow limits of life would disappear, and the broad horizons that befitted a kingly perspective would belong to Saul. This was a blessing, and it was the gift of the Spirit, but it remains upon the plane of the unregenerate. It is quite a different heart from that which is mentioned, for example, in Ezekiel 36:26.

When Saul came to Gibeah, the band of prophets was there to meet him. The language seems to imply that the prophets were there for the purpose of meeting him (liq-ra-tho). The Spirit of God then rushed upon him, and he prophesied in the midst of the prophets. It was as though Saul had actually become one of the prophets. To the eye of the beholder there would have appeared no difference; "and behold, with prophets he prophesied" (I Samuel 10:11). Whatever the precise nature of this phenomenon may have been, Saul also was partaker of it. He would here at least in no wise have been distinguished from the other prophets. Whatever the nature of the ecstatic inspiration which had come over the other prophets, and under the influence of which they probably gave expression to the overflowing feeling that filled their hearts, it had come also upon Saul. Only we must note carefully that it was not mere contact with the prophets which brought about such inspiration; it was the onrushing of the Spirit of God.

When the people who had known Saul saw him, they asked, "Is Saul also among the prophets?" The very asking of such a question supposes that the previous life of Saul had been quite different. Saul was one of the last whom they might expect to find in the company of prophets. One of those who was present then asked concerning the prophets "And who is their father?" This question has been interpreted in various ways. Probably, however, it is tantamount to asking whether the father of the prophets was also a prophet. In other words, did the gift of prophecy come upon these men by way of inheritance? Was it theirs as a birthright? The questions would imply a negative answer. The prophets did not receive this gift by way of heredity. Rather, it was a free gift of God Who bestows it upon whom He will. Therefore, since the prophets themselves did not thus receive it, must we be surprised that Saul has also received it? If God could freely bestow this gift upon the prophets, could He not also bestow it upon such a one as Saul, who up to this point had shown a disposition alien or at least indifferent to that of the prophets?

The Arresting Power of the Spirit Upon Saul

The second passage to which we must give consideration is I Samuel 19:19-24. Fearing the hand of Saul, David fled and came to Naioth. Word was then brought to Saul, who sent messengers for the express purpose of arresting David. They sought to follow out his bidding, and saw a company of prophets who prophesied, and Samuel was standing as one appointed over them. From this statement it would be precarious to seek to draw too many inferences. The word which expresses Samuel as one appointed over the prophets may have a reflexive force, so that we might translate, "one who had appointed himself." It would be unwarranted, however, to draw from this the conclusion that Samuel himself had established a prophetic group in Ramah. No doubt Samuel stood in relation to this group as a president to a body, but the text itself does not permit us to say this. Nor can we state positively whether Samuel himself was actually engaged in prophesying. All that the text says is that he was standing at the head of the prophets. Precisely what this means, we cannot say.

At any rate, when they had seen the body of prophets, the Spirit of God came upon the messengers of Saul, and they also engaged in prophesying. Here again we must emphasize that it was not contact with the company of prophets which produced the condition of prophesying, but rather the coming upon the messengers of the Spirit of God.

When this was made known to Saul he sent a second group of messengers, and the results were the same, and this was followed by a third group. Saul then determined to go himself. The Spirit of God came also upon him, and as he went, he prophesied until he came to Naioth in Ramah. There is no mention of Saul first meeting the company of prophets and then prophesying. Rather, as Saul was on his journey in quest of David, the Spirit came upon him, and he continued that journey under the compelling influence of the Spirit, prophesying as he went.

It is then stated that even Saul stripped off (way-yiph-shat) his garments, and even he prophesied before Samuel. The implication is that not only the messengers of Saul, but also the prophets themselves had stripped off their garments as they prophesied. The action is expressive of the ecstatic condition in which the prophets were placed by the overcoming power of the Spirit of God. Of Saul alone, however, it is related that he fell down naked all that day and all that night. From this we may rightly infer that in this particular act Saul was alone, and that there is a reason why this was so.

The action of Saul's was not one which commonly came upon those who were in the ecstatic condition. The seizure of the Spirit was more powerful in the case of Saul than in that of the messengers, for Saul had more stubbornly resisted the will of God. Hence, Saul would be compelled to recognize that God was more powerful than he, and that to resist God's will would be folly itself. The overmastering influence which came upon Saul was evidently designed to convince him that he could not struggle against God and so to subdue him and break his hard heart. The action of the king in sending the messengers to apprehend David was really a defiance of God, since Saul had previously experienced the workings upon his heart of the Spirit. His sin therefore, stands out in stronger light, and hence the severity of the measures employed to arrest him and, if possible, prevent his absolute destruction.

As a result of this experience people began to say, "Is Saul also among the prophets?" The origin of this proverb had occurred earlier; now, however, as a result of the present circumstances, it receives a renewed meaning, and is again employed. To the bystander, the strange condition of Saul was like that of the prophets when the Spirit came upon them. For this reason, even though it is not here expressly stated that the prophets fell down naked and lay thus all day and night, it may be assumed that at times this was the case. To the bystander, Saul's condition was reminiscent of the condition which at times came upon the prophets, and for this reason they asked, "Is Saul also among the prophets?"

It will be well at this point to consider what may be learned concerning the companies of prophets during Samuel's time. Since, according to I Samuel 3:1 the Word of God was rare in those days when Samuel was yet a child, we may assume justly that the bands of prophets were not yet in existence. They arose during the lifetime of Samuel, after his childhood. In all probability they owed their origin to him, although the Scripture does not explicitly declare this. There are reasons, however, for believing that Samuel was the human founder of these prophetic bodies. For one thing, the designation employed in I Samuel 19:20, may teach that Samuel was self appointed over the prophets. At any rate, whether this be so or not, he is pictured as the leader of the group. Its direction, at least, was under him. During Samuel's lifetime we may witness the downfall of the sanctuary at Shiloh. The ark of the covenant was taken away by the Philistines, and thus the representation of the very presence of God in the midst of His people was removed. With the fall of the sanctuary and the attendant priesthood, there arose a serious situation. Idolatry and apostasy made their appearance, and there was need for a strong leadership that would protect the rights of the theocratic nation.

It was necessary therefore, that the nation should be brought to a recognition of its apostasy. No one, apparently, stood in a position of such high respect as did Samuel, and it was evidently he who thus brought into being the bodies known as schools of the prophets. Thus an attempt was made to check the declining religious life of the nation and to bring it back to the law of God. We are probably not far wrong if we assume that it was Samuel whom God used in the establishment of these bodies.

Although these groups worked under the direction of Samuel, he probably did not live with them, for in I Samuel 7:17 we are told that he had his own house in Ramah, and this house seems to have become the center of his religious activities. It appears that there was a group of prophets who resided in Ramah, but whether they had common dwellings or not, it is difficult to say. In fact, we are not really justified in asserting that all the prophets lived in Ramah. As for the group mentioned in I Samuel 10, nothing whatever is said about its dwelling place. We cannot therefore conclude that there were two or more distinct groups of prophets, one at Gibeah and one at Ramoth. The Scripture is strangely silent upon this question. It may be that there was a group of prophets which more or less worked under Samuel's direction, in loose organization, and would be with him whenever he needed them. More than that the text does not permit one to say.

One of the spiritual exercises in which such groups engaged was that of prophesying together. They did not meet for the purpose of teaching one another how to prophesy, for prophecy is a gift of God and may be imparted only to those of His choice. At the same time, God did as a matter of fact employ those to be the recipients of this gift who were fitted therefor in mental and spiritual disposition. The prophets were men of like mind. Since they were raised up for the purpose of calling the nation back to repentance, it would seem that they themselves would be students of the Law of God and of His earlier revelations to His people. Indeed, it may be to this source that we are to look for the composers of those parts of the canonical books which we know as the Former Prophets.

The prestige of Samuel evidently proved to be a blessing. Saul never dared, so far as we know, to make an attack upon the body of the prophets, nor does there appear to have been hostility toward them upon the part of the nation itself. As far as we know, they were permitted at this time to carry on their work free from opposition on the part of state or people.

Sons of the Prophets

After the death of Samuel the prophetical bodies seem to have died out, not to reappear until the time of Elijah and Elisha. There was not, as far as is known, any hereditary group or succession of groups during this particular period. No allusion to such groups is found in the Scriptures. At the times of Elijah and Elisha they appear only in the ten northern tribes, and not at all in the southern kingdom. This is indeed strange, if there had been an hereditary succession from the days of Samuel. Furthermore, they now receive a new designation, namely, sons of the prophets. This expression shows that at this time the prophets stood in much closer and more intimate spiritual relation to their spiritual fathers than was the case with the companies who prophesied under the direction of Samuel.

We first learn of a group of prophets during the reign of Ahab. At this time, the worship of the Tyrian Baal had been introduced by Jezebel, and there was great need for the nation to be called back to repentance and to the true God. Only a stern figure such as Elijah could make a sinful people hearken, and in connection with his ministry we find the prophets. Jezebel herself had recognized the power of these groups, for we are told that she had cut off the prophets of the Lord (I Kings 18:4). Obadiah had taken one hundred of the prophets and had hid them in groups of fifty each. When later Obadiah meets Elijah he addresses him as master. Thus it appears that there was a spiritual leadership on the part of Elijah which was recognized by Obadiah.

Not only Obadiah but even King Ahab recognized the leadership of Elijah. Elijah had no hesitation in appearing before the king and commanding him to gather together the prophets of Baal and of the Asherah. That there is a profound difference between the prophets of the Lord, such as Elijah and Obadiah together with the prophets under them on the one hand and the prophets of Baal and the Asherah on the other, hardly needs to be stressed. The entire context makes this difference prominently clear. Consequently, there is no justification for regarding the actions of the Baal prophets as characterizing all prophets or prophetical groups. The difference between the two is essentially a religious one. The prophets of the Lord belonged to Him, and He controlled them as He desired. The prophets of Baal, by means of self imposed exercises, sought to produce the needed stimuli and excitements.

The opposite position has, of course, been maintained and in its support appeal has sometimes been made to I Kings 20:35. In this passage one of the sons of the prophets commands his companion to smite him. Here, it is said, in an example of self wounding in order to bring upon oneself the necessary ecstasy. This conclusion, however, does not follow. For one thing, there is here no instance of a self inflicted wound. Rather, the prophet calls upon his companion to do the smiting. And the reason why he does this is not to bring upon himself a condition of ecstasy, but rather by means of symbolism to show to Ahab what would happen because Benhadad had been released.[6]

This passage is also of interest because it introduces us to the expression "sons of the prophets." Much has been written upon this phrase, and there is no particular point in duplicating it here. It would seem, however, as though the word "son" is not intended to express actual sonship, but rather a close connection such as might be termed discipleship. The prophets were sons in the sense that they stood in a close and intimate relationship to the great master prophets, Elijah and Elisha. This intimacy of relationship had not been expressed during the days of

Samuel, when the prophetic bodies existed, since at that time, there does not appear to have been public and royal opposition. Now, however, during the time of Elijah, Jezebel had cut off many of these prophets, and Elijah himself was regarded as an enemy of the nation. It is probably this official hostility which brought the prophets into a closer relationship with their masters, a relationship which is expressed by the word "sons."

In 2 Kings 2 the sons of the prophets at Bethel are mentioned, and also those at Jericho. Again, in 2 Kings 4:1 we learn that these men may have been married. From 2 Kings 6:1 it appears that the sons of the prophets had a common dwelling place. It must be confessed that the information which is given concerning these groups is meagre. Hence it is not well to build elaborate theories as to the nature of the sons of the prophets. They appear as the background against which the great prophets, Elijah and Elisha, carry on their work. In the light of what is revealed in Numbers 11, we may assume that they were assistants in making known the will of God at this particular time to the nation. When the great writing prophets appear upon the scene, the "sons of the prophets" largely disappear.

CHAPTER VI

The Prophet and the Church

I F we are properly to understand the position of the prophet in ancient Israel, it is necessary to consider the relationship in which he stood to the established religious cult. Did he stand in an attitude of hostility toward the priest and the functions of the priest, or rather, did he work side by side with the priest as his support and colleague? Further, was the prophet himself an official representative of the cult? These questions are being discussed today, and to them we must briefly turn our attention.

It will be well to begin with a consideration of the last question, namely; was the prophet an official representative of the cult? The emphasis upon this subject has been comparatively recent. In the third volume of his studies in the Psalms Sigmund Mowinckel drew attention to this question, and since then others have followed him.[1] The most cogent presentation of the thesis, however, has come from Aubrey Johnson, who has written an important monograph upon the subject, and has marshalled from the Old Testament considerable evidence in support of his position.[2] We shall probably best arrive at an understanding of the question by means of a careful consideration of some of this evidence.

The Monograph of Johnson

It will be remembered that when Saul first enquired where he could meet Samuel, he was told that because of a sacrifice, Samuel had come to the city. From this fact, Johnson derives the conclusion that Samuel the Seer was a "cultic specialist closely associated with the sanctuary."[3] It is, of course, perfectly correct to say that Samuel had come to the city for the

95

purpose of sacrificing at the high place. The young women who met Saul replied to him, "He has come today to the city, for there is a sacrifice today for the people on the high place." There seems to be no doubt whatever, but that Samuel had charge of the sacrifice to be offered. Does it however, follow from this that Samuel was a cultic specialist? Rowley has aptly pointed out that in this very narrative Samuel tells Saul to await him at Gilgal whither Samuel will come to offer sacrifices (1 Samuel 10:8).[4] Hence, it would seem from this that we cannot conclude that Samuel had official connections with the sanctuary at Ramah alone.

Samuel was the religious leader of the people at the time. He was, of course, a *nabhi,* but he also performed priestly functions. Indeed, in the prophecy of the man of God unto Eli it had been announced, "And I will raise me up a faithful priest, that shall do according to that which is in mine heart and my mind" (1 Samuel 2:35a). It was the great task of Samuel to hold the nation together in his capacity as religious leader during the time of transition between the period of the judges on the one hand and that of the monarchy on the other. In order to accomplish this end Samuel went to different points in the land for the purpose of conducting religious services and offering sacrifices. It is but natural to conclude that he would offer such sacrifices at an established sanctuary or high place.

We have no warrant for supposing that these high places were necessarily officially established cults.[5] Perhaps they were originally used by the Canaanitic inhabitants of the land. Since the coming of Israel, however, the priesthood seems to have been of a very restricted nature. Doubtless Samuel himself had appointed priests to serve at some of the high places, but this is only supposition. We really know almost nothing about these high places as they existed during the days of Samuel. At any rate it seems to give an incorrect perspective to speak of Samuel as connected with these places of sacrifice. Rather, they were connected with him. That is, he as the spiritual leader of the entire nation went about from place to place, as he saw need. He was in a class by himself, and what is said of Samuel cannot be used with respect to the status of other prophets in connection with the cultus.

As further evidence that the seer was a cultic specialist attention is directed to the fact that Gad the Seer commanded David to seek God's forgiveness by means of sacrifice, which, of course, was a cultic act.[6] Gad commanded David to rear an altar unto the Lord and upon this altar to sacrifice so that the plague might be stayed from the people. To conclude from this however that Gad was a cultic specialist is surely to read into the Scriptures what is not found there. It should be noted in the first place that Gad received his command by way of revelation from the Lord (2 Samuel 24:19). Gad therefore, in proclaiming this message to David, was fulfilling the function, not of a cultic specialist, but of one who speaks the words of a superior to another, that is, he was acting as a prophet. The content of the command was not of Gad's own devising, but was a revelation from the Lord. Now, from the fact that the content of the message had to do with sacrifice and the offering of sacrifice upon the part of the king, it does not follow that the one who offered the message himself was connected with any shrine or altar for sacrifice. The prophets themselves were not working in open hostility to the priests, but rather, the one complemented the other. Hence, from this particular passage it is difficult to discover any particular relationship in which the prophet stood to the cult.

Johnson calls attention further to the fact that it was through the agency of this same Gad that the commandment concerning the musical service in the Temple was made known.[7] In 2 Chronicles 29:25 David, Gad, the king's seer and Nathan the prophet are mentioned side by side as the ones through whom the commandment of the Lord came with respect to the musical service of the Temple. If then the conclusion be drawn from this passage that Gad was a cultic specialist, it follows that the same was true also of David and of Nathan. Perhaps, in a certain sense, they were all of them cultic specialists. Much depends upon the precise sense in which one wishes to employ the term.

These three men are classified together as prophets (2 Chronicles 29:25), "for so was the word of the Lord by his prophets." It appears then that this is another case where the Lord gave commandments concerning the arrangement of the Temple service, and that these commandments were delivered by the hands of the prophets. Hence, the men who delivered these commands were performing the functions of prophets, and that is really all that can be said about their function. They were each of them prophets of the Lord. What the precise relationship of each to the Temple and its organization was, cannot be determined upon the basis of this passage.[8]

1. Elisha and the Shunammite

When the Shunammite woman wished to seek the aid of Elisha, her husband said to her, "Why goest thou to him today? It is neither New Moon nor Sabbath" (2 Kings 4:23). Upon the basis of this text it is assumed that we are in the presence of a cultic association.[9] The prophet, it is claimed, was usually visited upon a festival day; hence, he must have been himself connected with the cult.

It will be necessary therefore to examine this passage rather carefully. When the son of the Shunammite woman died, she brought him up and laid him upon a couch in the chamber of the Man of God, Elisha, and then called her husband to have prepared an ass so that she might make the journey to Elisha. It should be noticed that she gives no thought whatever to the day, but rather seems perfectly assured that because of her great need, the prophet will hear her. Indeed, so great is her confidence that she even believes the prophet capable of restoring to life her dead son. That there is anything unusual in seeking the prophet at such a time seems not to have entered her mind.

The husband however, replies, "Why goest thou unto him today? It is not the New Moon and it is not the Sabbath." Possibly the husband did not know that the boy had actually died. Perhaps in speaking as he did, he had no idea of the seriousness of the situation.. Perhaps also, he did not have the faith of his wife. If he knew of the boy's death, he may have doubted whether the prophet would be able to help, and hence, could see no point in troubling the prophet at this particular time.

The husband's words are indeed revealing. For one thing they make it clear that, even in this difficult time, the people were endeavoring to live in accordance with the prescriptions of the Mosaic law. According to the law of Moses, the Sabbath was to be a day of holy convocation (*miqrah-qodesh*) and the new moon a time of sacrifice (see Leviticus 23:3; Numbers 28:11ff.) Without doubt, then, the pious in Israel, even among the ten tribes, resorted to the houses of the prophets on these days for the purposes of worship and for holy gatherings. And the reason why they gathered at the houses of the prophets was that the Levitical priesthood at this time was not functioning to any great extent, and the prophets served as the spiritual leaders of the people.

When Elisha saw that the Shunammite woman was coming, he sent his servant Gehazi to meet her. Far from being unwilling to see her because it was not a festival day, he was very willing to see her. And when she finally came before him he was also ready to hear her, for he perceived that her soul was in bitterness, although he himself did not know the reason. It does appear then, we may say by way of conclusion, that at this period of Israel's history, the normal thing was to visit a prophet's house on a festival day. It does not follow, however, that the prophet was necessarily connected with any particular shrine.

The question may arise as to why Elisha should be visited at Mount Carmel. Johnson points out that this was the site of an early and famous 'high place' and that, in itself, this was sufficient to prove that Elisha was connected with the sanctuary.[10] It is of course perfectly true that at Carmel there was an altar of the Lord which the Israelites had torn down. When Elijah cried unto God from Horeb, he said, ". . . for the children of Israel have forsaken Thy covenant, thine altars they have torn down, and Thy prophets they have slain with the sword . . ." (1 Kings 19:10). Specific mention is made of one of these altars which had been torn down, namely, the one at Carmel, ". . . and he repaired the altar of the Lord which had been torn down" (1 Kings 18:30).

What, however, was the meaning of the altar at Carmel? This altar may have been erected even before the building of the Temple at Jerusalem. More likely, however, it was one of a number of altars which had been built by the devout in Israel during the time of the disruption of the kingdom. The king would have prohibited such worshippers from going to Jerusalem to the sanctuary; in Israel, Jeroboam had decreed that men should worship at Dan and Bethel. Hence, those who could not follow the commands of the king might well have erected altars at various places throughout the land where they could approach the true God whose service was desecrated by the apostasy of the northern tribes.

2. The Religious Condition in Israel

Such altars would of course not be acceptable to those who followed the apostate spirit of Jeroboam and his successors. Hence, we may well imagine, zealous followers of the apostate tribes would have torn them down. Apparently it was an act of fanaticism. Whether such altars had any legitimation in the first place is a question that probably cannot be answered. At any rate, their destruction brought forth from Elijah his anguished cry. Hengstenberg aptly remarks: "What pious Protestant would not have been filled with horror and detestation at the destruction of the crosses in France, without unconditionally approving the disposition that caused their erection, or the superstition with which in a multitude of cases they were regarded."[11] At any rate, Elijah considered the destruction of these altars as an equivalent to forsaking the covenant.

At the time of the contest with the priests of Baal, Elijah repaired the altar on Mount Carmel, which was one of the altars torn down by the apostate Israelites. Zealous for the new worship of the calves, and following the independent spirit of Jeroboam and the north, they could brook no opposition to the calf worship of Dan and Bethel. But at the time of the great contest with the Tyrian Baal, Elijah repairs this altar, an act which may be regarded as a tacit rebuke against the divided condition of the nation and the apostate religious worship of Dan and Bethel. It is very interesting to note that Elijah took twelve stones, according to the numbering of the sons of Jacob, and thus repaired the altar. His action spoke out in eloquent rebuke to the low religious conditions of the nation. Thus, it was from an altar which was dedicated to the Lord, that Elijah would take his stand. Is it not to be expected that Elisha, upon whom a double portion of Elijah's spirit had fallen, would also seek to foster the worship of the true God at an altar that was dedicated to Him? It is very interesting to note that Elijah has no connection with the official religion of the time. With Dan and Bethel he will have nothing to do. It is rather to an altar dedicated to the Lord that he repairs, and doubtless he had resided there for some time. From this, however, can it be inferred that he was a cultic prophet? In answer to the question we must note that, like Samuel and Elijah, Elisha was far more than a prophet. He was a spiritual leader of the times. His functions were many and varied. As a spiritual leader, and not necessarily as a prophet, he would be found working near the altar. Where else, we may well ask, would a religious leader of the time carry on his work efficiently?

This also explains the reason why Elijah performed what Johnson calls a "sacrificial scene" at the altar that he had repaired.[12] Elijah prepared the sacrifice, not because he was a cultic specialist, nor because he was somehow connected with that particular altar, but as a leader of the people who prayed to God to intervene and manifest His great power before an unbelieving nation. Elijah was a prophet, but he was more than a prophet. He was the spiritual leader in an apostate nation, who stood between the time of the founding of the monarchy and the period of the great writing prophets. From the act performed on Carmel one fact shines forth clearly.

Elijah, when he performed the duties of a spiritual leader, would not identify himself with the great shrines of the day, Dan and Bethel. He stood by an altar of the Lord, the God of the twelve tribes. His act was a remarkable rebuke against the official cult, the only cult in the Israel of that time of whose existence we have any knowledge.

It is perfectly true that in his complaint before the Lord Elijah does link together the altars of God and His prophets. In fact, he enumerates three complaints. The Israelites have forsaken the covenant; they have torn down the altars, and they have slain the prophets. By tearing down the altars and slaying the prophets they have thus forsaken the covenant. It does not follow from this statement however, that we are able to draw any conclusions with respect to the relationship between prophets and altars. The altars were the places where the priests offered sacrifice on behalf of the people. The prophets were those who brought the Word of God to the people. The priests represented the nation before God; the prophets represented God before the nation. The priest and prophet were the two great foci of religious life. What Elijah is really saying is that the people have so destroyed the true religious life of Israel that they have actually forsaken God's covenant.

A word of caution must also be injected with respect to drawing conclusions concerning the prophets of Israel from the activities of Baal prophets or other non-Israelitish prophets. The prophets of Baal may have held certain positions in the cultus of that god; it does not follow, however, that the prophets of the Lord held similar positions. We can learn about the prophets of Israel, not from phenomena outside of Israel, but only from the statements of the Scriptures.

3. The Jerusalem Prophets

It is the contention of Johnson that the Jerusalem prophets were actually members of the Temple personnel.[13] In support of this position he appeals to passages in which the prophet and the priest are found coupled together. Thus, Jeremiah once stood in the Temple court and before the priests and prophets announced the destruction of the city, unless the people repented. He was consequently accused by priests and prophets and by the people, but the magistrates refused to condemn him. From this passage however, it is difficult to tell what the relationship was in which the prophets stood to the Temple. They were in the court of the Temple when Jeremiah spoke, but so was Jeremiah and so were the people. Evidently, as Johnson himself admits, there was a large audience. From this it does not follow that those who were in the Temple court had any necessary connection with the Temple itself. For, while the prophets and priests are mentioned together, it should be noted that the people, in each instance, are included with them. Thus, it is Jeremiah on the one hand who is presented over against the people and the prophets and the priests.

For our part we would leave the question as to the precise relation between the prophets and the Temple unanswered. We do not think that sufficient evidence has been given in the Scriptures to enable one to pronounce with certainty upon the matter. Johnson's monograph, however, serves as a very wholesome antidote and corrective to the attitudes which became prevalent under the school of Wellhausen. According to this school, there was an almost irreconcilable antagonism between prophet and priest. The prophets decried sacrifice and the cult, and taught on the other hand a "spiritual" religion. This viewpoint has been held long and widely. To one who would take the Scriptural statements at their face value, it is a viewpoint which seems to be utterly without merit. Conservative scholars have protested against it all along but their voices went unheeded. Now, even those who do not accept the complete trustworthiness of the Word of God are beginning to oppose the once dominant theory.[14] Johnson's monograph serves as a wholesome corrective to the extravagant view of the older liberalism. It does cause us to see that there was indeed some connection between the prophets and the place of sacrifice. What this conection was, however, we for our part, are unable to say. We are unable to follow Johnson in his contention that the prophets were cultic specialists.

In this connection we must remember that the entire prophetic institution was a gift from God. It was not an expression of the religious nature of the people, but a Divine gift. The prophets were raised up of God; they did not emerge from the national religious consciousness. As the spokesmen of God, they uttered their messages wherever God commanded them to do so. At times this brought them into the Temple court; at other times it brought them into connection with other shrines. More than this, however, it is not wise to say.

Haldar on the Prophets

Johnson's monograph restricted its discussion to the Old Testament itself. Alfred Haldar extended the inquiry to the entire Ancient Near East.[15] Although he did not see Johnson's work until his own was ready for the press, his position is essentially the same. He believes that the prophets and priests were cultic officials, whose duties should not be too sharply differentiated, and in support of this position he brings forth a wealth of well-documented, comparative material. One is amazed at the erudition and wide reading which is represented by Haldar's work. If we are really to understand the relation between priest and prophet in Israel, thinks Haldar, we must find our clue in the relation between the two types of cultic functionary in ancient Mesopotamia, for in their functions the Hebrew priests and prophets were the same as the Mesopotamian functionaries. As Porteous well remarks: "The Hebrew priests and prophets are, that is to say, to be regarded as essentially species of a widely spread genus and the weight of emphasis is laid on similarity rather than on difference."[16]

If it can be shown that the *nabhi* did indeed practice divination and that his position in the religious life of ancient Israel was somewhat like that of the *mahhu* priest in Babylonia, then Haldar would seem to have proved his point. If the *nabhi* stood in relationship to the priest in Israel, as did the *mahhu* to the *baru,* we must conclude that the *nabhi* was indeed a cultic official.

1. The *Baru* and *Mahhu* Priests

As is well known there was in ancient Babylonia a group of religious priests who were called *baru*. The word comes from the Akkadian verb meaning "to see," and denotes a seer. Like the Hebrew designation, *ro'eh,* the term has no reference to any particular method of "seeing."[17] The *baru* was simply one who saw the will of the god.

Although the etymology of the word itself throws no light upon the mode of "seeing" engaged in by the *baru* priests, nevertheless, there is extant evidence which makes it clear what the functions of these priests were. The *baru* was one who saw by divination, and who consequently pronounced or uttered oracles for the god. There were different means of practicing divination. Thus, by the observance of oil and water in a divining cup (*makaltu*) the *baru* might learn the will of the god. Again, the omen might be obtained by observing the entrails and markings of the liver of a sacred animal. Likewise, through observation of the heavenly bodies or celestial phenomena and the flight of birds and such like, divination might be practiced. Finally, the will of the god was thought to have come in dreams, and these dreams must be interpreted.

In the *baru* priesthood we have a body of diviners, who employed the well known means of antiquity for obtaining omens. At the same time, these men seem to have acted in a wider capacity in that they could also take part in ecstatic rites. Their functions were somewhat broad in nature, and they were certainly not confined to any one means of divination. Hence, Haldar and others have stressed what they call a cumulation of functions, a description which seems to be quite accurate.[18]

Side by side with the *baru* priests, however, was another body which was designated by the name *mahhu,* a word derived from a verb meaning "to rave," and evidently signifying an ecstatic. This seems to be supported by a text from the Kouyunjik Collection which may be translated:

> I am smitten down like a *mahhu*
> That which I do not know, I bring forth.[19]

Not only, however, was the *mahhu* an ecstatic, but he could also perform some of the functions of the *baru*. Like the *baru* he also could employ the dream and the interpretation of omens. The distinction between the functions of the two groups, then, was not hard and fast.

There is one point, however, wherein a profound difference appears between these priests of ancient Mesopotamia and the prophets of Israel. The functions of divination in Mesopotamia were regarded as a science, to be practiced only by the initiated and the instructed. Those who were uninitiated could have no part nor share in the priestly ritual and mysteries. Through instruction one becomes "firm in knowledge."[20] Haldar appeals to a tablet to show that the priest was regarded as one who possessed the knowledge of the initiate:

> "The secret of the great gods;
> Let the knowing one show to the knowing one.
> Let the unknowing one not see.
> It is an abomination of the great gods."[21]

In this remarkable passage the priest or initiate is called "the knowing one" (mudu). He may show the mystery or secret knowledge only to those who are initiated. Those who do not know, i. e., the uninitiated, must not see such knowledge. For them to see it is an abomination in the sight of the great gods. The knowledge of divination was thus regarded as something which belonged only to a certain group, the initiate, and it is at this point that we meet one of the striking differences between the religion of Babylonia and that of Israel. The prophets of Israel were not looked upon as a group of initiates who possessed secret or mysterious knowledge. They were regarded as men upon whom the call of God had come and who spoke the message which He gave to them.

This fact is strikingly illustrated, for example, by the call of Amos. It was while Amos was about his everyday business that God commanded him to go and prophesy. He was not told to go to some prophet in order that he might learn certain mysterious knowledge which would be of help in interpreting and delivering oracles. He was told rather to prophesy, and this he did, to the consternation of the priest Amaziah.[22] Indeed, one may search carefully all that is said in the Old Testament concerning the call of the prophets, and there is not one word to support the view that they passed through a period of instruction in order to obtain certain knowledge which would be necessary for them, if they were properly to discharge their functions. They depended, not upon special instruction at the hands of initiates, but upon direct revelations from the one living and true God.[23]

Not only were the *baru* priests of Mesopotamia regarded as a body of initiates, but it was also requisite for him who would become a *baru* to pass through a special initiation. By this initiation he would gain cultic purity and would "see the glory of divination and receive a great name."[24] These initiatory rites bore the name *namburbu,* and included ablutions, anointings and cleansings.[25]

Again, we must insist that nothing like this is found in the Old Testament with respect to the prophets. It is perfectly true that the Old Testament priesthood had to undergo certain rites of purification and preparation, but such is not at all the case with the prophets.[26] At this point also, a wide gulf emerges between the cult of Mesopotamia and the divinely revealed religion of the Old Testament. The prophets were raised up of God, not to be members of some guild or class or association, but to speak forth His word.

2. Were the Prophets Diviners?

Far more important, however, is the question whether the prophets of ancient Israel ever did actually practice divination. If it can be shown that divination was as a matter of fact one of their legitimate functions, then the case is greatly strenthened that they may have been cultic officials in the sense of the *baru* and *mahhu* priests. It will be necessary therefore, to devote some attention to those passages in the Old Testament where, according to the advocates of the cultic-prophet view, the prophets do actually engage in any of the "technical methods of divination."[27]

In defense of his thesis, Haldar points out that the ancient Hebrew religion was deeply influenced by the Canaanite. He thinks that the Hebrews took over the Canaanitish temples and clergy and even modelled their own priesthood on that of the Canaanite clergy. As a result of adopting this position he is unwilling to give too much historical value to the accounts of Moses' founding the Hebrew priesthood. These, he says, are not to be taken too literally. Moses appears, according to Haldar, as the mythical founder of the Hebrew priesthood, somewhat like Enmeduranki in respect to the *baru* priesthood. Moses is described in the tradition in terms of the king ideology. Thus, he is called priest and prophet, watcher of the temple herds and one who kept his father-in-law's herds on the sacred mountain. Then too, like the deified king, Moses is god. Thus he appears as the royal cult founder, and hence, according to the Hebrew tradition, the priesthood was from the earliest times connected with the sacral kingship.[28]

One who is not familiar with the emphasis that is being placed at present upon the sacral kingship in the writings of contemporary Scandinavian scholars may be somewhat shocked to read Haldar's estimate of Moses. However, Haldar is not alone in this, and the idea of a sacral kingship as a common possession of the ancient Near Eastern world is an idea that must be reckoned with. For our part, we would assert without hesitation that we do not believe that such a view of the king was ever held in ancient Israel. We believe that the close relationship which existed between the prophets and the king is to be explained in another manner. The kingship in Israel was utterly unique. The king of Israel was not regarded as divine, but rather as the man who should rule after God's own heart.

It should be noted that Moses appears throughout the Bible as an historic figure. When Moses tends the flocks of Jethro, he is not to be conceived as tending the temple flocks. It is true that the title *rb nqdm* appears in Ras Schamra as a designation of one who is also called *rb khnm* (the high priest). Whatever

the practical significance of this designation may be in Ras
Schamra, however, we are not justified in drawing the conclusion from its presence in Ras Schamra that therefore Moses
was the shepherd of temple flocks.[29]

Nor can we say that Moses, like the deified king, is god. The
passages to which Haldar appeals, (namely Exodus 4:16ff. and
7:1) are not intended to represent Moses as a god or as divine.
To interpret them thus is to read into them that which was
never intended. These passages serve an entirely different
purpose. They are to emphasize the fact that Aaron is to be the
spokesman for Moses. As spokesman he is to stand between
Moses and the people, just as the prophet stands between God
and the people. Moses, therefore, as a result of this function
of Aaron, will be placed in a position relative to the people
such as God occupies when He speaks through His prophets.
Aaron between Moses and the nation will be in the position of
prophet.

Likewise the designation, mount of God, (Exodus 3:1) cannot be used to support the idea that Moses was shepherding
sacred flocks. The term is used simply by way of anticipation,
because of the remarkable appearance of God that was later to
take place here. To the reader of Scripture, these wondrous
events connected with Mount Sinai would be well known, and
hence, for the sake of the reader, Moses, the author of this
passage, uses this phrase by way of anticipation.[30]

We cannot, therefore, agree that the Hebrew priesthood was
patterned after that of the Canaanites, and that Moses is to be
looked upon only as a mythical founder. We accept rather the
teaching of the Scripture that Moses was an historical person,
and that the role played by him in the founding of the priesthood was precisely that which is laid down in the books of the
Pentateuch.[31] This does not mean that we refuse to recognize
similarities between the religion of Canaan and the religious
cultus of the Hebrews. We do recognize such similarities, but
we refuse to accept them for more than they are worth.

At this point a note of caution must be injected. There is a
grave danger in constantly seeking for smilarities, and from
these drawing conclusions as to relationship and identity. We

may list similarities between two different religions, and then draw an utterly erroneous conclusion. An example will suffice to illustrate this point. Christians assemble for worship in buildings; Moslems assemble for worship in buildings. Does it follow, however, that Christianity and Mohammedanism are essentially the same? Christians listen to sermons in their worship; Moslems listen to sermons in their worship. Does it follow that the officials of the Christian Faith and those of the Mohammedan are essentially the same? There is a great danger that when the investigator has listed the similarities which undeniably exist among various religions, he will therefore conclude that his task is complete.

If we are really to arrive at the truth we must consider not only the similarities but also the differences which are to be found among the different religions. It is only when we do this that we come to a proper understanding of them. In the writings of the Scandinavian scholars of the present day, there is too much emphasis upon similarity. These similarities, however, are superficial and of a surface nature. They may well be characterized as accidental. The differences between the Divinely revealed religion of ancient Israel and the religions of the nations round about is as profound as is the difference between Christianity and other competing religions. To ignore these differences is to close one's eyes to all the truth. The study of similarities is interesting and profitable; the study of differences, however, will bring us to the truth. When we seriously contemplate the differences which existed in the cultus of ancient Israel and those to be found in the worship of Canaan we begin to understand that one is a religion revealed by God whereas the other is an expression of the sin darkened heart of the unregenerate man.

a. Micah and the Levite

In the light of these introductory remarks we can explain the claim that the prophets of Israel practiced divination. Indeed we must go further and ask whether divination was a lawful practice even for the priests. By way of example Haldar appeals to Judges 18:5, where the children of Dan speak unto the priest that Micah had hired and say, "Ask of God, that we may know." Then follows the response of the priest: "Go in peace, before the Lord is your way which ye go."

In order to understand this episode and its bearing upon the problem before us, we must look briefly at the background. Micah is presented in the book of Judges as one who seems to have blended together the worship of the true God and the service of idols. He had, we are told, a house of gods and he made an ephod and teraphim, and then consecrated one of his sons to be his priest. Apparently Micah was one of those who would worship God in an idolatrous manner. In so doing, he followed not the Divine command, "Thou shalt not make unto thee any graven image" (Exodus 20:4a), but rather went his own way. So much, then, for the man who had hired the Levite.

Why a Levite should be journeying about, we are not explicitly told. Different suggestions have been offered, but we are inclined to the opinion that this rambling Levite was one who was not content with his lot in Bethlehem. At any rate, he came to the house of Micah and was hired to be a priest. Strangely enough, he accepted the offer and permitted Micah to consecrate him.

When the Danites came into Ephraim they recognized the Levite and evidently thought him to be a legitimate priest. Their question, however, is not asked in a spirit of devotion. "Ask the gods," they request.[32] There is no indication in their question that they would approach Jehovah. In all probability they only think of making their request after the Levite has told them of his position. Their language was probably influenced by the Levite's own description of his gods. We may paraphrase their thought somewhat as follows: "Here is our opportunity; this man is a priest and he can consult the gods. He has several of them. If we approach him, he should be able to obtain some information for us." In such a spirit and with such an attitude, so it seems to the present writer, did these Danites speak to the Levite. Without doubt he employed his usual method of consulting the teraphim, whatever that method may have been, and then gave his answer. It is a fairly safe answer, "Go in peace, before Jehovah is your way in which ye go" (Judges 18:5b). The priest mentions the Name of Jehovah. There is no evidence, however, that this oracle was actually revealed by Jehovah. The priest, we believe, was one who acted upon his own initiative; who, while pretending to be a true priest of Jehovah, yet worshipped Jehovah in an idolatrous manner.

We are in perfect agreement with Haldar that here is an example where Israelites approached a priest expecting him to obtain an oracle for them. However, we cannot regard this priest as a member of the legitimate priesthood which God had instituted. The practices in which he engaged were Divinely prohibited; he was not a true priest of Jehovah.

b. Other Examples

The next example to which Haldar appeals is that of the priest of Nob, Ahimelech, asking Jehovah on behalf of David.[33] The description is given in the words of Doeg the Edomite who reports to Saul that he saw Ahimelech asking of Jehovah for David. In the defense of his actions, Ahimilech acknowledges what he has done and asks (verse 15) "Did I begin to ask of God for him today?" Thus the priest makes it clear that this is by no means the first time that he has approached God to ask the will of God for David. From this, however, we are not to draw the conclusion that Ahimelech was a particular type of priest like the Akkadian *sa'ilu,* but simply that in thus approaching God, Ahimelech was fulfilling part of his priestly duties, which did include approaching Jehovah to obtain information by means of the Urim and Thummim.

Haldar appeals to Deuteronomy 33:8ff. to show that the Levites are described as diviners, and that in connection with their divinatory rites, incense and sacrifices are mentioned. With much that Haldar writes we find ourselves in agreement; we cannot, however, accept his conclusions. He proceeds upon the assumption that since there are formal similarities between the description of the Levites given in this passage of Deu-

teronomy and certain Akkadian phrases, therefore the Levites
were diviners of the same type as those of Babylonia. This
conclusion by no means follows. It is to be expected that certain formal similarities will be present, and it is possible that
Haldar is correct in his estimate of these. He points, for example, to the phrase "and the work of his hands do Thou
favor" (Deuteronomy 33:11b) as being comparable to similar
pronouncements in certain Babylonian texts. Again, he points
to the words, "judgment" (mishpat) and "law" (torah) as
being virtual synonyms, each designating the oracular response
of God. We also agree with Haldar when he points out that
the *torah* and *mishpat* are identical with the word of Jehovah.
There is here present in Haldar's writings, we believe, a sound
exegetical instinct at work, and at least in a formal sense, we
are able to agree with him. Our point of difference appears in
that we believe the law and judgments which the Levites
declare to Israel and to Jacob are a revelation directly given
by God, who has revealed Himself to sinful man in a special
way for his salvation. Haldar, on the other hand, would
seek to make of one piece the religious phenomena of Babylonia
and those of Israel. To do this, we believe, is to do injustice to
the evidence.[34]

According to the Bible, the Urim and Thummim were used
for obtaining judgment.[35] It is the opinion of Haldar, however, that in addition to these, sacrificial divination was also
employed by the priests of Israel for receiving an oracle.[36]
Haldar appeals to the words of Psalm 86:17, "Show me a
token ('oth) for good," and remarks that this token ('oth) is
the usual expression for the sign from which the oracle is read.

For our part, we believe that such an appeal to this Psalm
is entirely unwarranted. The speaker here is not a diviner
who is seeking a favorable omen which he can interpret. He is
rather one, — we believe it to be David, — who cries out to
God under deep distress. He prays for a sign of good, so that
his enemies may see. Thus, if God will give to him such a
token, his enemies will see that God has truly been with him
and helped him, and so will be ashamed of their opposition to
him. Such, it seems to the present writer, is the simple mean-

ing of this beautiful Psalm. To appeal to the token as a favorable sign from which an omen may be read is to read into the text what is not found there.

Appeal is also made to Psalm 5:3 as "a clear instance of sacrificial inspection."[37] We may translate the relevant words: "In the morning I arrange for Thee and keep watch." In verse 3a, the Psalmist declares that God will hear his voice in the morning.[38] The meaning is amply clear. He would begin the day with prayer to God. His cry to God goes forth with the early morn. Likewise he would approach God through the sacrifice. The word which we have translated by "arrange" is used elsewhere of laying the wood and pieces for the sacrifice (Leviticus 1:7, 8, etc.).[39] As the day began to dawn the priest was to lay the wood for the morning offering of a lamb (Lev. 6:5; Num. 28:4). In this Psalm the morning prayer and the morning sacrifice are compared. The Psalmist's prayer is as a spiritual sacrifice. In the morning he will prepare this spiritual sacrifice, watching for an answer. It is perfectly true that the word "arrange" does have reference to sacrifice. It is not true, however, that there is even the faintest suggestion of inspection of the sacrifice for the purpose of obtaining an oracle or omen. The suppliant, we believe, was David. In any case, he was a humble believer in Jehovah, who would begin the morning by lifting his voice of praise as a 'sacrifice to God. There is not the slightest indication that the suppliant was a priest.

In 2 Kings 16:15 we read the phrase, ". . . and the brasen altar shall be for me to enquire by." This passage is difficult to interpret, for the precise significance of the words "to enquire by" is not clear.[40] Haldar thinks that the phrase denotes a rite by which the king, perhaps through the priests, would divine. It is perfectly true, that if divination by entrails is to be performed, an altar is needed. However, it does not follow that if there is an altar and sacrifice, divination by entrails is to be employed. And since the words "to enquire by" are, despite Haldar, not used in the Old Testament of omen divination, we should be very careful about interpreting them in such a way in this particular passage. If we retain the translation "to enquire by," it may be indeed that Ahaz had in mind some religious service, such as prayer, which he himself was to perform. It should be noted that this account of the altar is omitted from Chronicles, and that instead we read, that Ahaz offered sacrifice "to the gods of Damascus who smote him, saying, The gods of the kings of Aram helped them; I will sacrifice to them that they may help me: and they were the ruin of him and of all Israel" (2 Chronicles 28:23). It may be that Ahaz, therefore, did seek by prayer at the altar to obtain the favor of these heathen gods. Whatever be the precise meaning of the phrase, we may be sure that this was not the Divinely legitimatized religion of the Hebrews, and that Ahaz in this case was acting upon his own. The passage therefore, cannot really tell us much about the religious life of Israel.

There is however, another interpretation of the phrase which is worthy of consideration. The phrase may be translated "for deliberation." Its meaning would then be that Ahaz would reflect upon the altar before proceeding further with his arrangements. It appears, therefore, that the precise meaning is not as patent as might be desired. At any rate, we do not seem to be warranted in deducing from it a clear case of omen divination.

In Psalm 27:4 we read: "One thing have I desired of the LORD, that will I seek after; that I may dwell in the house of the LORD all the days of my life, to behold the beauty of the LORD, and to enquire in his temple." Do we have here an example of divination, as Haldar declares?[41] A mere glance at the text should make it clear that such is not the case. When the Psalmist asserts that he would behold the beauty of the Lord and enquire in his temple, he is not expressing a desire for divination from omens in the temple. The phrase which we translate "to behold" means to feast upon with the sight. It is expressive of a gaze or beholding that is lingering and clinging and pleasing. "To enquire" in His temple is simply a designation of contemplative meditation. The enquiring in which the Psalmist would engage is performed in meditation and prayer.

It should be noted further that again we have a Psalm which expresses the aspirations and longings of the believing heart for communion with God. The words are not those of a priest who desires to engage in divination, but rather of the ordinary man who would approach his God through prayer. When the natural, face-value meaning is so satisfactory, there is little reason for adopting an interpretation so unnatural as that proposed by Haldar.

c. Alleged Examples of Prophetic Divination

We have considered in some detail these passages adduced by Haldar to show that the priests of Israel engaged in sacrificial divination and we have found that such an interpretation is not warranted by the passages themselves. It now remains to consider whether the prophets of Israel ever engaged in such practices. Haldar seeks to defend this position by pointing out an equation of the priest with the seer. To do this he appeals to Isaiah 28:7, ". . . the priest and the prophet have erred through strong drink, they are out of the way through strong drink; they err in vision, they stumble in judgment."[42] In this passage the priest and the prophet are mentioned as leaders of the people. They have this much in common; both of them do see visions and give judgment. In the performance of these duties they have become extremely lax, and are drunken at their tasks. More than this, however, we may not assert. The passage teaches that both priest and seer did have visions and gave judgment. It does not teach that the two were to be equated. There were certain tasks which the priest alone might perform, and there were certain tasks which the prophet alone might perform. In one particular their tasks coincided, namely, the seeing of visions and the giving of judgment.

Very interesting is Habakkuk 2:1, "I will stand upon my watch, and set me upon the tower, and will watch to see what he will say unto me, and what I shall answer when I am reproved." Haldar assumes that the "watch" and the "tower" (*mishmarti* and *matsor*) are the places of omen inspection, as though the prophet, when he desired to receive an oracle went to a certain place to inspect the omens.[43] It is with a certain

sadness of heart that one thus sees this profound text evis-
cerated of its meaning. In referring these words to something
external, Haldar is doing nothing new. Long ago, Ferdinand
Hitzig thought that the prophet went to some steep and inac-
cessible place so that he could be far away from people and
alone with his thoughts.[44] Such an interpretation, however,
does not get at the heart of the passage. The words are to be
understood in a figurative sense. The prophet is not talking
about going to some particular place of watch to receive a
message; rather, he is thinking of retiring to the inmost re-
cesses of the heart to meditate upon the words of God. The
figure seems to be taken from the custom of ascending a high
place to look into the distance. Thus, a watchman stood upon
a tower in Jezreel and beheld the company of Jehu approaching.[45] By means of this inner reflection and contemplation, the
prophet prepares himself that he may hear the word of Jehovah.

Very similar is the prophecy in Isaiah 21:6-10. Haldar believes however, that this passage gives a description of the
"divination corporation" in action.[46] In verse six the king
(my lord) orders the speaker (i. e., the leader) to permit the
seer to take his stand to observe the omens. If he sees pairs
of certain animals, he is to attend closely. Apparently the
oracle is to be obtained from the movements of the animals
which the seer observes. In support of this view Haldar makes
out quite a convincing case to show that the word in verse
eight which has generally been translated "lion" should really
be translated "one belonging to God" and that it designates
the seer who is mentioned in verse six.[47] Thus, verses 8-10
constitute, on Haldar's view, the response of the seer to the
leader.

The word "lion" has caused difficulty to the commentators.
It has been the custom to translate "like a lion," thus signifying the manner in which the watchman replied to the
prophet. The other view has been to make the words "a lion"
form part of the answer which was given by the watchman. Of
these two views the former seems to be preferable. The watchman, if we adopt the former of these two views, replies with
a lack of patience, complaining to God that he must stand so

long at his post without seeing anything. If, however, the word which is commonly translated "lion" should really have the sense, "man of God," there could be no objection. The sense then would simply be: "And the man of Jehovah cried."

It remains however to consider the heart of the view which Haldar presents. Does this remarkable prophecy of Isaiah really set forth the seer as seeking to obtain an omen from the movements of animals? For our part we are unable to accept such an interpretation. We believe that a careful examination of the passage will show immediately how erroneous such an interpretation really is. In the first place, it should be noted that the one who speaks to the prophet in verse six is not the king, but the Lord.[48] It is true that the word here used is not the covenant Name, Jehovah; it is, however, one of the names of God and as spelled here is never used of anyone but God. Secondly, the one who speaks is the prophet Isaiah himself, not the leader of some divination corporation. In verse two the prophet has announced that a grievous burden has been declared unto him and then goes on to say that as a result of this burden, he is distressed. He then proceeds in verse six to give the reasons for his concern. This he does by announcing that the Lord has given him a command to station a watchman.

The watchman to be stationed is of course an ideal figure, so that the prophet may employ this device for reciting or relating his message. We are not to think of some watchman actually mounting a place of watch to behold the Babylonians. Rather, by this figure of speech the prophet brings to the attention of his hearers the fact that Babylon is fallen. The watchman is to look for pairs of animals. He replies to God, however, in a complaining maner (verse six), indicating how he keeps his post. Finally, in verse nine, the answer is brought forth by the appearance of a chariot of men and a couple of horsemen that Babylon is fallen. The details are indeed difficult, but there is no evidence whatever that the watchman was to obtain an oracle by observing the movements of the animals.

That which militates most strongly against Haldar's thesis, however, is the fact that even before the prophet, in obedience to the Lord, sets the watchman, he knows the message which the watchman will give. The opening verses of chapter twenty-one contain a clear intimation of the message later to be proclaimed. This is strengthened by the announcement of the prophet's reaction to the message. He would not have been so upset, had not the message been of some momentous character. Then too, the picture of the banquet in Babylon which appears in verse five shows that something of truly momentous character is about to take place. The watchman then takes his station to behold the approaching enemy, namely the Medes and Persians. He does not watch to obtain an oracle, but to behold the advance of the enemy. Then he announces clearly what had been intimated before, the fact that Babylon will be destroyed. Isaiah the prophet then states (verse ten) that this is a message which has come to him from the Lord of hosts. These words of verse ten are not to be regarded as the words of the watchman, but rather as those of the prophet. They have reference, not only to the episode of the watchman, but to the entire preceding part of the chapter. Hence, it is the prophet himself who has received the message which included the episode of the watchman. The episode of the watchman itself was a part of the revelation granted to the prophet.

As a result of his investigations Haldar concludes that in Israel there must have been a complete counterpart to the corporations of the *baru* in Mesopotamia and to their ritual.[49] From a study of the passages which Haldar adduces and which we have briefly considered above, we are unable to share this opinion with him. That there was divination practiced in Israel we are of course ready to grant. The discussion of the place which such divination occupied in Israel must, however, be reserved until we have completed a survey of Haldar's treatment.

After a discussion of the *ro'eh, hozeh* and other functionaries whom he would classify as belonging to the associations of the priests (*kohanim*), that is, those whom he would consider as the Israelitish equivalent of the *baru* priests, Haldar passes on to a discussion of the *nebi'im*. Since we have already considered the meaning of this word we shall here simply note what Haldar has to say. He believes the etymology of the word to be clear, and derives it from the root *nb'* as meaning "speaker."[50]

Haldar rightly rejects the view that the prophets condemned sacrifice. Far from condemning and repudiating sacrifice, the prophets themselves took part in the sacrificial ceremonies. Their most important function, however, consisted in the giving of oracles, and the characteristic feature of this oracle giving was ecstasy.[51]

Ecstasy, we are told, was symbolized by the breath of Jehovah (*ruach Yahweh*), just as in Mesopotamia the breath of the god is also mentioned. The heart or essence of ecstasy seems to be a concentration of the attention which is of so intense a nature that other impressions are removed from the consciousness. To bring upon this state, the inhabitants of ancient Mesopotamia and the Semites of the North West employed artificial methods and so, thinks Haldar, did the prophets of the Old Testament likewise.[52] In this state of ecstasy the prophets of the Old Testament gave their oracles, and thus they corresponded to the *mahhu* priests of Mesopotamia.[53]

In addition to this, the *ro'eh* interpreted oracles by observance. Thus, according to Haldar, the *ro'eh* really stood in relationship to the *nabhi* as did the *baru* to the *mahhu* in Mesopotamia. Between the two there was a very real difference, but each partook of the functions of the other. To show that a sharp line cannot be drawn between the functions in the cult Haldar appeals to Isaiah 28:7, which we may translate:

And also these have gone astray through wine;
And through strong drink they have erred;
Priest and prophet, they have gone astray through strong
  drink
They are swallowed because of the wine
They err because of strong drink
They go astray in seeing (a vision)
They reel in the giving of a decision.

If the word *ro'eh* which we have translated "seeing" simply means the observation of omens, then, without question, Haldar has proved his point. That the word is used in such a sense, however, is a matter which cannot be proved. In our discussion of this word above, we have shown that the word does not have such a connotation.

More convincing is an appeal to Micah 3:11 which we may translate as follows. "Her heads judge for bribes, and her priests give instruction for hire, and her prophets divine for silver; yet they lean upon Jehovah saying, Is not Jehovah in our midst? no evil will come upon us." A cursory reading of this passage, indeed, of the entire chapter would give the impression that divination was a legitimate function of the prophets, and that the prophet Micah was condemning not the divination in itself but rather the abuse of this gift by the seeking of money. It is necessary therefore, to devote some consideration to the statements made in this third chapter of Micah.

Micah's condemnation of the prophets in chapter three depends upon what he had earlier said in chapter two, verses six and eleven. In these verses he made it clear that the nation prefers those who prophesy to them according to their own wishes. They are unwilling to pay heed to those who come with a message from Jehovah, but if a man with none of the credentials of a true prophet should express his willingness to prophesy of wine and strong drink, the people would hear him, and he would become their prophet. It is obvious, therefore, that Micah is not talking about prophets who actually have received commissions from Jehovah such as he himself had received. He is condemning rather those who outwardly appeared to be true spokesmen of Jehovah, but in reality had received no revelation from Him. These men he characterizes as the "prophets that make my people to err" (Micah 3:5). To these there will be no vision, since God will not reveal Himself unto them. Likewise, their divination will amount to nothing, since it will be dark to them. God will not head them at all, and hence all their claims to prophecy and divination mount to nothing.

The time will come when they will be confounded, and their confusion will be manifest. They are those who have set themselves up in the name of Jehovah. They claim that they lean upon Him. Their claims however are false, since they do not know Him at all. Hence they carry on their practices, prophesying and divination, merely for the sake of gain, as did Balaam. Those whom Micah condemns therefore, are not prophets whom Jehovah has raised up, but those who claimed to prophesy in the Name of Jehovah, yet were without a true call.

At this point it is necessary to stress again most carefully wherein we differ from Haldar and others in our interpretation of the prophetic phenomena which appeared in ancient Israel. Haldar and most modern scholars seem willing to lump together all prophetic phenomena and to regard them as of one piece. Since some prophets practiced divination, many scholars are willing to conclude that divination was a legitimate practice or function of all Israel's prophets. For our part we cannot accept any such method of procedure. As we have sought to make clear in the preceding pages we believe that God revealed Himself in a special manner to the prophets. He chose these men and set them apart to perform a special work for Himself. Only those whom He thus called were true prophets.

We do not deny, however, that there were those, even as there are unbelieving ministers of the Gospel today, who claimed to be prophets. These men gave themselves out as recipients of a revelation from Jehovah; they said that they were accredited prophets. In reality, however, they were men who had had no revelation at all, but who rather, looked merely unto themselves for whatever messages they might have to declare. Without question these false prophets practiced divination. Hence, we are perfectly in agreement with Haldar when he says that there were those in Israel who bore the designation *nabhi* and who also practiced divination. On that point we have to quarrel whatsoever. Where we differ is in our refusal to admit that divination was a legitimate practice of the Divinely accredited prophets. In other words we must face the fact that in Israel there were prophets both true and false and we must also examine most carefully what constituted the difference between the two. In the following chapter we propose to make such an examination. At present we would simply call attention to the fact that Haldar has overlooked this all important distinction. In his study of Micah 3 he does not pay heed to the fact that the prophets whom Micah condemns are not true prophets of Jehovah.

In 2 Kings 17:13 the prophets are reported as condemning Israel with the words: "Turn ye from your evil ways, and keep my commandments and statutes, according to all the law which I commanded your fathers, and which I sent to you by the hand of my servants the prophets." According to Haldar the law (torah) of which mention is here made is the term for an oracle obtained by technical means. It is of course true that there is a certain correspondence between the Hebrew word *torah* and the Babylonian *tertu*.[54] The *tertu* was an oracle which the seer had received, but it does not follow that the *torah* was an oracle derived by technical means. The word simply means "instruction," and when applied to a message delivered by a *nabhi* indicates that the *torah* was a revelation from God. It is perfectly true that the prophets did deliver the *torah* which they had received from Jehovah. They received this *torah* however, not by the ordinary technical means of divination, but rather as a direct revelation. The similarity with the *tertu* of Babylonia is really only of a formal nature.

In writing the above we have sought to deal with the most important and convincing evidence adduced by Haldar. His work is an extremely refreshing contrast from the school of Wellhausen. He has certainly shown that the prophets did not stand in rigid and unyielding opposition to. the sacrifices of the Law. He has also shown that there were formal similarities between the priests of Mesopotamia and some of the religious functionaries of Israel. At least the false prophets in Israel did appear to function somewhat like the priests of Mesopotamia. Since, however, no distinction is made by Haldar between the true and the false prophets of Israel, he has not proved his point. Those whom God raised up to be His spokesmen did not constitute a formally organized group like the *baru* of Mesopotamia. There is really no evidence in the Old Testament that the true prophets were organized in any formal way. Each prophet, although in the Divine economy he was under Moses, was nevertheless directly responsible to Jehovah for what he did and said. We conclude therefore, that the idea of cult prophetism, as espoused in modern times, cannot be proven, for it fails to make the distinction between true and false prophets.

CHAPTER VII

Prophets False and True

THE study of Old Testament prophecy is rendered more difficult and complicated by the fact that in ancient Israel there were different kinds of prophets. Thus, Jeremiah declares: "Then the LORD said unto me, The prophets prophesy lies in my name: I sent them not, neither have I commanded them: they prophesy unto you a false vision and divination, and a thing of nought, and the deceit of their heart" (Jeremiah 14:14). From this verse certain conclusions may be drawn. 1. There were prophets with whom Jeremiah would not associate himself. He belonged to one class, namely those who had truly received the word of the Lord, and they belonged to another class, those who had not received that word. 2. According to Jeremiah, certain prophets claimed to have been recipients of Divine revelation. They looked to God and appealed to the Lord's Name as an accreditation of their message, whereas as a matter of actual fact, the Lord had not sent them. 3. These prophets whom Jeremiah denounced looked for the source of their message not to the Lord, but to their own deceitful heart. The message, then, according to Jeremiah, was of purely human origination. It was not Divine but human. 4. Lastly, the message of these prophets was one of vanity and deceit, and consequently one that was not to be trusted. In the eyes of Jeremiah such prophets were men who had no right to the prophetic office.

What, on the other hand, would have been the opinion of these men concerning Jeremiah himself? Would not they have considered themselves legitimate prophets of Israel and have regarded Jeremiah as a dangerous and harmful disturber of the peace? We are not entirely ignorant of the manner in which such men would have acted toward Jeremiah nor of the attitude which they would have entertained with respect to him. In the twenty-sixth chapter of his prophecy, he himself relates how the prophets and others declared that, because of his denunciations of Jerusalem, he must die. There was an irreconcilable antagonism between Jeremiah on the one hand and many of the prophets on the other.

It has been the custom to call these opponents of Jeremiah and others like them false prophets. Such a term of course bears with it a strong element of condemnation, and perhaps there are those who feel that, since we have no defense of these men, such as they themselves could make, we are in no position to discuss them with any objectivity. For our part, we are unable to agree with the unamed scholar, mentioned by Davidson, who expressed his regret that the productions of these men have perished and that as a result we must listen only to the judgment of their adversaries and not to their own defense.[1] Davidson admits that it would be interesting to examine some fragments of their literary labors but he proceeds very wisely to conclude that such fragments were probably not worthy of being preserved. It may be suggested also that these false prophets did not leave anything in writing.

If we acquiesce in the usage of history and label these men false prophets we need not fear doing them an injustice. Nor need we doubt for an instant the trustworthiness of the Biblical judgment upon them. The basic question which now faces us is simply, Shall we accept the testimony of the Bible at face value? And this is to come to grips again with the old question of the nature of the Scriptures. This is not the place to enter into a long defense of the trustworthiness of the Bible nor to seek to show that the Bible is after all the Word of God. For our part we believe most firmly that it is the Word of God and that it is entirely to be trusted in all of its statements, and hence, we have no hesitancy whatever in accepting at face value all that the Bible has to say about these false prophets and for that matter, all that the Bible has to say about anything else.

We face the investigation then, confident that the records which we have are trustworthy and reliable. Indeed, were it not for these sacred Scriptures, we would know nothing whatsoever about the false prophets or the true. When we thus discover that there were actually irreconcilable prophets and groups of prophets we begin somewhat to realize the complexity of the problem which faces us. It now becomes clear that we cannot simply declare that prophecy was originally Canaanitish. We must ask rather, which prophecy was Canaanitish in origin, for it may possibly be that what we call false prophecy had its roots in Canaan. There is however, a vast gulf fixed between false and true prophecy,[2] and if the one came from Canaan, it is very clear that the other did not. Likewise, in considering the question of cultic prophecy in Israel, we may very well grant that certain types of prophets were intimately connected with the official cult, whereas others were not. Certain types of prophets may indeed have resembled the *mahhu* and *baru* priests of Mesopotamia; on the other hand, such resemblances need not have applied to all who were designated prophets.

These preliminary considerations bring us to the thought that we must do more than speak of prophets and prophecy in Israel as such. We do not deal adequately with the situation by the use of such terms. If we are faithfully to describe the prophetic phenomena we must pay strict heed to the fact that there were different types of prophets. It is a failure to differentiate adequately among the types of prophets that has led some scholars to lump the Israelitish prophets together and to treat them as all of one piece, to regard them all as being essentially the same in kind, although, admittedly, differing from one another in degrees of ecstasy, and particularly of ethical perception.

The False Prophets

For our part we believe that there was a vast cleavage among the prophets of Israel, a cleavage so great that it placed in one category all those who had actually been called into the prophetic office in a special way by the supernatural call of the sovereign Jehovah, God of Israel and Creator of Heaven and earth, and that it distinguished these prophets, who alone were deserving of the name from all others, however much they may have differed among themselves in respect to secondary matters, who had not received a special supernatural call from God. Those who belonged to the former class, men such as Isaiah and Jeremiah, did not of their own volition decide to become prophets. They were called by a solemn, efficacious, supernatural call to perform a special mission for the true God and to declare unto the nation His very words. Other religious leaders who took unto themselves the designation of prophet and who had not been called of God belonged to another category, which in many respects was imitative of the first, but which was separated from it by a profound gulf. It is this latter class which we shall designate false prophets, since its members were those who had not actually received a call from Jehovah.

There are basically but two ways of considering the relationship in which these groups stood to one another. In the first place we may regard true prophecy as an outgrowth of false. We may say in effect, as many do say, that some men in the lower group, by means of their deeper and keener spiritual perception, rose above their fellows and became known as the truly great prophets. This, we may note, is the common way of explaining the origin of the great prophets in the nation Israel. On the other hand, we may regard true prophecy as a genuine work of God for His people, and false prophecy as a degeneration from the true. Upon this position the great prophets did not arise from a lower group; they were raised up of God. The lower group — to use the designation for the present in the broadest sense — was not the source of the higher. It is this latter interpretation which we think to be correct. True prophecy is not an outgrowth of the false; but the false is a deterioration and perversion of the true.

In asserting that false prophecy is a degeneration of the true we have adopted a position which has not found wide acceptance in the ranks of modern scholarship. In one way or another, modern scholarship looks upon the true prophecy of the Old Testament as in some respect an outgrowth of the false. Sometimes the distinguishing feature is thought to be found in the mode of reception of the prophetic message. Thus, Obbink, for example, acknowledges that the technical means for obtaining information, so prevalent in the ancient near-east, were found in "Jahvism" also, although in a modified form.[3] The great prophets, however, which, according to Obbink, represent the purest "Jahvism," know a form of revelation which is not found in heathenism, namely the clear reception of the message without vision, dream or any of the other technical methods then in use. With the true prophets the vision was restricted to the inaugural vision by which they were called to be prophets. With the ecstatic bands of Canaanite prophets, therefore, the great prophets of Israel have nothing to do.

This analysis of the situation, however, will not stand. For one thing, it should be noted that the great prophets never condemn other prophets because of ecstatic phenomena or because certain methods of obtaining information have been employed. Ecstasy and vision are not the criteria which the true prophets employed to distinguish themselves from those whom they would condemn. Furthermore, it is not in accord with fact to say that the great prophets received visions only in their inauguration or induction into the prophetic office. To note but one example, there are five visions recorded in the last three chapters of Amos, the very section of the book in which the account of his call is stated, yet there is no account of any vision received at the time of his call to be a prophet. In addition to this it cannot successfully be denied that some of the strange "irrational" elements which characterized the earlier prophecy are also to be found among the great writing prophets. If therefore, we are to seek that which caused a cleavage between the true and false prophets, we shall not find it in the mode of ascertaining information. "Ecstatic" behaviour was not the possession of false prophets alone.

A more cautious approach is suggested by Albright, who mentions that it may have been partly as a reaction against pagan "ecstaticism" that the movement of true Israelitish prophetism arose.[4] Again, however, it must be repeated that the Israelite prophets did not condemn ecstatic phenomena as

such. They did condemn idolatry and the worship of false
gods, together with messages which were the product of the
prophet's own mind, but they did not, so far as the evidence
is extant, condemn any prophet because of his "ecstatic" behaviour.

"Spirit" and "Word" Prophets

Very unique is the theory of Mowinckel in which he seeks
to discover a distinction between the pre-exilic prophets who
possessed the "word of Yahweh" and the earlier prophets
whose inspiration was derived from "the spirit of Yahweh."[5]
It was this possession by the *ruach* or "spirit of Yahweh"
which produced in the earlier prophets their ecstatic behaviour,
and which was repudiated by the later prophets.

Neither Amos, Zephaniah, Nahum, Habakkuk nor Jeremiah
make any mention of the spirit of Yahweh, yet, according to
Mowinckel, their consciousness of the prophetic vocation is in
some respects stronger than in the ordinary *nabhi*.[6] In Micah
3:8, where the Spirit of the Lord is mentioned, Mowinckel
would, wrongly, we think, delete the words as a gloss.[7] It is
only with Ezekiel that we find the "spirit of Yahweh" mentioned as the source of prophetic inspiration, and again in some
of the literary, post-exilic prophets. Some of the older, reforming prophets, however, expressly reject the idea of prophetic
inspiration as from the *"ruach* Yahweh." Thus, we are told,
Hosea condemned the man of the spirit as "wild with folly,"
and Micah contrasts himself as a man "full of power, judgment
and might" from the prophets "who deal in lies and wind
(*ruach*)."

Herein, therefore, according to Mowinckel, lay the difference. The ecstatic prophets had the "spirit of Yahweh," whereas the great prophets received the "word of Yahweh." As Rowley has pointed out, however, at the first account of a cleavage
among the prophets, Jehoshaphat requests of Ahab, "Enquire, I
pray thee, at the word of the Lord today" (1 Kings 22:5).[8] Apparently, the "word" of God was claimed as a common possession of both sides. Micaiah commanded the king to hear the
word of the Lord, and he also accused his opponents of being

possessed by a lying spirit. Rowley very aptly remarks that what Micaiah's successors meant was that it was necessary to test the spirits.[9]

It will be of some advantage to give brief consideration to a few of the passages which Mowinckel adduces, for by such a means we can evaluate more justly and satisfactorily the distinction which he would seek to make. In the first place, then, we may turn to Jeremiah 5:13. According to Mowinckel, this passage expresses the prophet's scorn of the prophets who possess the *ruach* (spirit). They do not have the word, and so Jehovah will turn them into wind, or nothingness. The passage however, must be subjected to careful consideration before this interpretation may be accepted. According to the context in which the verse is found, Jeremiah has rebuked the nation for disbelieving the Lord and for denying that the threatened calamities would come to pass.

Then follows the verse with which we are now concerned. It is a strange verse, and we may render literally: "And the prophets shall become wind, since the speaking is not in them (or, and the speaking, etc.), thus it shall be done to them." Are these words to be regarded as constituting part of the disbelief of the people, or are they rather a threat uttered by Jeremiah himself? According to Mowinckel, the latter interpretation is preferable, and the verse is then to be regarded as out of place.[10] On this interpretation we find the people condemned for asserting that the threatened judgments will not come to pass nor eventuate. Jeremiah then proceeds to condemn those prophets who have been faithless in announcing the will of God. They shall, he declares, become mere wind, without God's word.

There is serious question, however, as to whether this view of the passage is the true one. A more time honored interpretation has been to consider verse thirteen as constituting part of the statement of the disbelieving nation. "Not only will these threatened judgments not come upon us," we may paraphrase the thought on this construction, "but you prophets who have been threatening us with these calamities will yourselves fail. You will no longer speak, but will become as wind." There are certain advantages in favor of this construction.

For one thing, it does not require a rearrangement of the verses, such as seems necessary upon the other interpretation. Secondly, it is perfectly in line with the sinful attitude of the people. "Your own sword hath devoured your prophets, like a destroying lion" (Jeremiah 2:30b). Lastly, it brings to the fore that which was most offensive to the nation, namely, the speaking of the prophets. It was the message of rebuke and condemnation which the sinful nation would not hear. Hence, verse thirteen is really an example of wishful thinking. "If the prophets become mere wind, then they cannot speak to us of condemnation."

While, therefore, we prefer this latter interpretation we accept it with some reserve because of the difficulty of the verse itself. It is not a distinction between two kinds of prophets which is given here, but rather a picture of prophets who can no longer speak, since they have become wind. Wind, as employed here is obviously a symbol of confusion. Instead of a clear word, the prophets would speak nothing; they would be filled with wind. Hence, it is not a distinction between prophets who had a clear word and those who had the spirit, but rather between the word of the prophets and confusion itself.

It must be noted that in the Hebrew text itself a strange word is used, which we have rendered in the translation by "speaking." This form closely resembles the Hebrew expression for "word," but at the same time, it is distinct. The Hebrew text does not speak of prophets who do not have the word, but of those in whom there is not "the speaking." There is no sufficient reason as many have suggested, for emending the text. The Greek translation (Codex B) reads, "Our prophets were for wind, and the word of the Lord was not in them." Jerome has translated, "The prophets had spoken into wind, and there was no answer in them, therefore these things have come upon them." As will readily be seen, however, these translations are of little help in meeting the difficult problem which is posed by the presence of the word "speaking."

Difficult as is the presence of this word, we prefer to allow it to stand, observing the rule that the more difficult reading should prevail. Jeremiah, we may say by way of summary, is not distinguishing between two classes of prophets, those who have the spirit and those who have the word. He is simply making a contrast between confusion and the word of the Lord. It is true that there are other words in the Hebrew language which might have been employed instead of *ruach*, but the use of this word does not in the least indicate that Jeremiah was seeking to depreciate prophets who were possessed of the spirit (*ruach*). This passage therefore would not seem to support Mowinckel's contention.

Very interesting, also, is Micah 2:6, which, according to Mowinckel, presents Micah as quoting a current phrase, but which he would not, since the verse describes the prophets as speaking ecstatically, apply to himself. In verses one to five Micah has set forth the announcement of coming doom. Such a prophecy, however, was not what the nation wanted to hear, and it met with opposition. Not only the people, but also the false prophets uttered opposition to it. In verse six, the words of these opposing false prophets are given. " 'Prophesy not,' they prophesy; if they do not prophesy to these, the shame will not depart." The false prophets prophesy, and the content of their message is found in an address to the true prophets. To the true prophets, they say, "prophesy not." If, however, the true prophets do not prophesy to these false messengers, the shame which has been proclaimed will not depart. The verse is extremely difficult, but the rendering which we have given seems to be most free from objection.

According to Mowinckel, the word which we have translated "prophesy not" is one which literally means "to speak ecstatic words so that one froths at the mouth."[11] With this interpretation we cannot agree. The root idea is simply *to drop* or *to drip,* and when the word is used of human discourse, or Divine, for that matter, it is employed figuratively as, for example, when Job says, "my speech used to drop upon them" (Job 29:22). Surely, there is not the slightest hint of ecstasy in such a passage. It is perfectly true that the word *hittiphu* is used of prophesying, and in Micah 2:6 it does apply to the false prophets. It is, however, used also of Ezekiel, and the idea expressed by the word is found in Deuteronomy 32:2, a passage which presents the basic thought.

What is of particular interest in this connection is the occurrence of a parallellism in verse seven between the *ruach* of the Lord and the Lord's words. It is of little concern how we translate the word *ruach;* that which is of concern is the fact that it appears in parallel construction with "My words." "Is the spirit of the Lord straitened?" the prophet asks. These punishments which are to come are not His only doings; His mercy can also be shown. His words also do good to the one who walks uprightly. If, in other words, true repentance is to be found, the mercy of the Lord will be manifested. His *ruach* is not straitened, so that other deeds are precluded from following, and if one walk in obedience to Him, His words will be of blessing. Both the *ruach* and the words are pictured as from God and as bringing blessing to the man who walks uprightly. Such a usage of *ruach,* in parallel connection with mention of the words of God, is a strong argument against the division which Mowinckel seeks to make.

Micah 3:8 would seem to constitute an objection to Mowinckel's position. Here the prophet very definitely contrasts himself with the false prophets and speaks of himself as full of power which comes from the Spirit of the Lord. Mowinckel, however, does not understand the passage in this sense. He believes that, as they now stand, the words *"ruach* Yahweh" are to be construed with the verb, as though Micah were saying, "I am filled with strength, and with the Spirit." Consequently, he would delete the words, *"ruach* Yahweh" as a gloss.[12] It should be noted, however, that these words appear in both the Septuagint and the Vulgate. As far as textual evidence is concerned, there is no reason for deleting them. Furthermore, when they are properly translated, the difficulty disappears. If we paraphrase the passage "I am filled with power, which power comes from the Spirit of the Lord," we have a rendering that well expresses the original and at the same time removes one of Mowinckel's principal reasons for regarding the words as a gloss. This verse, therefore, stands as a strong obstacle in the path of accepting a rigid distinction between spirit-prophets and word-prophets.

It may not be out of place briefly to consider one more passage which is treated by Mowinckel. It is found in the prophecy of Jeremiah, and as translated in the Authorized Version reads, "The prophets that have been before me and before thee of old prophesied both against many countries, and against great kingdoms, of war, and of evil, and of pestilence" (28:8). This verse is used by Mowinckel to show that all the earlier genuine prophets were prophets of evil.[13] Prophecy must, so the argument runs, have a relation to ethical standards. Those who have preached of good, and therefore that which men wish to hear, are prophets false indeed. The true prophet, on the other hand, has preached of evil.

However, as Aalders has well pointed out, these words do not set forth a general rule or principle, but speak of a particular instance.[14] They do not teach that all true prophets, always, have prophesied only of evil, as though that were the hall-mark of such a prophet. Rather, they form the background against which Jeremiah is denouncing the words of Hananiah. Hananiah has just prophesied of good. He has declared that the vessels which Nebuchadnezzar had taken from Jerusalem will be returned within two years. "Very well," says Jeremiah in effect, "if this prophecy is true, let us see the fulfillment. Let the captivity come to an end in two years, and we shall know that you, Hananiah, are speaking as a true prophet. Nevertheless, you do well to listen to what I, a true prophet, am saying. In times when calamities and evil were on the horizon, the true prophets have not hesitated to speak the truth, and to foretell evil. They have not changed their message, because of a desire to please the nation. The true prophets have spoken fearlessly of the evil to come, just as I am now doing. The fact that you, at such a time of impending evil, have chosen to speak forth a message of hope and good, is evidence that you are not in line with the actions of true prophets in times past. If your prophecy comes true, we shall believe you. Otherwise, you show yourself to be a false prophet."

Some such force seems to attach to the biting scorn which attends Jeremiah's words. They are adapted to a particular situation, and in the light of this particular situation we must understand them. Not to do so is to impute to them a sense which they were never intended to bear. We cannot regard this verse as constituting a principle of distinction by which all false prophets were seen to have proclaimed a message of weal, whereas true prophets were identified by a message of woe.

This examination of Mowinckel's hypothesis has been somewhat brief. At the same time it has served to show that some of the principal passages upon which he depends for support do not in reality lend the desired support. The distinction between spirit-prophets on the one hand and word-prophets on the other is one that is not found in the Old Testament. The true prophets did indeed speak the word of the Lord; they also were possessed of His Spirit. If we are to discover the point of identification between the false and true prophets we must look elsewhere.

Micaiah the Son of Imlah

Perhaps the best place to begin an investigation of the distinction which existed between the false and true prophets is with a study of the first passage in the Bible in which this distinction is to be found, namely, the remarkable prophecy about Micaiah the son of Imlah, which appears in the twenty-second chapter of First Kings.[15] The background of the prophecy is found in the fact that Ahab the king of Israel had suggested to Jehoshaphat king of Judah that he go with him together in battle against Ramoth-Gilead to take it from the king of Syria. To this proposal Jehoshaphat gave his full assent.

Before proceeding to battle, however, Jehoshaphat desired that Ahab should enquire of the Word of the Lord. Ahab, therefore, gathered together the prophets, about four hundred men. This action is adduced by Haldar as evidence that the king is envisaged as a leader of an association of cult prophets.[16] It is quite possible that these prophets were in the actual pay of Ahab, and that they were associated with the royal court. They seem at least to have been in his service and available at his call. Whether he himself was a leader of such a cultic association, however, is another question, and one which cannot be answered decisively.

As far as these prophets themselves were concerned, they were not true prophets of Jehovah, nor were they bands of prophets such as those described in connection with Samuel and Elijah, nor were they prophets of Baal, but, prophets of Jehovah who was worshipped as standing upon the form of a calf.[17] In response to the king's question as to whether he should go to war or not, they answered with one voice in the affirmative, giving just the message that the king wished to hear.

Interestingly enough, Jehoshaphat is not satisfied with this response. He seems to recognize that these prophets have not actually received their message from Jehovah, and so he asks whether there is not still another prophet of the Lord. We may not know all that was involved in the asking of this question, but it may well have been that the king's conscience was troubling him. In his heart of hearts he must have known that he was doing wrong. He, the king of Judah, should have had nothing to do with the king of the apostate nation Israel. Perhaps he is seeking for further justification of his course. We do not know. We do know however that he was not satisfied with the words of the Ahab-prophets (if they may thus be described); in their words he did not recognize the voice of Jehovah.

In response to Jehoshaphat's question, Ahab informs him that there is yet one more prophet, namely, Micaiah the son of Imlah. The question is sometimes asked why Elijah was not called. In answer however, we may note again the question of Jehoshaphat, "Is there not here a prophet of the Lord?" Elijah had gone into retirement, and at all events seems not to have been in the vicinity. Micaiah evidently dwelt near at hand, where he would readily be available. He is the only true prophet who is present, and for that reason Ahab mentions him rather than Elijah. Ahab, however, has no use for

Micaiah. "I hate him," he says, "for he does not prophesy concerning me good but evil." At first sight this attitude of the king strikes one as being churlish and childish. One is reminded of the words of Agamemnon against the sooth-sayer Chalcas:

> Prophet of evil; thou dost never speak to me what is good:
> It is always dear to your heart to prophesy what is evil;
> Thou hast never spoken nor accomplished anything good.[18]

No doubt there is something of childishness in Ahab's words and attitudes. We must look more deeply, however, if we are to understand the real reason for his dislike of Micaiah. Evidently he was imbued with the ideas of ancient superstition which believed that the prophet had some control over the divinity. Micaiah's attitude and actions, then, might be regarded on the part of Ahab as rooted in a desire to bring harm to the king. Believing that the prophet would have the power to accomplish this, he therefore lived in hatred of him. Jehoshaphat, however, rebukes the king's words by saying, "Let not the king say so," and a messenger is sent to summon Micaiah.

Meanwhile the false prophets continue prophesying before the king, and one of them, Zedekiah the son of Chenaanah, made horns of iron, declaring that with them Ahab would push Syria until it was consumed. It is possible that while engaging in this symbolical action, Zedekiah was seeking to embody the prophecy about Joseph, given in Deuteronomy 33:17, in which the horns of Joseph were said to be like the horns of a wild ox. The implication of Zedekiah's action was that the blessing which belonged to Joseph would also come to Ahab as he went against Ramoth-Gilead.

In the meantime the messenger who had been sent to fetch Micaiah was busily engaged in giving Micaiah some coaching in preparation for his meeting with the kings. This episode may be far more instructive than at first sight appears to be the case, for it shows that in the eyes of the messenger, at least, there were prophets who wanted to know in advance in what direction the wind was blowing. Without doubt the messenger believed that he was doing Micaiah a favor. In his eyes, Micaiah was no

different from the other four hundred prophets, and a word
in advance could put him upon the right track so that he would
prophesy what the king wanted to hear.

The messenger, however, mistook his man. Micaiah was
not in the least interested in knowing what the king wanted to
hear. His reply to the messenger stands out as a great classic
expression of fidelity to a high commission. "As the Lord
liveth; that which the Lord says unto me, that will I speak."
One cannot read these noble words without the conviction that
Micaiah was deeply conscious of the seriousness of his vocation.
His words call to mind the remarkable statement of the Lord
in Deuteronomy, "I shall put my words in his mouth, and he
shall speak all that which I command him." One who could
speak as did Micaiah was one who knew well that God had
called him to be a prophet, and he was also one who was fully
determined to be faithful to that honor which God had bestowed
upon him.

When the king asked Micaiah what he should do, he received
the reply, "Go up and prosper, and the Lord will give it into
the hand of the king." It is a strange reply, and gives the impression that the prophet had gone back upon the word which
he had just spoken to the messenger. Such, however, was not
the case. Some have thought that he spoke as he did merely
to show how he would speak if he were guided only by personal considerations. It is as though he had said, "If I were
to consult only my own wishes, I would urge you to go ahead
with the expedition." More likely, however, we have here
words of devastating scorn. "You ask whether you should go
up against Ramoth-Gilead? Well and good, you shall have
an answer such as you deserve. You shall have a prophecy
that fits in well with what everyone else is saying." As Machen
so admirably paraphrased the thought, ". . . the prophecy of a
parrot that speaks only what others speak, the prophecy of a
courtier who speaks only what will win the favor of men."[19]

Ahab recognized immediately the irony that lay in Micaiah's
words. "How many times must I adjure thee," he said, "that
thou speakest unto me only truth in the name of the Lord."
Micaiah's action thus constituted a stern denunciation of the

king and set Micaiah apart as one who would not preach to
win the favor of a monarch but who would declare only the
word of the Lord. Then Micaiah answers, and with his answer there is a great change. There is now no mere repetition
of words which the king wished to hear, but a depth of dignity
and beauty such as characterized great and true prophecy. "I
saw all Israel scattered upon the hills, as a flock of sheep which
have no shepherd; And the Lord said, These have no masters,
let them return each one to his house in peace."

This did not please Ahab, and he remarked to Jehoshaphat,
"Did not I say that he does not prophesy good unto me, but
evil?" Micaiah then proceeded to explain to Ahab what it was
that lay in back of the messages of the false prophets. "And
he said, Wherefore, hear the word of the Lord, I saw Jehovah
sitting upon His throne, and all the host of heaven standing
by Him, from His right and from His left. And Jehovah said,
Who will deceive Ahab, that he should go up and fall in
Ramoth-Gilead? and one spake thus and another thus. And the
spirit went out and stood before Jehovah and said, I shall deceive him, and Jehovah said unto him, Wherewith? And he
said, I shall go out and be a spirit of deception in the mouth of
all his prophets. And He said, Thou shalt deceive and also
thou art able. Go and do thus. And now, behold! Jehovah
hath sent a spirit of deception in the mouth of all thy prophets,
and Jehovah hath spoken evil concerning thee."

We have translated the passage somewhat literally so as to
bring out certain points which are obscured in the ordinary
English translations. In vision Micaiah sees the Lord upon
His throne. It is a picture which reveals the absolute sovereignty of God in His providential dealings. It was His
design that Ahab should perish at Ramoth-Gilead and that the
means which would lead to his destruction were to be found
in a deception of his mind, produced by the words of the false
prophets. It is as though the prophet had announced to the
king, "You are evil, and part of the judgment which is to come
upon you because of your ungodly life is a deception of your
mind which will ultimately result in death." The message is a
strong reminder to us of the fact that all things which come to

pass in time have been decreed by God. And in His strange Providence, He who is Himself holy and pure and not the Author of evil, had decreed that the death of Ahab should take place at Ramoth-Gilead and that it should be the result of a false message having been preached to him and accepted by him.

When therefore we read the words, "Who will deceive Ahab?" we must remember that we are being given a glimpse into the decretive will of God before that will has actually been carried out in God's providential works. He who will find fault with this representation of God is finding fault, not only with this representation, but with the fact that God has included evil in His eternal decrees.[20]

The one who is ready to deceive Ahab is described as the spirit. Calvin and others have held that the reference is to Satan himself, and that the situation is somewhat analogous to the prologue of Job. However, the definite article seems to preclude a reference to Satan. It is better to regard the lying spirit as the personified spirit of prophecy itself. Thus, in Zechariah 13:2 we read, "I shall cause the prophets and the unclean spirit to pass out of the land." Likewise, the Apostle John speaks of the "spirit of truth and the spirit of error" (1 John 4:6). The idea finds expression also in 2 Thessalonians 2:11, "And for this cause God shall send them strong delusion, that they should believe a lie." There is then a spirit of prophecy as such, without reference to a distinction between true and false prophecy. Thus there will come upon the false prophets a spirit of delusion or of falsehood which is sent from God and under the influence of which they will declare a message that is not in accord with the truth. On this occasion at least, even the false prophets were subject to an influence that was beyond their own control and which they could not withstand. They were the recipients of an impulsion which was evil in nature and which could lead them to utter only that which was contrary to the truth. Micaiah sums up the matter in verse twenty-three, "And now, behold! Jehovah hath put a lying spirit in the mouth of all these thy prophets, and Jehovah hath spoken evil against thee."

Very interesting is the reaction of Zedekiah to this analysis of Micaiah. Enraged, he smites Micaiah upon the cheek and says, "Whence has the Spirit of Jehovah passed from with me to speak with thee?" The action of the angered prophet of Ahab reveals that he was not inspired from the Spirit of the true God, else he would not have resorted to tactics such as he did, but rather would have awaited with patience and suffering whatever should come upon him. At the same time, we may possibly understand his anger as due at least in part to the fact that he regarded Micaiah's statements as a true exposure. He was well aware that the message which he had proclaimed was not one of his own devising. It was a message, rather, which he was compelled to speak. The source of his inspiration was not the Spirit of God, but a lying spirit; nevertheless, it was a source outside of himself. Zedekiah evidently felt that Micaiah had exposed him, and hence he must strike the prophet. His true nature thus manifests itself.

From a consideration of this remarkable prophecy there are several points which we may note. In the first place those who are regarded in the Bible as false prophets did at times indeed associate together about a common center, such as the king's court. In the second place those who were regarded as false prophets in this episode were men who were willing to speak a message that was pleasing to the king in order to seek his favor. This is seen from the manner in which the messenger sought to persuade Micaiah to do likewise, and it is also seen in the fact that these prophets spoke with one voice, as though there had been an agreement before-hand.

At the same time the false prophets were men who could be deceived. A spirit of falsehood could come upon them and so overpower them that they became the slaves of that spirit and spoke in accord with its dictates. The question therefore arises, Were these prophets false because a spirit of deception had come upon them and consequently had rendered them false, or rather were they evil men already and because they were evil, the spirit of deception found ready lodgment in their hearts?

Prophets Who Were Deceived

The answer to questions such as these can be found only by a consideration of the principles which govern the Divine economy. Time and time again God had promised to send various punishments upon His people because of their sins. And perhaps it is but a narrower application of this idea to assume that falsehood may have been sent upon certain men because they were themselves already false. They were men who did not endeavor to walk in accordance with the Law of God, and so their minds did become prey to a delusion. Under ordinary circumstances these men were apparently ready to preach to the king a message which he wanted to hear. They were, therefore, men whose primary interest was not the truth, and consequently, the spirit of delusion came upon them and made them its subjects. Although the term "false prophets" does not occur in the Bible itself, nevertheless, these men showed that they were not true prophets by the fact that they readily spoke what the king wanted to hear, and their own evil nature made them fit subjects for the entrance of a spirit of falsehood which could be detected by those who knew the truth.

It does not follow however, that every time a false prophet spoke, he was under the special influence of a spirit of delusion. Perhaps there were those who spoke simply from ignorance of the truth or from a perverse heart. Very instructive is the passage found in Hosea 9:7, 8, "The days of visitation have come; the days of recompense have come; Israel will know. The prophet is a fool; the man of spirit is mad, because of the abundance of thine iniquity, and great is the enmity. Ephraim was a watchman with my God, as for the prophet, the snare of the fowler is upon all his ways, enmity is in the house of his god." This passage is confessedly difficult, and interpretations have varied. At the same time, the central message appears to be clear. Hosea is pointing out to his nation that the days of the visitation of Divine judgment will come, and that the people will learn that their prophets have deceived them. In that day Israel will understand that the guides upon whom she depended, the prophet and the man of the spirit, have proven to be untrustworthy. These men had evidently prophesied to the effect that days of recompense and visitation would not come, a message which the people were willing enough to hear. They were, therefore, false prophets, and the spirit mentioned cannot be the spirit of truth but rather a spirit of falsehood which characterized those who thus spoke. The man of the spirit is like the man mentioned in Micah 2:11 who walks in the spirit and falsehood. From these words of Hosea we may learn that those who throughout the course of Israel's history prophesied messages foretelling only good were men who were inspired of a false spirit.

The prophet goes on to say that Ephraim does indeed look out for revelations and messages, and does this by the side of the true prophet of God. Ephraim will then learn that its own prophets have not been true, but that they were like the snares of a bird-catcher, who lead the nation on to its destruction. What Hosea is teaching is that there existed in ancient Israel a body of men who bore the name *nahbi* and "man of the spirit," but who were not entitled to such designations. The true *nabhi* was raised up of God and the "man of the Spirit" was a man upon whom the Spirit of God had come. It was necessary for ancient Israel to probe more deeply and to learn to discern the false from the true. Many who bore these designations were living a lie; they had not been raised up by God, and the spirit which was in them was not the spirit of truth but of falsehood. They spake messages, therefore, which did not originate with God, but which were the product of an evil spirit and could but deceive the nation.

False prophecy in the Old Testament however, is not always attributed to the direct influence of a spirit of falsehood, such as deceived the prophets of Ahab's court. Sometimes the false prophets are mentioned as those who speak merely from their own heart and sometimes it is the effect of their prophesying which receives the stress. In Isaiah 9:14ff. the tail of the nation is said to be the prophet that teacheth lies and thus causes the people to err even unto destruction. Ezekiel mentions those who prophesy out of their own heart and follow their own spirit when in reality they have not received a revelation. They are said to see vanity and to divine lies (Ezekiel 13:9). In other words they acted as though they were true prophets, whereas, as a matter of fact, no revelation from God had come to them. These prophets, as Ezekiel points out in another passage, had deliberately lied (Ezekiel 13:7). They claimed that God had actually spoken, whereas He had not spoken.

According to Micah 3:5, 6 these men were messengers of falsehood in that they proclaimed a message of peace when there was no peace, and because of this falsehood, the day would become black over them. Zephaniah characterizes such men as "light and treacherous persons" (Zephaniah 3:4). Jeremiah goes to the heart of the matter when he points out that they were men whom God had not sent. We may translate his words literally: "And Jehovah said unto me, Falsehood do the prophets prophesy in My name; I have not sent them and I have not commanded them and I have not spoken unto them; a vision of falsehood and divination and nought and the imagination of their heart they prophesy unto you. Therefore thus saith Jehovah concerning the prophets who prophesy in My name when I have not sent them, and they say, Sword and evil will not be in this land; by the sword and by the evil those prophets will be consumed." From this passage it appears very clearly that the false prophet, whatever else may be said about him, was a man who had not received his message from Jehovah. Whether that message was the direct product of the inspiration of a lying spirit or whether it was the product of his own heart — and there seem to have been instances of both — the false prophet proclaimed a message that was not in accord with the truth because he had not been sent by God, and the Word of God had not been placed in his mouth.

The existence of these false prophets and their ministry was responsible for great calamity in ancient Israel. In a truly classic passage Jeremiah lifts up his voice against them and the evil which they have done. With respect to them, he says, his heart within him is broken. His bones shake, and he compares himself to a drunken man, one whom wine hath overcome. The prophets are profane, he continues, and their wickedness is found in the house of Jehovah. In the prophets who dwelt at Samaria, Jeremiah says that he has seen folly, since they prophesied by Baal. The prophets of Jerusalem also have committed folly, " . . . they commit adultery, and they walk in lies, and they strengthen the hands of evil doers, so that none returns from his evil; all of them have become to me as Sodom, and its inhabitants as Gomorrah" (Jeremiah 23:14b). Again, " . . . for from the prophets of Jerusalem there has gone forth alienation to all the land" (Jeremiah 23:15b). Therefore, the nation is commanded not to hearken to such prophets, since they speak merely the vision of their own heart, and not one which comes from the mouth of Jehovah. "God did not send them," we may paraphrase, "yet they ran; He did not speak unto them, but they, despite this fact, uttered their prophecies. They had not stood in the council of God, and therefore they could not cause the people to hear God's words. God, however, knows full well what they are saying. He is not a God who is merely near at hand and not far off. He hears the claims of these false messengers who proclaim lies in His name, by constantly saying, 'I have dreamed, I have dreamed.' Such men are prophets, but they are prophets of the deceit of their own hearts, and by means of their dreams they have caused the people to forget the Name of Jehovah. If a man does indeed have the word of Jehovah, he should speak it, for that word is like fire and like the hammer that breaks the rock in pieces. Had Jehovah's word been spoken, the nation would not have gone astray, but rather would have been convicted of its unrighteousness.

"These false prophets, however, actually steal My words from their neighbors. They use their tongues, and utter, 'He saith.' They prophesy lying dreams; they utter lies, and their boasting is vain. God, however, did not send them, nor did He command them, and consequently, they are of no profit to the nation. They have perverted the words of the living God. Hence, upon the sinful nation is to come an everlasting reproach and a perpetual shame, which shall not be forgotten."

Such a scathing denunciation makes it clear that there was antagonism between these false prophets and a man such as Jeremiah whom God had actually sent. On their part, confident that the word would not perish from the prophets, they sought to conspire against him. During the beginning of the reign of Jehoiakim the priests and prophets, upon hearing a messenger of condemnation from the mouth of Jeremiah, laid hold on him, saying, "Thou shalt surely die" (Jeremiah 26:8b). "Why," they asked him in effect, "hast thou prophesied, comparing the temple to Shiloh, and declaring the utter destruction of this city?" An episode such as this makes it clear that the false prophets were men who depended for the source of their messages upon human wisdom and not upon Divine revelation. According to their best thought, without a doubt, Jeremiah's messages appeared to be foolishness. He was giving utterance to messages of doom and calamity, whereas, as far as one could tell, such messages were not really warranted. Hence it appears that the false prophets often spoke forth words of hope, and could not brook contrary predictions.

Even when appearances might not seem to warrant a message of hope there were those who nevertheless believed it best to refuse to admit any consideration of complete destruction and punishment. Consequently, during the fourth year of the reign of Zedekiah, after Jehoiachin had already been taken captive, and two assaults had been made upon Jerusalem, a certain false prophet, Hananiah the son of Azzur the prophet, declared that within two full years the vessels of the temple would be returned. This prophecy he uttered in the name of Jehovah the true God. To this message of falsehood Jeremiah rose in opposition. "Very well," he said in effect, "if you have prophesied the truth, let the Lord fulfill the prediction. A prophet should speak in accord with the truth. Prophets in previous times have uttered their messages concerning war and evil and pestilence. Such prophecies are not at all unusual. If a man ventures to prophesy of peace, he can only be recognized as a true prophet, if Jehovah fulfills his message."

Thus far we have considered only those prophets who were false in that they spoke lies in the name of Jehovah. There were also men who spoke in the name of other gods and thus deceived the people. One of the condemnations which Jeremiah (2:8) uttered against the nation was that the prophets had prophesied by Baal and walked after those things which do not profit. Such men are not to be regarded as belonging in the same class with the prophets of Baal who were present at the contest upon Mt. Carmel. These latter were not Israelites; they made no profession of allegiance whatever to the God of Israel. They were devotees of the god of another nation. Not so, however, those whom Jeremiah condemns. These were Israelites who claimed to be prophets. However, so meagre was their understanding of the true nature of prophecy, or possibly, so perverse was their nature that they would utter prediction not in the name of the God of Israel but in the name of Baal. It was against such as these that Moses had uttered his remarkable warning in Deuteronomy. Even if such a prophet or dreamer of dreams performs signs and wonders, yet utters his messages in the name of a god other than Jehovah, the people were not to hearken unto him. In His inscrutable providence God permitted such deceivers to appear in order to test the love of His own nation.

The Distinction Between True and False Prophets

Upon the basis of the rather brief survey just given it will now be possible to say a word respecting the relationship which existed between the false and the true prophets. As we have seen, it was not a case of the one being an ecstatic and the other not, nor of the one having the spirit whereas the other had the word of Jehovah. The point of distinction lay not in the external realm, but rather, as Rowley has recently stressed, in the realm of the spirit.[21]

That which distinguished the true from the false prophet lay in the fact that the true had received a message from Jehovah, whereas the false had not. The question is one which can be answered aright only upon the basis of a truly Christian-theistic

position. To arrive at the correct answer therefore, it is necessary to postulate the existence of Jehovah as the true God, who
could reveal His will unto His servants the prophets. He who
is the Creator did, in accordance with His own desire, reveal
His secret unto the prophets, and they in turn gave utterance
to that which had been spoken to them. It is necessary that we
thus carefully and insistently stress the need for positing belief
in the actual objective, metaphysical existence of the God of
Israel, for it is beside the point to speak of a God who reveals
if no such God exists. True prophets, therefore, were not
merely men who thought that Jehovah had spoken to them.
If we limit our definition of the true prophets as men who were
conscious of having received a message from Jehovah, the God
of Israel, and if we go no further, we have not reached the
heart of the matter. The true prophet was not only conscious
of having received a revelation from Jehovah; he had, as a
matter óf actual fact, received such a message. Jehovah, the
God of Israel, had spoken His word to the prophet. Any view
of prophecy which does not come to grips with the question of
revelation and the existence of God has failed at the outset.

The false prophets, on the other hand, had not received messages from God. They prophesied, but the messages which
they uttered were of human origination, and not Divine revelations. The visions which they experienced were not imposed
upon them in a special supernatural manner, as was the case
with the true prophets, but were visions which came from the
human heart alone. Therein lay the mark of distinction. The
true prophets had received special revelation from God; the
false prophets had not.

Why then, it may well be asked, were there false prophets?
Why did men dare to proclaim that their words had come
from God when such was not actually the case? To answer
these questions we must remember that, as a true prophet has
said, "the heart of man is deceitful above all things and
desperately wicked."[22] Why do ministers of the Gospel today
speak in the Name of Jesus Christ and yet deny the doctrines
of the Christian Faith? What leads a man who does not believe to enter the ministry? These are questions that involve

the individual human heart before God. No doubt there are many reasons why those who are not called of God to preach His Word are nevertheless to be found standing in the pulpits of the country. Be that as it may, by their preaching of a false gospel and their encouraging of human ability and goodness, they deceive many.

Perhaps not all of the false prophets of ancient Israel were deliberately deceitful; it is quite possible that many of them were themselves deceived. It is possible for a man to think that he has the word of God, when he actually has not. A man who has truly received a revelation from God may know that such is the case; but a man who has received no such revelation may indeed be deceived. No doubt some of the false prophets were men of such a class.

Many of them however are set forth in the Bible as wicked men. They were drunken (Isaiah 28:7), and they uttered a message that would find favor with their hearers. They were corrupt, blind leaders of the blind, who felt secure in their position.

Ewald has pointed out three respects in which it is possible for a prophet to become corrupted, respects which, he thinks, adhere in the very nature of prophecy itself.[28] In the first place he calls attention to the unusual phenomena which sometimes accompanied prophecy and which are commonly designated by the word ecstasy. Such ecstasy, whatever its precise nature may have been, should have been under the control of the prophet, yet it may very easily have passed over into uncontrolled frenzy. Secondly, as we have pointed out, whereas the true prophet knew well that he had received the word of Jehovah, the false prophet had not undergone such an experience. Conceivably he might have believed himself to have been the recipient of Jehovah's word, whereas such had not really been the case. Lastly, there may have been a tendency for prophecy to become a mere profession. There may have been those who had been associated with the bands of prophets, mentioned in Samuel and Kings, who would be inclined to regard prophecy as nothing more than a profession, and if it were possible for such men to serve in the pay of the king, they would naturally seek to do so.

The real reason for the existence of false prophecy, however, is to be found, not in such external circumstances, but rather in the corruption of the human heart. The fallen heart has, despite its depravity, retained the *semen divinitatis* and seeks to give expression to some kind of religion. After all is said and done there is little real distinction between the false prophet and the soothsayer of antiquity. Hence, the phenomena which characterize the false prophets in Israel may doubtless also have characterized such men in other countries. And in Israel there would naturally be a tendency for the false to imitate the true. True prophecy came forth in the Name of Jehovah; it is to be expected that false prophecy would for the most part do the same thing. True prophecy however, was not imitative; it was unique. False prophecy was of one piece with that whole web of superstitious practice which bound the ancient world. There were essential resemblances between the *mahhu* and *baru* priests and the false prophets of Israel, as there were accidental resemblances between these priests and the true prophets.

If however, the distinction between the two was such as we have maintained, it may well be asked how the Israelite of old could distinguish between them. Certain hints have already been mentioned. If a prophet spoke in the name of any god other than Jehovah, he was not to be obeyed. If he should speak in the name of Jehovah and his message did not come to pass, he would be shown to be false, as was the case with Hananiah, who predicted the return from captivity within two full years. True prophets therefore would be accredited as such by the fact that their messages came to fulfillment. In the case of those who uttered Messianic prophecies, we may assume that, since their local messages were accredited and fulfilled, they were thus shown to be trustworthy and would be believed when they spoke of the distant salvation.

There is however, another factor which must be taken into account. It is a factor which is really more fundamental than the considerations which have just been mentioned. When

the incarnate Son of God was upon earth He spake of His
sheep as follows: ". . . they know his voice. And a stranger
will they not follow, but will flee from him; ᵢᵤr they know
not the voice of strangers." And again: "Every one that is
of the truth heareth my voice" (John 10:4b, 5; 18:37b).
With these words we come into the very heart of the question.
Those who are of the truth, who are "My sheep," whether they
live in New Testament times or at the present day or whether
they lived during the Old Testament age, know the voice of
God. The Lord is their shepherd, for in His sovereign particular love, He has absolutely elected them unto everlasting
life. They are His people, purchased by the shedding of the
precious blood of Jesus Christ, and they hear His voice. The
redeemed know the words of God and they follow them.

In ancient Israel the true "church of God" ("for he is not
a Jew which is one outwardly" . . . Romans 2:8a) would know
the voice of God speaking in the true prophets and would turn
from the words of false prophets, not recognizing in them
God's words. Those who walked in humble obedience to the
Law of God, who loved Him with all the heart and who looked
for the consolation of Israel and the coming of the Desire of
nations, would recognize their Father's voice, just as the
humble Christian believer of the present day, untutored and
uneducated though he may be, yet knows the Word of God
and can detect it from those messages which are not in harmony with the Voice of God.

Here then, we must rest the case. Two kinds of prophets
existed side by side in Israel — the true and the false. The
true came forth with a message from Jehovah, a message for
the benefit of the nation. The false uttered a message of human
origination, and consequently, one which could not meet the
deep needs of the people and which could not be for its ulti-
mate good. Any serious attempt to account for the origin and
nature of prophecy in Israel must take full account of these two
groups and of the profound gulf which separated them. The
one was from man; the other from God.

CHAPTER VIII

Were the Prophets Writers?

I N what has been said thus far, we have sought to defend the position that the prophetic movement in Israel was of a unique nature, and that this uniqueness was to be found in the fact that it was an institution raised up of God. The prophets were recipients of Divine revelation and not merely religious leaders with gifted insight. Our investigation cannot be regarded as completed, however, until we have come to grips with another problem. Granted that the prophets were special messengers of the one living and true God, wherein lies their relevance for us today? Were the prophets spokesmen for God who were concerned only with contemporary problems, or did they also have a message for future days?

There are those who have stressed the thought that the prophets uttered messages which concerned only their own times. This was the position of the older liberalism, and we may note a classic expression of it in the words of A. B. Davidson: "The prophet is always a man of his own time, and it is always to the people of his own time that he speaks, not to a generation long after nor to us. And the things of which he speaks will always be things of importance to the people of his own day, whether they be things belonging to their internal life and conduct, or things affecting their external fortunes as a people among other peoples."[1] Davidson further declared "That a prophetical writer always makes the basis of his prophecies the historical situation in which he himself is placed."[2]

If these statements of Davidson accurately characterize the Old Testament, we may readily see that there can be no such thing as true prediction.[3] If the words which the prophet uttered were always spoken to his own and not to subsequent generations, it would seem that there is no such thing as Mes-

153

sianic prophecy, for Messianic prophecy is prediction in its highest and best expression.

The position which Davidson has so clearly stated has also found favor among more recent scholars. As a result of the labors of Hermann Gunkel, the school of "form-criticism" has gained great prominence. In his own studies of Genesis and the Psalms Gunkel laid stress upon the need for discovering the "life situation" in which the original utterance of the prophet was given forth.[4] It has come to be almost an axiom of modern scholarly research that in the study of the prophetical books one must, before he can correctly interpret an oracle, find the situation in life — i. e., the historical situation, in which the oracle first came to expression, and which called it forth. One need but consult any recent work upon the prophets and he will discover that it is based upon this underlying fundamental.

There is, however, another way of evaluating the prophets. According to the consistent representation of the Scriptures, the prophets did not speak only to their own generation, nor were their messages called forth merely because of certain historical situations. There is of course a certain sense in which it may be maintained that an historical situation did form the background for the prophetical messages, in that the great need of the people in the promised land was for the direct voice of God. And because the need of the nation was so great, God did raise up the prophetic institution. The continued sinful character of Israel called forth the many denunciations which the prophet uttered. But this is quite a different thing from the position that the prophets were merely men of their own time and that their messages, individually, were each called forth by some local situation.

The picture which the Old Testament gives is quite different from that which is postulated by the modern school of interpretation, as may be seen, for example, by an examination of the remarkable prophecy of peace and salvation uttered by Isaiah (2:2-4). The subject of this prophecy has to do with that which takes place in the latter days. "When these latter days come," we may paraphrase the thought, "they will find the mountain of the Lord's house established in the top of the mountains." The phrase "the latter days" is clearly eschatological, and refers to the end part of the days.

Without a doubt this prophecy was uttered against the dark background of the present sinfulness of the nation. Indeed, it is made the occasion for an appeal to Judah to come and walk in the light of the Lord. But it is absolutely impossible to discover any particular situation in the life of the nation — other than the general condition of sinfulness — which gave rise to the utterance of this particular promise. If these words are a real prophecy of the future, then Isaiah is clearly speaking forth a message which has to do with later generations. He is, in other words, describing a condition which will take place long after he himself and his contemporaries have departed from the scene of earthly existence.

Here again the whole question of the nature of prophecy meets us. Are we to consider this message as expressing merely the hopes of the prophet, or shall we rather look upon it as an actual prediction of things which would surely come to pass? The seriousness of the message and the analogy of the Scripture lead one to adopt the latter alternative, and if we do adopt this latter alternative we are compelled to assert that the prophet was speaking not only of his own time, but of one long subsequent to himself.

This same evaluation of the work of the prophets is stated very clearly in the New Testament, and we need do no more than appeal to a few examples. John declares that Isaiah was speaking of the unbelief of the people of Christ's day, and that he prophesied when he saw Christ's glory. The life situation which called forth Isaiah's utterances, therefore, was the glory of Christ. Isaiah saw that glory and spoke of Christ. Peter was very bold to assert that ". . . all the prophets from Samuel and them that followed after, as many as have spoken, they also told of these days" (Acts 3:24). The apostle Paul begins his epistle to the Romans by mentioning the Gospel which God had "promised afore by his prophets in the Holy Scriptures" (Romans 1:2). There is no need to multiply examples. A mere cursory glance at the New Testament should convince anyone that its writers did indeed believe that the prophets were speaking of the Messianic salvation.

If the New Testament is correct in such an evaluation it follows that there was a good reason for the preservation in writing of the prophetical utterances. If these words were not merely confined to some local situation, but were words of life given by God, we may readily understand that in His wise providence God made provision for their preservation. If however, the New Testament view is not correct, we are faced with the problem as to why and how these words were committed to writing. Matthews, for example, who very definitely excludes the supernatural element from prophecy, looks upon the writing down of the prophecies as an innovation upon the prophets' part.[5] This was, he thinks, a movement away from what was transient and ecstatic toward that which was ethical and reflective. The words were deemed to have permanent value, and so were committed to writing. The older liberalism generally has set forth elaborate theories as to the composition of the prophetical books, and there is no point in entering into a discussion of them here.

A new feature was injected into the discussion, however, by the insistence of Gunkel upon the spoken word as the unit of tradition. We should not even think of pen and ink, he maintained, but only of the spoken word.[6] H. S. Nyberg, in his important *Studien im Hoseabuche,* took up this thought and maintained that before the exile there was very little of the Old Testament in written form.[7] There were circles and groups which handed down the tradition, and only after the exile did the written Old Testament appear. The prehistory of the Old Testament literary material was therefore for the most part oral in character, and the question of obtaining the very words which the prophets spake was not to be settled upon the grounds of literary criticism but rather upon those of the history of tradition.

These views of Nyberg were applied to the prophetical books in particular by Birkeland[8] and also by Engnell who would associate the prophets with the cultic groups, and who has asserted the bankruptcy of literary criticism.[9] In answer to

Engnell Mowinckel has written a strong plea for a combination of literary critical methods with the study of the history of tradition.[10] These, thinks Mowinckel, together with the history of form, must all be employed in the interpretation of the prophets and in the endeavor to reach the actual words which lie behind the various strata of tradition.

A most refreshing note has been added to the debate by the appearance of a study devoted to the question of transmission among the Arabs. This was conducted by Widengren for the purpose of informing those Old Testament scholars who do not possess a first hand knowledge of the Arabic literature.[11] By an examination of the situation in pre-Islamic times Widengren shows that transmission among the Arabs was not limited to the oral word alone but that poems were better preserved if they were written down. Oral transmission, he points out, has exerted a disastrous effect upon the faithful handing down of ancient poetry. By extending the survey to include the Koran and early Islamic literature Widengren concludes that ". . . it is wrong to contrast oral and written tradition too much in an ancient Semitic culture" (p. 56). When he turns to the prophets of Israel, Widengren comes to essentially the same conclusion. He thinks that the prophets were acquainted with writing, and often wrote their prophecies themselves. Sometimes they may have dictated, and sometimes the prophecies may have been transmitted for a short time and then written down by disciples of the prophets. Those parts which survived the longest in oral form were probably the biographical parts.

There is much worthwhile material in Widengren's pamphlet, and it is a work which is deserving of careful study. Although we cannot accept the basic approach to the study of prophecy which it presents, nevertheless, it is in our opinion one of the most stimulating works which has appeared in recent times. It has been answered by Engnell who again states his position, and since Engnell is apparently the spearhead of the "Uppsala School," we shall do well to set forth his position as he has last expounded it.[12]

Engnell seeks to make it clear that he does not maintain that the entire Old Testament was transmitted by way of oral tradition. He holds rather that the two modes of transmission, oral and written have largely run side by side and should not be played off against one another, as though the one necessarily excluded the other. He does believe, however, that most of the Old Testament was not committed to writing until the time of the exile or later. In support of this position he points to the analogy of the transmission of other literature from the Near East. More important than this, however, is the internal analysis of the Old Testament literature itself. It is along this line, thinks Engnell, that the problem is to be solved, and not merely by appeals to Arabian literature or to the texts of Ras Schamra.

Oral transmission, he points out, does not necessarily involve the completely accurate preservation of the tradition but is rather a living remodelling. At the same time, the fact that the Old Testament is a sacred book ("the absolutely peculiar position of the O. T., owing to its religious 'life situation' and its cultic confinement, its character of being a sacral, a holy literature") gave to oral transmission a capacity for resisting alterations and corruptions. Hence also, any comparison with a profane literature is fallacious. If we are to do justice to the understanding of the Old Testament, we must, thinks Engnell, engage in a just evaluation of the role of oral transmission.[18]

When is the orthodox scholar to stand in this debate? For our part we rejoice in the emphasis which Engnell places upon the uniqueness of the Old Testament. Unlike, him, however, we find that uniqueness to consist not in the religious or sacral character of the Old Testament, but rather in the fact that it is a revelation from God to man. And since this is so we are unable to enter the ranks of the debate which the Scandinavian scholars are now waging over the relative merits of oral and literary tradition. As a conservative, we naturally find comfort in many of the remarks which Engnell has to make against the method of literary criticism, as it has been practiced by the school of Wellhausen and others. We believe, however, that the principles of form-criticism which underlie Engnell's works are also erroneous. The writing of the Old Testament is sui generis. It stands apart from all else, and hence we can discuss the question of the composition of the prophetical books only upon the basis of what those books themselves have to say.

When therefore we approach the books of the prophets we immediately make the discovery that there is a remarkable silence about the question of composition. There is a heading over the individual books, and we, for our part, believe that those headings are trustworthy in their statements and that they were inserted over the books in all probability by the prophet himself. Actual statements concerning the writing down of the prophecies are very few in number. Isaiah is told to take a great scroll and to write upon it with the pen of a man (8:1). This is a symbolical action, and throws little light upon the question of the writing down of the prophetical books. The prophet is also commanded to "Bind up the testimony, seal the law among my disciples" (8:16). He is also commanded to go and write in a table and note in a book, that it may be for the last day, for a time for ever (Isaiah 30:8). The roll which was revealed to Ezekiel was covered with writing (Ezekiel 2:9ff.), and Ezekiel is commanded to write the law of the Temple and its ordinances (Ezekiel 43:11, 12). Likewise Habakkuk is commanded to write his vision and to make it plain upon tables (Habakkuk 2:2).

It is from Jeremiah however that we learn most. In one passage (30:2) the command comes to him to write in a book all the words which God has spoken to him. In the thirty-sixth chapter we are given the account of how Jeremiah, at the command of God, dictated to his scribe Baruch the words of his prophecy. When Baruch was asked how this took place, he replied, "He pronounced all these words unto me with his mouth, and I wrote them with ink in the book" (Jeremiah 36:20). It was this scroll which Jehoiakim burned in the fire, having cut it up piece by piece with his pen knife. Hence we are told, "And Jeremiah took another roll, and he gave it unto Baruch the son of Neriah the scribe, and he wrote upon it from the mouth of Jeremiah all the words of the book which Jehoiakim the king of Judah had burned in the fire, and there were yet added upon them many similar words" (Jeremiah

36:32). Finally we are told that Jeremiah wrote ". . . in a book all the evil that should come upon Babylon, even all these words that are written against Babylon" (Jeremiah 51:60).[14]

In the light of this scanty evidence there are at least certain conclusions to which we may come. For one thing the writing was for the purpose of preserving the message. The message was not a mere oracle to be uttered and forgotten, as was the case with thousands of the heathen oracles. Again, we are probably warranted in using the example of Jeremiah as normative. As he was commanded to write down his prophecies, so, we may assume, did the other prophets also write. Indeed, the question may very well arise whether some parts of the prophecies were ever uttered orally. It may indeed be that Isaiah actually preached the last twenty-seven chapters of his book, but it would seem more likely that he composed these prophecies in writing, looking forward in vision to the time when the nation would be in bondage and in need of a deliverer.

More than this we can scarcely say. In the light of the available evidence, however, we appear to be most warranted in declaring that the prophets themselves, as inspired organs of the Holy Spirit, did commit their messages to writing, so that they would be preserved from perishing and might remain for the edification of future generations of the people of God.

CHAPTER IX

The Prophets as Recipients of Revelation

I T is now necessary to consider more carefully than we have done heretofore the claims which the prophets made for themselves, and in approaching this question we must do more than limit the discussion to a consideration of their supposedly supra-normal experiences. Eissfeldt, for example, speaks of the nature and significance of the supranormal experiences of the prophets as being a psychological question.[1] However, to speak thus is to delimit the issue at the outset. The so-called supranormal experiences of the prophets cannot be considered in isolation from other factors.

The Unique Character of Old Testament Prophecy

If we are to pay serious heed to the words of the prophets we are driven to the conclusion that they believed themselves to have been the recipients of revelation from the God of Israel. There is a wondrous ease with which they speak forth in the assurance that Jehovah has first spoken to them. They come before the nation, not as religious leaders who have a word to speak in their own name, but rather as those who are compelled to give utterance to a word which has come to them from Jehovah. Jehovah was the God of Israel who existed in independence of the prophets, and with whom they could hold real converse. Jehovah had spoken, and in that belief lay the compelling motive for action. The first question therefore, to be considered in any proper analysis of the position of the prophets as recipients of revelation is the psychological conviction which they themselves had that God had actually spoken to them. Whence came this conviction? Was it the result of a delusion, or was it the product of a deliberate at-

tempt to deceive? Or, strange as the thought may be to the
modern mind — is the explanation which the prophets themselves give of their conviction based upon fact? Did God
actually speak to them as they claimed that He did?

Closely allied with this problem is another. In Israel we are
not dealing with a prophet who appeared now and then upon
the horizon, for in the history of Israel prophecy was no mere
isolated phenomenon. Rather we find a unique movement
which possessed remarkable continuity. Although Abraham
was called a prophet, and although now and then an isolated
prophet appeared upon the scene, from the time of Samuel
down to the close of the Old Testament period, the goodly
company of the prophets stood forth upon the religious horizon. The psychological conviction of which we have been
speaking was not limited to one or two men, not even to the
greatest, but rather characterized the entire history of the
prophetic movement. If an unnamed man of God may come
with tremendous earnestness before Eli and cry "Thus saith
the Lord" (1 Samuel 2:27), so also may Malachi introduce
his message as "The burden of the word of the LORD to
Israel by Malachi" (Malachi 1:1). Wherever we turn in the
Old Testament we find the prophets speaking forth in the
Name of Jehovah, and speaking with deep earnestness. How
is this continuity, which extended over several centuries, and
which is utterly without parallel in any nation of antiquity
other than Israel, to be explained?

In the third place, the student must pay attention to another
phenomenon, namely the body of predictions which characterized the entire prophetic movement. When these predictions
are taken together, it becomes apparent that there is a teleological trend to the whole. The prophets' are looking forward to
the "last days" when God shall visit His sinful people in blessing and salvation. It is not that eschatology characterizes the
utterances of isolated prophets, but rather that it is woven into
the very texture of the entire prophetic fabric. One cannot
read the words of the prophets without giving wholehearted
agreement and approbation to the inspired utterance of the

Apostle, "Yea, and all the prophets from Samuel and them that followed after, as many as have spoken, they also told of these days" (Acts 3:24).

Nevertheless, these three elements, so essential to any true understanding of the phenomenon, have often been overlooked. It has been held by some that the prophetic movement of Israel was but an outgrowth of something that was already present on the soil of Canaan. One of the most effective advocates of this view was Gustav Hölscher, whose work appeared in 1914.[2] According to Hölscher the home of prophecy was not the Arabian desert but rather the districts where culture and race were not pure Semitic. Prophecy was one of those religious and cultural connections which had bound Syria and Asia Minor since ancient times, and is, therefore, to be regarded as of Canaanitish origin.

The same view has been presented by Alfred Jepsen who appeals to the example of Wen-Amon at the court of Byblos.[3] Here he thinks, we have the elements of prophecy. It was during a dance, possibly an ecstatic dance, that the revelation came. The revelation was furthermore given during a sacrifice, and the "prophet" was found at the royal court. In addition to this example of Wen-Amon, Jepsen calls attention to the fact that the prophets of Baal also belonged to Canaan, and he also appeals to the inscription of Zakir of Hamath as evidence for the Canaanitish origin of prophecy.

In opposition to this view Alfred Haldar, as we have seen, believes that the phenomenon was widespread in the ancient world.[4] For our part we are not going to adopt either one or the other of these positions. As we have sought to make plain, we believe that the phenomenon found in the Old Testament was a revelation from God and did not grow out of similar phenomena to be found elsewhere. As far as the false prophets of Israel were concerned, we do agree that the phenomenon which they represented was found widespread in the ancient Near East, and therefore, to this extent, we would follow Haldar as over against Hölscher and Jepsen.

Were the Prophets Ecstatics?

In line with his view that prophecy was of Canaanitish origin, Hölscher advanced the view that the prophets of Israel were ecstatics.[5] Prophets and seers of all times, he tells us, including those of the Hebrews, have been known for their peculiar spiritual states, through which they were in possession of divine revelations. These experiences are customarily dealt with under the concepts of ecstasy and vision, and are more or less bound up with emotional excitement. Hölscher proceeds to an elaborate discussion of the nature of ecstasy, adducing many examples from Arabic literature, and declaring that such ecstatic experiences are found throughout the pages of the Old Testament.

It is obvious that such an approach regards the prophetic movement as of one piece with other examples of "prophecy." Indeed, Hölscher says that the prophets are to be understood psychologically, and that the investigator must free himself as much as possible from religious-historical concepts. For Hölscher, therefore, the study is really a psychological one.[6] It is an elaborate and profound attempt in which he has been engaged, but since he has limited the field of investigation, we believe that he has not arrived at the truth. Our principal concern now, is not whether there was "ecstasy" in the activity of the prophets, but rather that Hölscher has felt it necessary to regard the question as merely psychological and thus to turn aside from an explanation of the prophetic conviction to be the recipients of Divine revelation.

Hölscher's work is probably the most elaborate and thorough presentation of the position that the prophets of Israel were engaged in ecstatic performances. After a long discussion of the nature of ecstasy, he proceeds to the examination of many Old Testament passages, and in these he thinks that he finds the examples which support his position.

Philo and "Ecstasy"

That the prophets were ecstatics was not first suggested by Hölscher. Before him, men like Giesebrecht,[7] Knobel[8] and

Stade[9] had advanced the same idea. The view however, is really much older. We shall probably find the first presentation of it in the writings of Philo. In his discussion of Genesis 15 Philo identifies the deep sleep which fell upon Abraham as an ecstasy.[10] This ecstasy, he says, may take different forms. It may be a madness which produces mental delusion (*paranoian*). It may be extreme amazement at sudden and unexpected events. On the other hand it may be mere passivity of the mind, but in its best form it is a divine possession or frenzy (*entheos kato-koche te kai mania*) such as came upon the prophetic class.

It is this last kind of ecstasy which according to Philo is found in Genesis 15. What came upon Abraham was an experience that was inspired and God-possessed (*enthousiontos kai theophoretou*). Philo goes on to say that when the divine Spirit comes, the mind is driven from its home (*exoikidzetai*), since mortal and immortal may not share the same home. It is this experience which regularly comes upon the prophetic class.

It will be seen that what Philo has done is to take the terminology of the Greeks which described frenzy and to apply this terminology as a description of the inspiration of the Scriptural prophets. It may be remarked in passing, however, in view of the loose manner in which the term ecstasy has been used by some modern writers that Philo is deserving of credit for his careful discrimination in the employment of the word.

This word ecstasy, which was first used by Philo in connection with the deep sleep (*tardemah*) that fell upon Abraham has been widely current in modern writings upon the prophets. Following the impetus given by Hölscher, men such as Gunkel,[11] Jacobi,[12] Theodore Robinson,[13] Lindblom,[14] Hertzberg[15] and Adolphe Lods[16] have looked upon the prophets as ecstatics. The word has not always been employed with precision, and Lindblom has pointed out that there are two kinds of ecstasy.[17] One of these he calls "absorption" (*Verschmelzungsekstase*) in which the prophet's personality is fused together with God. The other type, called "concentration ecstasy" (*Konzentrationsekstase*) is one in which the soul is so deeply concentrated upon a single object that normal consciousness is obscured. It is this latter, thinks Lindblom, which was applicable to the prophets.

The theory of ecstasy has by no means been universally accepted. It has been subjected to thoroughgoing and searching criticism at the hands of both Heschel[18] and Seierstad.[19] Others also have raised their voices in opposition, and since these arguments are easily accessible, it will not be necessary to repeat them here. Our consideration of the question cannot rest merely upon the narrow point as to whether the prophets were or were not ecstatics. To limit the field of discussion in such a manner is to confine it to the realm of the psychological, and such a procedure, we believe, is not truly scientific. We shall not therefore, enter the ranks of the contestants with respect to this question. We prefer to ground our examination upon a broader basis. When the examination is thus conducted, we believe that we shall be in a position to discern in how far ecstatic experiences characterized the activities of the prophets.

Hattusilis' Claim to Revelation

In the beginning of this chapter we noted that the prophets of Israel regarded themselves as the recipients of Divine revelation, and it is this psychological conviction upon their part which we are called upon to evaluate. The task is made more difficult because the prophets do not stand alone as those who thought that they had received a message from God. Others also have made the claim. By way of example we may appeal to the statements of Hattusilis as they are found in his Apology.[20] A careful study of this interesting document will put us in a better position to evaluate the words of the Old Testament prophets.

The author of this Apology was Hattusilis the Third who is seeking to defend his action in taking the throne. It is a document characterized throughout by a certain religious feeling. Hattusilis begins by extolling the divine power of Ishtar and utters the hope that there will be reverence to Ishtar in the future among his descendants. While Hattusilis was yet a child, Ishtar by means of a dream spoke to his father Mursilis saying that the days of Hattusilis were short and that he would not live unless he became a priest of Ishtar. In obedience to this message Mursilis placed Hattusilis in the service of Ishtar as a priest, and thus he served her, prospering and being guided by her hand.

When the father Mursilis dies,[21] the elder brother Muwattalis became king and appointed Hattusilis to a certain governorship. In this position he had success because, he says, his lady Ishtar constantly favored him. When others were aroused to jealousy, Ishtar appeared to him in a dream and said, "Fear not that I shall abandon you to a hostile deity." She was true to her promise and always rescued Hattusilis from his enemies, supporting him with her divine power in times of illness. She always held him by the hand. She never passed him by nor left him to the hand of an enemy nor to those who envied him and opposed him at law. In fact she even placed his envious enemies in his hand so that he destroyed them utterly.

When Muwattalis saw that Hattusilis had no designs upon the throne he recalled him and placed all the infantry and the charioteers of the land of Hatti under his hand. In this position Ishtar constantly showed her favor so that he conquered the lands of the enemy and drove the enemy from his own land. At the command of his patron deity Muwattalis left his home Hattusas, and then various subject lands began to rebel. Against some of these rebellious lands Hattusilis was sent, and since Ishtar went before him, he defeated them. This, he says, was his first manly deed, and in this campaign for the first time Ishtar proclaimed his name. In further battles also the favor of Ishtar remained with Hattusilis.

When one of the enemies, a man by the name of Armadattas, saw Ishtar's favor, he became envious of Hattusilis and sought to bewitch him. Hattusilis, however, worshipped the goddess, who commanded him to marry the daughter of a priest and who gave to them the love of husband and wife. The goddess also issued a command: "You and your house must be subject to me," and the goddess dwelt within the house which they were making.

At no time did the goddess forsake Hattusilis. When an indictment was brought against him, she showed her divine power by finding witchcraft in the accuser, Armadattas, and making him lose his case. This continued favor of the goddess aroused the envy of Urhitesupas, who was in authority in the land of Hatti, and who sought to take away various lands from Hattusilis. Since Hattusilis was the priest of the storm god of Nerikkas, he was unable to take away the city of Hakpissas. For seven years Hattusilis was submissive, but at length, when the city of Hakpissas was taken, he declared war, calling upon Ishtar to decide as to the righteousness of his cause. "Come! Ishtar of Samuhas and the storm god of Nerikkas shall decide the case for us."

For some time Ishtar had been promising the kingship to Hattusilis, but now she appeared to his wife in a dream with the following revelation: "Before your husband I shall go. All of Hattusas shall be led with your husband. Since I have regarded him highly, I have never at any time abandoned him to hostile judgment nor to a hostile enemy. I am now going to exalt him and to make him a priest of the sun-goddess of Arinnas. You are to make me, Ishtar, your patron deity." This promise, we are told, was abundantly fulfilled by the goddess, who constantly showed her divine power in support of Hattusilis. As for the enemy, Urhitesupas, she shut him up like a pig in a sty. A certain house was given to Ishtar, who, thereafter, showed favor after favor.

Prosperity now seemed to be in the hands of Hattusilis. Ishtar took him as a prince and placed him upon the throne. In return he gave to Ishtar the house of Armadattas and other things also. These he consecrated and gave to the one whom he regarded as his goddess. He closes the Apology with the wish that anyone who in the future should take away from Ishtar any of these things should be an opponent at law of Ishtar. In the future, whoever ascends the throne, "let him show reverence toward Ishtar of Samuhas among the gods."

We have outlined the content of the Apology with some detail because it is one of the documents from the ancient world in which there are apparently serious claims to have received a revelation. It is our task to evaluate these claims, and in so doing two problems must be faced. First of all, there is the psychological problem. How did Hattusilis come to believe that the goddess Ishtar had spoken to him? Secondly, there is the theological problem, namely, did the goddess Ishtar actually speak with the king? Unless we are willing to face both of these questions, we cannot possibly arrive at a just evaluation of the document.

In the first place we may say that of the two the psychological problem is the less important. There are several explanations as to why Hattusilis believed that Ishtar had spoken to him, if he actually did have such belief. There is of course the explanation — although it is not a legitimate one — that Ishtar actually did speak with the king. If that were so, then of course, Ishtar was a real goddess, and certain very important consequences follow. It may be, on the other hand, that Hattusilis' language was merely a certain court style; it had no real meaning, but was merely used in order to give to the Apology a certain convicting force. It is also possible that the king, living at a time of gross superstition, spoke under the influence of that superstition. His words, upon this assumption, would be but idle expressions, devoid of any true meaning. It is also possible that the words of the king were the expressions of ignorance and thoughtlessness. In other words they may have been uttered lightly, as mere empty phrases or clichés. It is not always easy to discover the reasons why people use religious language. The motives which guide their actions are often difficult to ascertain. By isolating the psychological problem and considering it alone, however, we shall not be able to arrive at the truth. The present writer inclines to the belief that the words which the king employed were little more than empty phrases which gave a certain polish or religious slant to the Apology. This, however, is only a private opinion. We certainly cannot be dogmatic upon the subject.

If we are really to get to the heart of the matter, we must come to grips with the theological problem. That problem revolves about the questions whether an actual revelation was granted from Ishtar and whether or not there is an actual Ishtar. As soon as we have posed these questions we have seen their answer. The document of Hattusilis obviously is based upon a polytheistic background. Ishtar is regarded not as the only goddess but simply as the goddess of Hattusilis, as one among others. Not even Hattusilis himself thinks of her as the only goddess. The whole structure of this heathen (for it is such) pantheon lacks reality. Ishtar is not; she does not possess an objective, independent, metaphysical existence. To put it in the simplest of terms: there is no Ishtar. Consequently, since there is no Ishtar, there is no revelation from her, and Hattusilis, whatever may have been the reason for his employment of the language which he used, did not actually receive a revelation from Ishtar. The study of the reasons why he thought he received such a revelation (if we are really going to give to his words any serious content whatever) may be very interesting, but it is comparatively unimportant. Whatever may have guided the king in the choice of his language, we know that as a matter of actual fact, he was not the recipient of any favors or revelation from Ishtar.

The Psychological Conviction of the Prophets

This brief survey of the Apology may prepare the way for the study of the psychological conviction which the prophets of Israel had. If we isolate this question however, from the deeper theological question we may arrive at interesting possibilities, but we shall not arrive at the truth. And the reason why we shall not arrive at the truth is that the prophets themselves have told us how they came to their convictions. They have told us that God did speak to them. Here, however, the case takes on a new slant when we realize that we are face to face, not merely with one man, but with an entire body of men who lived over long periods of years, each of whom claims that God has spoken to him.

We must therefore, come to grips with the theological question. Did God actually speak with the prophets? In other words is the Christian life and world view correct or is it not? There are certain very fundamental and basic presuppositions upon which this Christian view of the world rests. It presupposes for instance the existence of that God who is a spirit, ". . . infinite, eternal, unchangeable, in his being, wisdom, power, holiness, justice, goodness and truth."[22] This God exists in utter independence of anything outside of Himself, for He is the creator of all things visible and invisible. He is, we may say, self-contained and utterly self-sufficient. Furthermore, it is a postulate of the Christian position that this God, who has created, has also revealed Himself. He has revealed Himself in the very constitution of the created universe, but He has also, in wondrously loving fashion, revealed Himself in the Bible. The Bible, therefore, according to the Christian position, is God's spoken Word. Now, when we pay serious heed to the claims of the Bible, we discover that it claims to be God's word, not only in isolated instances, but fully and completely, in all its parts. Therefore, the constant assertion of the prophets that God has spoken with them is not to be reduced to the level of the banal words of an Hattusilis, who says that an Ishtar has spoken, but rather is a serious claim that the one true God has spoken. There is, in other words, a seriousness in the claims of the prophets, which appears nowhere else. If we accept Christian theism, we must admit that God did speak with the prophets.

It will be impossible to consider every claim to the recipiency of revelation which is found in the prophetical books. We shall simply confine ourselves to the prophecy of Isaiah and then seek to evaluate the language. We may, therefore, note the following:

Isaiah 1:1 *the vision . . . which he saw*
  1:2 *for the Lord hath spoken*
  1:10 *hear the word of the Lord*
      give ear unto the law of our God
  1:18 *saith the Lord*

1:20 *for the mouth of the Lord hath spoken*
1:24 *therefore, thus saith the Lord*
2:1 *the word which . . . he saw*
2:15 *saith the Lord*
2:16 *moreover the Lord said*
5:24 *rejected the law of the Lord of hosts*
     despised the word of the Holy One of Israel
6 *the entire chapter contains words spoken by God*
     to the prophet
7:3 *the Lord said to Isaiah*
7:7 *thus saith the Lord*
7:10 *and the Lord spake again*
8:1 *and the Lord said unto me*
8:3 *and the Lord spake unto me*
8:11 *for the Lord spake unto me with a strong hand*
9:8 *the Lord sent a word*
10:24 *thus saith the Lord*
13:1 *the burden . . . which Isaiah . . . saw*
14:22 *saith the Lord of hosts*
14:24 *the Lord hath sworn, saying*
14:27 *Lord hath purposed*
14:28 *was this burden*
15:1 *burden of Moab*
16:13 *this is the word that the Lord hath spoken*
17:1 *burden of Damascus*
18:4 *thus hath the Lord said unto me*
19:1 *burden of Egypt*
19:17 *purpose of the Lord*
20:2 *at that time the Lord spake*
20:3 *and the Lord said*
21:1 *burden of wilderness of sea*
21:10 *that which I have heard from the Lord*
21:11 *burden of Dumah*
21:13 *burden upon Arabia*
21:17 *for the Lord hath spoken*
22:1 *burden of valley of vision*
22:12 *the Lord did call*
22:14 *revealed Himself in my ears*

22:15   *said the Lord*
22:25   *saith the Lord of hosts*
23:1   *burden of Tyre*
23:11   *the Lord hath given commandment concerning Canaan*
24:3   *the Lord hath spoken this word*
25:8   *the Lord hath spoken it*
28:13   *shall the word of the Lord be unto them*
28:16   *thus saith the Lord*
28:22   *have I heard from the Lord*
28:26   *his God doth instruct him*
28:29   *cometh from the Lord*
29:10   *Lord hath closed your eyes*
29:13   *and the Lord said*
29:22   *saith the Lord*
30:1   *saith the Lord*
30:2   *asked at my mouth*
30:6   *burden of the beasts of the south*
30:8   *go! write*
30:12   *thus saith the Holy One*
30:15   *thus saith the Lord God*
31:4   *saith the Lord to me*
36:10   *the Lord said unto me*
37:6   *thus saith the Lord*
37:21   *thus saith the Lord*
37:22   *this is the word which the Lord hath spoken*
37:33   *therefore thus saith the Lord*
38:4   *then came the word of the Lord to Isaiah*
38:5   *thus saith the Lord*
39:8   *good is the word of the Lord which thou
          hast spoken*
40:1   *saith your God*
40:5   *for the mouth of the Lord hath spoken it*
40:25   *saith the Holy One*
41:13   *saying unto thee*
42:5   *thus saith God the Lord*
43:1   *thus saith the Lord*
43:10   *saith the Lord*
43:14   *saith the Lord*

43:16 *thus saith the Lord*
44:2 *thus saith the Lord*
44:6 *thus saith the Lord*
44:24 *thus saith the Lord*
44:26 *confirmeth the word of his servant*
44:27 *that saith*
44:28 *that saith of Cyrus*
45:1 *thus saith the Lord*
45:11 *thus saith the Lord*
45:13 *saith the Lord of hosts*
45:14 *thus saith the Lord*
45:18 *for thus saith the Lord*
48:17 *thus saith the Lord*
48:22 *saith the Lord*
49:1 *the Lord hath called me*
49:3 *and he said to me*
49:5 *saith the Lord*
49:6 *he saith*
49:7 *thus saith the Lord*
49:8 *thus saith the Lord*
49:18 *saith the Lord*
49:22 *thus saith the Lord*
49:25 *thus saith the Lord*
50:1 *thus saith the Lord*
50:5 *hath opened my ear*
51:22 *thus saith thy Lord and thy God*
52:3 *for thus saith the Lord*
52:4 *for thus saith the Lord*
52:5 *saith the Lord*
54:17 *saith the Lord*
56:1 *thus saith the Lord*
56:4 *for thus saith the Lord*
57:15 *for thus saith the high and lofty one*
57:19 *saith the Lord*
57:21 *saith my God*
58:14 *for the mouth of the Lord hath spoken it*
59:20 *saith the Lord*

59:21 *saith the Lord*
       my words which I have put in thy mouth
61:1 *anointed me to preach good tidings*
63:8 *for he said*
65:8 *thus saith the Lord*
65:13 *thus saith the Lord*
66:1 *thus saith the Lord*
66:5 *hear the word of the Lord*
66:9 *saith the Lord*
66:12 *for thus saith the Lord*
66:20 *saith the Lord*
66:21 *saith the Lord*
66:22 *saith the Lord*

A cursory glance at the above list will make it clear that the prophet labored under the conviction that the words which he was uttering were actually indicted of God. Oftentimes the personality of the prophet even recedes completely into the background, and the speaker appears to be God Himself. Almost naturally, for example, one reads words such as "I have blotted out, as a thick cloud, thy transgressions, and, as a cloud, thy sins: return unto me; for I have redeemed thee" (Isaiah 44:32). The usage of the personal pronoun in the first person clearly refers to God Himself. Nor is such a phenomenon unusual. It appears throughout the prophecy, and is interwoven naturally with the utterances which the prophet speaks forth as having been given to him by God.

From all of this it appears that the prophet believed that he had been the recipient of an objective revelation. He did not think that he was uttering words which had found their origination in his own mind, but rather that he had received a message which God had given to him. At certain times he stresses this aspect of revelation, as when he says, "for the mouth of the Lord hath spoken it," or, "the Lord spake to me with a strong hand." Likewise, clauses such as "the Lord hath sworn, saying," or "this is the word that the Lord hath spoken," or "thus hath the Lord spoken to me" may very legitimately be appealed to as stressing the objectivity of the revelation. The perusal of a list, such as is given above, is very rewarding, for it reveals, beyond any legitimate question, that there is, running throughout the entire prophecy, an underlying and basic claim that the words which came to the prophet were the product of Divine revelation.

If therefore, we are to consider the psychological question of the prophetic conviction, we may note that the answer to the problem, in so far as we are able to determine it from the words of the prophet himself, is that he believed himself to be the recipient of words which had been placed in his mouth or spoken to him by God. With this psychological problem the theological is intimately bound up; indeed, the two cannot actually be separated. The answer to the psychological problem must be determined along lines which are consonant to and in harmony with basic Christian-theistic presuppositions, or else it must be answered against the background of the assumption that man, and not God, is king in the realm of being and knowledge. When this question therefore is studied against the background of Christian-theistic postulates, we are compelled to say, as the New Testament and the historic Church of all the ages has said, that the prophets believed themselves to be the recipients of Divine revelation because as a matter of fact they actually were the recipients of Divine revelation.

The Method of Prophetic Revelation

The question of course arises whether in every instance the prophet heard these Divinely uttered words with the physical ear. And it is at this point that we enter a realm of great mystery. The prerequisite of ordinary hearing, the ear, is physical, but hearing in itself is psychical. It may be that God could cause the words which He spoke to be heard or impressed upon the mind of the recipient so that he was aware of the impression without the use of the physical organs of hearing. This would seem to be true of the words which God spake to Isaiah in the remarkable vision recorded in the sixth chapter. It may also have been true of other messages which God im-

planted in the prophet's mind.   On the other hand, at times
the physical organs were employed as when the prophet speaks
of the Lord revealing Himself "in my ears" (22:14).

It is also apparent, not only from the above list of phrases
from Isaiah but also from the express statement made to
Miriam and Aaron that God revealed His words by means of
vision or sight.   Here, even more than was the case with
hearing, it would seem that the prophet beheld without the use
of the physical eyes.   Very instructive in this case is the language that is employed of Balaam.[23]   It became evident to
Balaam, we are told, that the Lord was pleased to bless Israel.
Therefore the soothsayer did not seek after enchantments as he
had done on previous occasions but rather lifted up his eyes
towards the encampment of Israel, and the impression which
he received from this sight served as a preparation in his
heart for the reception of the Spirit of God who was to come
upon him.   With respect to the two earlier utterances of
Balaam we are told that the Lord had placed a word in his
mouth.[24]   Apparently this was an instance where Balaam heard
within him the word of God without the use of the bodily ear
and without a trance or condition of ecstasy.   Now however,
the Spirit of God comes upon him and his bodily eyes are
closed so that with the inward eye, the eye of mental perception, which the Spirit has opened, he may behold the message
of God.   He is thus in a condition of Divinely imposed ecstasy
or trance.[25]

The description is introduced by the phrase "the oracle of
Balaam," which indicates here that the oracle is Divinely
revealed.   Furthermore, the soothsayer speaks of himself as a
man whose eyes are closed, and as Hengstenberg has pointed
out, "Balaam describes himself as the man with closed eye
with reference to his state of ecstasy, in which the closing of
the outer senses went hand in hand with the opening of the
inner."[26]   The physical eyes were closed so that all perceptions
from the outward world of sense would be excluded from the
mind of the seer.   This closing of the eyes is evidently to be
regarded as the result of a Divine compulsion.   To the spec-
tator Balaam would have appeared to be in a trance or at least

to be unconscious, and such a Divinely imposed condition we may loosely denominate ecstasy. It was a condition brought upon the subject not by himself, nor even by the intensity or power of the concentration of the mind, but by God, so that the complete attention of the subject might be centered upon the message which he was to receive.

It is while he is in this condition that Balaam sees the vision of the Almighty.[27] He sees not with physical but with internal eyes. The compulsion of the Spirit is so great that, like Saul, he falls down physically, and the inner eyes are opened. It is of course impossible to state how a man in such condition, with physical eyes closed and fallen prostrate, under a mighty Divine compulsion, could actually see a vision which God gave to him. Superficially the vision may have resembled a dream in that while one experiences a dream he sees events portrayed before him. However, the vision in itself is to be distinguished from a dream, and the only similarity would seem to be in the portrayal before the eyes of the mind of those things which God wished to impress upon the prophet's consciousness and understanding.

It is well to ask the question why there was imposed upon the recipient of revelation a condition which would exclude the sensory world from the consciousness. In all probability this had something to do with the personal equation itself. In the case of Balaam, who is consistently represented in the Scriptures as a heathen soothsayer, the spiritual condition of receptivity would certainly be at a low ebb. Hence, it was evident that the entire personality should be conquered and controlled while the Spirit communicated to Balaam His message. It would not necessarily follow that this should always be the case when visions were revealed unto the prophets. At the same time a certain amount of bodily subjection may have been present even in the revelations given to an Isaiah or an Amos. All of the true prophets were regarded as occupying in the theocracy a position subservient to that of Moses, and this fact doubtless explains the reason why the clearness and distinctness which characterized the Lord's speaking to Moses was not to be found in the visions and dreams granted unto the prophets.

There is a further factor to be noted. Superficially considered, we may discern a certain outward resemblance between the actions of the prophets and those of the heathen soothsayers. It will not do to say that in religious matters the false always imitated the true, for in this case the false sometimes antedated the true. There is perhaps another explanation at hand. When God gave His wondrous revelation through the prophets He did not give that revelation in a vacuum nor did He give it to a nation that was isolated from the remainder of the world. He gave it rather to a people who were well versed in the ways and practices of idolatry and superstition. It was probably a didactic purpose therefore which led to no sharp distinction in outward behaviour between the true prophets and the soothsayers who inhabited Canaan. The people would recognize that the prophets, by their actions, were men who told the Divine will. It was, we must remember, a backward and sinful nation with which the prophets had to deal, and only step by step could the great truths of redemption be presented. No very great formal difference, therefore, would characterize the true prophets or set them apart from the enchanters and diviners of Canaan. The difference lay in something else. The difference lay in the fact that the prophets spoke in the name of Jehovah and were accredited of Him when their predictions and messages came to pass.

Although there was this outward resemblance, there was actually a profound difference. The "prophets" of Canaan fell into ecstatic trances which were self-imposed; the true prophets of Israel were overpowered by the onrushing of the Spirit of God. In one case the human mind was in control; in the other the Spirit of God. All discussion of the nature of prophetic ecstasy must take this factor into account. The compulsion which overpowered the true prophets was Divinely imposed. Whatever suspension of the prophet's personality there may for the time have been, it came not from the man himself but from God.

The Suspension of the Prophet's Personality

Since, therefore, we regard the possession of the Spirit as a Divine gift and not humanly brought-on, we cannot agree with Widengren when he says that by means of listening to a harp player Elisha could "transfer himself into the ecstatic state, filled with the Spirit of Yahweh" (2 Kings 3:15).[28] We believe that a more careful reading of the passage in Kings will not yield such an interpretation. The verse may be translated literally as follows: "And now, take for me a ministrel, and it came to pass when the minstrel played, that the hand of Jehovah came upon him." This passage does not teach that the coming of the hand of Jehovah was the result of the playing of the minstrel. It says nothing more than that while the musician was playing, God's hand came upon the prophet. There was of course a reason why Elisha asked for the musician. Music has the power of soothing the mind and elevating it to make it receptive and meditative. The music would doubtless have made such a preparation that God might speak to a mind undisturbed by outside influences. In other words it would form a suitable background against which God might give His revelation. Consequently, as the musician was playing, and the mind of the prophet was restful because of the music, the hand of God came upon Elisha.

It is questionable, however, if we may legitimately use the word ecstasy in connection with this revelation. Although the term "hand of Jehovah" usually indicates God's strength, here it would seem to be nothing more than a synonym for revelation. As Elisha, because of the music, was restful and prepared in his mind, God spoke to him. It was evidently a case where the words were heard with the inner ear alone. They were heard by Elisha, therefore, but not by those who were about him. Immediately, however, he speaks forth the word which he has received. He does not fall into a trance or act as though in frenzy. Rather he speaks forth the word which he has heard with boldness and conviction, "Thus saith the Lord, make this valley full of trenches" (2 Kings 3:16). This passage is but furthe evidence of the fact that in giving His revelations to the prophets God did take the personal characteristics of the recipient into account. With Balaam, a heathen soothsayer, and with Saul who sought the life of David, there was a complete subjection of the personality, a Divine overpowering which subdued fully the recipient. With Elisha there is, at least upon one occasion, the need for a quiet and meditative frame of mind, in order that he may be properly fitted to receive the Divine revelation. But it must be stressed emphatically that, just as in the case of Balaam and Saul the physical state of unconsciousness did not bring on the Spirit, so with Elisha the playing of music did not bring on the hand of God.

Widengren's View of the Prophets

According to Widengren the prophetic leader who proclaimed the will of Jehovah was ". . . the oldest extant model of the charismatic leader and thaumaturge . . ."[29] He was, thinks Widengren, the type which is found at the beginning of the Christian era in such persons as, for example, Apollonius of Tyana, and Widengren even appeals to Otto's work, *Reich Gottes und Menschensohn,* where "Jesus is analyzed as the model charismatic."[30] The same type, we are told, is most cultivated in the dervish orders of Islam and in the legends of the Sufi saints. With respect to the great Islamic mystics Widengren finds no difference in the parapsychic faculties attributed to the leaders and to the dervishes in general. Hence, he feels that we should not treat the great prophets of Israel as distinct from the prophetic "fraternities" or "orders," and he arrives at this conclusion by an examination of the "parapsychic" powers found in the pre-exilic writing prophets.

This examination is thought-provoking, but throughout we find that the author does not pay serious heed to the claim of the prophets to be recipients of Divine revelation. Their experiences are simply regarded as upon one level with those of Islamic mystics and others. Hence, we cannot agree that Widengren has proved his point. Any investigation of the prophetic phenomena which does not pay full heed to the element of Divine revelation cannot be called scientific. A scientific investigation must take into consideration all facts, and to exclude the element of revelation is at the outset to limit or circumscribe the area to be studied to such an extent that the truth cannot thereby be reached.

Widengren appeals to the case of Ezekiel eating the roll, "And he said unto me, Son of man, cause thy belly to eat, and fill thy bowels with this roll that I give thee. Then did I eat it; and it was in my mouth as honey for sweetness" (Ezekiel 3:3). The visionary experience, we are told, has here a connection with the sensation of taste, and this sensation of taste ". . . is presumably connected with visions and auditions in a hypnagogic state."[31] Appeal is made to the statement of a Moslem visionary who described his condition in the following language:

And I found sweetness in my heart and my mouth. And I remained for eight days without eating food or drinking anything, until I was too weak for the prescribed prayer. But when I ate, this sweetness went away.[32]

Likewise, attention is called to a statement in the Slavonic Enoch:

Listen, my child, from the time when the Lord anointed me with the unguent of his glory, food was not in me, and my soul does not think of earthly sweetness, nor have I any desire for anything earthly.[33]

It should be noted however that Ezekiel, when God commanded him to eat the roll, had for some time been in an ecstatic condition. The prophet had already stated (2:2) that ". . . the spirit entered into me when he spake unto me, and set me upon my feet; and I heard him that spake unto me." Following this the Lord gives a somewhat lengthy revelation unto Ezekiel (verses 3-8) which culminates in the words, "Open thy mouth and eat that I give thee" (verse 8b). Ezekiel then beholds an outstretched hand and in the vision devours the roll that was extended to him. The roll, which symbolized the message of God for the nation, was not merely to be eaten but was to be taken into the very constitution of the man. It was while the prophet was eating the roll that he remarked upon its

sweetness being that of honey. In Psalm 19:10 the words of
God are also compared to the sweetness of honey and the drop-
pings of the honeycomb. It was the Word of God, and therefore it filled the prophet's heart with joy. Every word of God
is sweet, for he who hears God's Word knows that it is from
God Himself.

It should be noted however that there is no sense of taste
which accompanies the entire vision. The sense of taste is
restricted to the one symbolical act of eating the roll. In this
symbolical act the prophet serves as an illustration of the truth
conveyed in the Psalms: "How sweet are thy words unto my
palate; yea, sweeter than honey to my mouth" (119:103).
The "taste perception" cannot be explained as an accompaniment of the vision but merely the natural consequence of receiving the word of God. Nowhere else in the prophetical literature
is there any mention of a sensation of taste in connection with
a vision. To lower this remarkable prophecy of Ezekiel to the
level of Islamic mysticism is to miss its point entirely.

Widengren offers a very interesting discussion of the phenomena of levitation with respect to the question of the far
sightedness of Ezekiel. He believes that in the contemplation
of Ezekiel's experiences there are three factors which must be
taken into account.[34] These are hypnotism and autosuggestion,
the parapsychic phenomena of levitation and the exaggerating
influence of tradition. In certain cases, he thinks, the phenomena of levitation were so strong that the prophet actually
believed that he had seen events at a great distance with his
bodily eyes. Ezekiel, although actually in Babylonia, nevertheless thought that he was in Jerusalem. It was not in a vision
that Ezekiel thus believed himself to have been transported, but
rather in actuality. Such an experience, believes Widengren,
we are to explain upon the principles of levitation which are
known to us.

In the light of this suggestion, it will be well to consider
briefly these sections in the prophecy to learn from them what
we can. The first passage to which we may turn is Ezekiel
3:14. In the fourth verse of this chapter the prophet had received his commission to go to the Israelites. When this com-

mission is concluded (verse eleven) a wind lifts Ezekiel up, and while he is in this condition he hears the voice of a great rushing, "Blessed be the glory of the Lord from his place." It must be noted that that which lifted up the prophet was not the Spirit, for the word is used indefinitely, without the article, and is therefore to be translated "wind." While this wind is but the perceptible token of the Spirit's presence, nevertheless, it is in itself but a wind which God employed to bring the prophet to the scene of his labor.

How then are we to consider this transportation? There are three principal interpretations which may claim assent. It might be said that Ezekiel was actually carried in body from Babylonia to Jerusalem and so saw with the bodily eyes the things which he describes. It might also be maintained that Ezekiel, through powers of concentration, so excluded himself from the outward world that he became overpowered with the conviction that he was actually being transported to Jerusalem. The explanation of such an experience would probably be found along the lines of the principles of levitation, and such an explanation does serve to account for some of the parallels which Widengren adduces. Lastly, we might say that Ezekiel's experience was in vision or ecstasy.

Our answer to the problem must not be derived by a consideration of parallels brought from the Near East nor from a general appraisal of parapsychic principles, but simply from exegetical considerations alone. The only witness which we have to this strange experience of Ezekiel is the text itself, and so we must allow the text to speak. It seems therefore when we do engage in a proper exegesis of the passage that the experience of being lifted up by the wind was in vision. The Divine message to Ezekiel had not ceased, but while the prophet was in this strange state of being overcome by the Spirit, the wind carried him up. The experience therefore was not an actual bodily levitation, but a transportation in vision, experienced under the compulsion of the Spirit of God Who had come upon the prophet. This seems to be supported by the consideration that Ezekiel hears behind him the sound of a great rushing and the noise of the wings of the living creatures and the wheels.

Suppose however, that our exegesis at this point is incorrect. Suppose that the vision received by Ezekiel comes to its close with verse eleven of the third chapter, and that the episode which is then related takes place after the close of the vision. Must we then be reduced to the assumption that the prophet is speaking of a real bodily levitation? Can it not be that God has brought to bear upon the prophet so intense and compelling a concentration of his powers upon the subject of concern that the impression is really conveyed to Ezekiel that he is being transported through the air? If we adopt such an interpretation we find that we have at least a certain formal agreement with Widengren. He however would explain such an intense concentration as being due to principles of levitation which have also expressed themselves in extra-Biblical examples; we for our part believe that such a concentration would have been Divinely imposed and that consequently the experience would have been of an utterly unique nature. It would therefore have been a revelation which fell under the category of "vision," a word which has a very wide connotation, and might even include such an experience as we have described. In this case the far-seeing need not have been with the bodily eye but with the inner eye; it would, however, have been so intense that Ezekiel believed that he had actually seen, as indeed he had, the events which he relates.

A similar passage is found in the eighth chapter of Ezekiel, wherein it is again related that a wind lifted the prophet up between heaven and the earth. In this instance however, there can be no question but that the transportation took place while Ezekiel was in an ecstatic condition. In the first verse of the chapter we are told that the hand of the Lord fell upon the prophet. Then, while he was in this condition, he saw a likeness as the appearance of fire. From this likeness there came forth a hand, and took him by a lock of his head, and the wind lifted him up. Furthermore, in this instance, it is expressly stated that in the visions of God the prophet was brought to Jerusalem. In the light of this express claim we are compelled to regard the episode as having taken place while the prophet was yet under the compulsion of the Spirit, or, as we have loosely employed the term, in an ecstatic condition.

Of particular interest is the account of Ezekiel's experiences given in the eleventh chapter, which begins with the statement that the wind lifted the prophet up and brought him to the east gate of the Lord's house. If we assume that this statement introduces an episode distinct from the revelation given in the previous chapter, we are perhaps to understand this as an example of far seeing. However, we cannot make our decision upon the basis of this first verse alone. In verse five the Spirit of the Lord falls upon the prophet while he is at the east gate of the Temple. While the Spirit is upon him, Ezekiel prophesies, and during the course of his prophecy, one of those who heard him, Pelatiah the son of Benaiah, died. After further prophecy, the wind lifted the prophet up and brought him in a vision by the spirit of God unto Babylonia. The prophet then remarks, "And there went up from me the vision that I had seen" (11:24b). In the light of these concluding remarks, we are again compelled to assume that here also the entire proceedings took place in a vision or in the ecstatic state. There was then no real levitation, but an experience in ecstasy. The actual body of Ezekiel remained in Babylonia all the time, but in the ecstatic state which came upon the prophet, he was transported to Palestine. We cannot therefore agree with Widengren that hypnotism or autosuggestion had anything to do with the experience, but rather that it was Divinely imposed. We certainly will not admit that the "exaggerating influence of legend" can be appealed to, for we regard the Scriptures as a revelation from God and not a mere remnant of Hebrew literature and tradition. Lastly, we do not believe that those phenomena which may possibly accompany experiences of levitation, as these have come to us with respect to Mohammed and others, had any bearing upon the case of Ezekiel.

It is true that the manner of the Divine revelation was adapted to the peculiar personality of the prophet. Ezekiel, as we may learn from his book, was introspective and serious.

Perhaps certain modes of revelation were more adapted to meet these personal characteristics than others. On the other hand, the very nature of the message to be given may have dictated the mode of revelation. How, exactly, could one who lived in Babylon give a message to those who lived in Palestine unless there were brought home to him in some vivid way the conditions of those whom he would reach? Certainly this ecstatic condition in which the prophet was transported so that he might see the inhabitants of Jerusalem was well adapted to enable him to declare his messages to them.

It is true that while he was preaching, one of his hearers fell dead. This episode, however, took place in the ecstatic vision. No doubt it came to actual realization as soon as the prophet's message was published, and perhaps it was this fact that made Ezekiel so importunate in his cry to God, "Ah Lord God! wilt thou make a full end of the remnant of Israel?" (11:13b). In conclusion therefore we believe that it is justifiable to interpret all the experiences of "levitation" recorded in Ezekiel as having occurred while the prophet was in an ecstatic state.

Prophetic Visions

Following Tor Andrae, Widengren believes that there are two kinds of visions.[35] One of these — that which is characterized by sharp outlines and not overburdened with detail — is said to be clear and plastic. The other type, as represented for example by Ezekiel, is said to be complicated. As an example of the first, we are referred to the great Temple vision of Isaiah. There can be no particular objection to thus classifying the visions which are recorded in the Bible. Our objection arises when a further step is taken and an attempt is made to bring them down from their exalted and unique character to a level with the "visions" of Mohammed and others.

The vision of Isaiah is very instructive, not because it will enable us the better to understand the visionary experiences of non-Biblical characters, but because it will indeed cast much light upon the nature of the visions which God gave to His servants the prophets. In the first place we may note that the prophet introduces the vision with the simple statement of the fact that he saw the Lord, and dates the vision by the nearest important event. When the prophet states that he saw the Lord, this is sufficient to show that the seeing was not with the bodily eye. Although the Lord appears in human form, yet He is seated upon a throne, high and lifted up. It is difficult to understand how this could have reference to the earthly temple, although the building in which the Lord appeared was one whose plan was based upon the Solomonic Temple. Isaiah would thus know that the building was a temple, but it was not the earthly one. What is important is that the Lord was seen in a building for worship.

It is difficult to say whether the prophet was completely in a state of trance or ecstasy. It may have appeared to an observer that the body of Isaiah lay prostrate in unconsciousness. Perhaps the outside world had so receded from the consciousness that only the presence of the Lord in the Temple occupied the attention of the prophet.

At any rate, Isaiah is perfectly capable of exercising his intellectual faculties. He understands the words of the seraphic choir, and is so impressed with the holiness of the Lord that he utters a cry of despair because of his own lack of holiness. Indeed, he is even capable of analyzing his sinful condition. When the symbolical assurance of the forgiveness of sins is granted, he understands its meaning, and is ready to reply to the Lord's request for one to perform a difficult mission. This vision makes it clear that the prophet, even though in the condition of receiving a vision, was nevertheless capable of conversation and intelligent discourse.

In our insistence that the revelations received by the prophets were genuine and that the recipients were men who actually were called of God to serve as His prophets there is a further point to be stressed. The uniqueness of the phenomenon takes on a decided emphasis when one notes the teleological thread which binds together the utterances of the prophets. It is not merely a brief unimportant oracle which we find on the lips of these men, but rather a great picture of a coming Redeemer. There is indeed a development and unfolding of the picture of the Person and work of the coming Messiah. When this remarkable fact is stressed, one immediately notes a profound difference between the Messianic prophecies of the Old Testament and those alleged messianic prophcies of Egypt. It is a remarkable thing that a book such as Hengstenberg's Christology, one of the greatest works of Biblical interpretation ever to have been written, could have been produced.[36] One wonders what a "Christology" of Egyptian Messianism would be. The very suggestion can produce but a smile, for it brings into strong focus the tremendous difference between the content of the prophetic revelation and the messages of the clairvoyants and soothsayers of the ancient world. It is this doctrine of the Messiah which must be explained. We may draw all the comparisons we wish between the experiences of the prophets and those of religious leaders of other nations and we have but scratched the surface. We may try to bring the prophets down to the level of other religious workers to analyze them, but by such a procedure we shall not arrive at the truth. The fact remains, ignore it as one will, that the prophets claimed to have received their messages from God. If this claim is not justifiable, we then have no explanation of the prophets and their activity. If they were not actually raised up of God in a special direct manner they were evil men and not to be trusted. They made the claim that God had spoken to them, whereas this was not the case. They were therefore deceivers and not to be believed. How could a product so great and good as Messianic prophecy have come from such an evil source? This is the question, and it cries for an answer. Upon the basis of modern naturalistic theories, it cannot be satisfactorily answered.

There remains but one alternative. It is to accept the claims of the prophets at face value. If we do this, we discover that all fits into its proper place. The wondrous message which came forth from the lips of the prophets was not of human origination. It came from God. The prophets were, as they claimed to be, men upon whom the power of God did come and who received the very words which He revealed unto them and then went forth in boldness to proclaim, Thus saith the Lord.

CONCLUSION

After the healing of the lame man the apostle Peter addressed those who beheld the miracle. It is not through our own power that this is done, he proclaimed, but through the Name of the risen Jesus Christ, whom ye in ignorance did slay. Ye did it in ignorance, as did your rulers, "But those things which God before had shewed by the mouth of all his prophets, that Christ should suffer, he hath so fulfilled. Repent ye therefore and be converted . . ." (Acts 3:18, 19a).

According to Peter the prophets spake of the sufferings of Christ. These prophecies have been fulfilled, he reasons, and since they have been fulfilled men should repent of their sins. Here in Israel was a phenomenon which could find no equal or parallel anywhere else in all the world. Here were men, raised up of God, who saw the salvation to be obtained by the Messiah. Here God did intervene in human history in a peculiar way.

This view of the apostle does not find ready acceptance today. The climate of the theological and philosophical opinion is more and more to remove the Christian Religion from its foundations in history and to place it in a supra-temporal and supra-historical realm. This procedure is based upon a philosophical position which is essentially anti-metaphysical and hence destroys once and for all true Christianity. For true Christianity is rooted and grounded upon something that God did for man in history. It is a religion that is historical throughout, and if this historical basis goes Christianity goes with it.

In the death of Jesus Christ of which Peter spoke, a sacrifice was offered which could and did atone for sin. As a preparation for this sacrifice God sent His servants the prophets through whom He announced to the sinful world the coming of the Redeemer. The prophets therefore, are not to be regarded merely as religious geniuses or leaders. To consider

191

them as such and nothing more, is completely to misunderstand them. Nor were their messages of human origination.
For prophecy, despite all that has been written to the contrary,
"did not come by the will of men, but holy men spake as they
were borne along by the Holy Ghost."

APPENDIX

Extra-Biblical "Prophecy" in The Ancient World

In the previous discussion we have given some attention to the work of the *mahhu* and *baru* priests of Mesopotamia. In order that we may more clearly understand and appreciate the unique character of Old Testament prophecy, we shall survey very briefly some of the examples of "prophecy" which have appeared in the ancient near east. The proper place to begin such a survey is with the recently discovered texts of Mari, in the Tigris-Euphrates valley.[1]

The first of the relevant texts from Mari is a letter written by a certain Itur-asdu, who relates that on the day on which he wrote to the king of Mari, Zimrilim, a man from Shakka came to him with a message. He was dreaming, he said, and wanted to go with another man to Mari. He did go to Terqa and entered the temple of Dagan, falling down prostrate before the god, who thus addressed him. "Have the kings of the Benjaminites and their people made peace with the people of Zimrilim which came over?" After a negative answer to this question had been given, Dagan continued, "Why do not the messengers of Zimrilim stay always before me, and why does he not grant a complete report before me? I would have given the kings of the Benjaminites a long time ago into the hands of Zimrilim. Now go! I have sent you. Thus shalt thou speak to Zimrilim. Send thy messengers to me and provide a full account for me. Then will I let the kings of the Benjaminites sprawl in a basket for catching fish and place them before you." As a result of being told this dream Itur-asdu is writing to Zimrilim, advising that he carry out the demands of Dagan.

In the first place it may be noted that the messenger from Dagan, although his name is given, Malik-Dagan, appears nevertheless without any official title. He is introduced merely

as a man from Shakka (awil sha-ak-ka^{ki}). At the close of the
tablet it is expressly stated that he is an ordinary man (qallum).
The message which Dagan gave to this man came to him
while he was dreaming. The language which he employed is
very similar to that used by the chief butler in Genesis in stating
his dreams.[2] In the dream Dagan utters his commands. There
is nothing in the message which corresponds to the "Thus saith
the Lord" of Scripture, although the messenger is told, "thus
shalt thou speak," a phrase which of course does appear in the
messages given to the prophets of Israel.

What is of interest, however, is the fact that Malik-Dagan
does not proceed to the king and deliver his message in the
name of Dagan. He goes rather to one of the king's officials
Itur-asdu, and this latter sends the commands to Dagan in the
form of polite recommendations. It is quite possible, as Von
Soden has suggested, that we have to do here merely with polite
court style, which forbade a more direct method of approach.[3]
Von Soden also suggests that in every case the official may not
have been convinced of the genuineness of the message. The
language used in the present tablet seems to support such a
view. In writing to the king Itur-asdu suggests, "And let my
master test this dream."[4] As for the messenger himself he is
to bring an offering unto Dagan (pa-aq-ra-am) and thus he
performs the work of a priest.

The question arises why Dagan asks Malik-Dagan about
the state of affairs between the Benjaminites and Zimrilim.
It is unlikely that these are merely rhetorical questions. In the
Scriptures the Lord asks rhetorical questions for the purpose
of calling man's attention to something. Such rhetorical questions of the Bible are very different in character from that
which is stated here. These questions appear to be asked for
the purpose of eliciting information. When Malik-Dagan
replies to Dagan and is on the point of leaving (i-na pa-ni
wa-si-ia), then Dagan speaks to him further. In the light of
this circumstance, it is very difficult to regard the questions of
the god as rhetorical.

At the same time the gods of Babylonia are supposed to have
knowledge of the affairs of men upon earth. Von Soden sug-

gests that the Canaanites of Mari may have regarded the god as so bound to his image in the temple at Terqa that he would not have been able to keep himself informed about the overall state of affairs and so would seek to elicit information from his messengers.[5] Whatever the answer may be, it is clear that Dagan is not presented as an omniscient god, but as one who must depend upon his messengers for information.[6]

It is true that Dagan delivers a message, and that Zimrilim is to obey the message whether he wishes to or no. It is also true that the message is to be delivered regardless of whether the king's subjects will also experience the god's disfavor. It is going too far, however, to say with Von Soden, that the message ends in a prophecy of salvation, conditioned upon obedience to the god's will.[7] All the message says is that if Zimrilim will fulfill the god's demands, Dagan will conquer the Benjaminites. This, however, is not a message which has to do with the end of time or a spiritual deliverance from sin, but merely a promise of amelioration for a local situation.

Von Soden has pointed out that the demands which are made upon the king are of a very external nature.[8] There is no question of personal love and devotion to Dagan, nor of any ethical demand. The god shows no concern whatever about the moral conduct of Zimrilim and his people. Likewise, it should be noted that the message of Dagan was merely a brief oracle, the contents of which were comparatively unimportant, having to do merely with a local situation.

A second tablet[9] from Mari was written to the king by a certain Kibri-Dagan who relates that on the day on which he wrote to the king, a *muhhum* of Dagan came to him with the following message: "The god has sent me. Write quickly to the king that they offer offerings for the dead (ki-is-pi) to the spirit (i-te-em-m (i-im)) of Jahdullim." Then Kibri-Dagan advises the king: "May my lord do that which seems good to him."

In this passage the messenger is designated by the title *muhhum*, which is probably an equivalent of *mahhum*. We are not told how the *muhhum* came to the conviction that Dagan had spoken to him, for in this text there is no revelation of a dream. At any rate, the message has to do with a matter of the cult, namely, the offering of a sacrifice to the spirit of the king's father, Jahdullim, who had been murdered. What is of interest is the manner in which Kibri-Dagan advises the king to do what seems good to him. Perhaps this is but a polite way of suggesting that the king do what the god has commanded. On the other hand, and more likely, Kibri-Dagan probably does not take the message too seriously and so does not expect the king to do so.

A third text concerns the building of a city gate. A *muhhum* had already spoken concerning the matter and now speaks again energetically (dan-na-tim). The text is broken and difficult to reconstruct, but it is clear that the message of the *muhhum* merely relates to the city gate and its construction.

It is interesting to note that this brief statement concerning the message of the *muhhum* does not occupy the entire tablet. The writer, Kibri-Dagan, first deals with other matters and then (sha-ni-tam) mentions the coming of the *muhhum*. This almost incidental reference to the *muhhum* is very interesting, for it shows that his arrival and the message which he proclaimed were not regarded with the same solemnity as greeted the messages of the Old Testament prophets. He is not identified as belonging to Dagan, but is merely mentioned as "that *muhhum*" or "a *muhhum*."

Another text presents a message from Dagan in which an animal sacrifice is commanded for the fourteenth day of the following month.[10] The recipient of the message, Kibri-Dagan, writes to Zimrilim, urging him to handle the matter as he sees best. The messenger is once referred to as "that man," although the designation *muhhum* probably appeared on a broken part of the tablet.

A tablet published in the volume *Studies In Old Testament Prophecy* contains a text in which the god Adad gives oracles by means of an *apilum* and *apiltum* (the feminine: the words refer to one who responds, answers).[11]

The letter seems to have been addressed to Zimrilim by one who first resided at Mari and then was sent upon a mission to Alahtum, situated in the region of Aleppo. In reality there

are two oracles which appear upon the tablet. Adad, who is
described as the lord of Kallasu, has spoken by means of oracles
(i-na te-re-tim), and demands the deliverance of certain animals. If they are not delivered, Adad will take away the throne
and city, but if Adad's commands are obeyed, throne upon
throne will be given. The respondents who are said continually
to deal with oracles have spoken this message. Indeed, so the
writer continues, the *apilum* of Adad is keeping watch over the
region of Alahtum.

The writer goes on to say that when he dwelt at Mari he
used to send to his lord everything that the "Respondents"
said. Now he lives in another country; should he not, however, even so write to his master everything that he hears and
that is told him? Otherwise, his lord might take him to task
for not having done so.

The tablet closes with another message. The *apilum* of Adad,
the lord of Halab, is said to have spoken to a certain Abu-halim
as follows: "Write to your lord," . . . "I am the one who will
give you the country of the east."

That which is particularly striking with respect to the first
oracle is that the writer seems to have heard of it more or less
by chance. Even though living in a different country, the
writer thinks that he should inform his master of such a message, since his master might otherwise take him to task. This
seems to imply that the *apilum* would not necessarily have seen
to it that the message was delivered to the king. He does not,
therefore, appear as a spokesman, the primary function of the
Hebrew *nabhi*.

As Lods has pointed out, the oracles are presented in the
exact terms supposedly employed by the god.[12] Even the introductory formula reminds one of the "Thus saith the Lord"
of the Old Testament. Adad of Kallasu, we are told, has
spoken in oracles thus (um-ma-a-mi). And of Adad of Halab
it is said: "Thus he has spoken" (ki-a-am iq-bi-e-em). Such
introductory formulae, therefore, as the Akkadian correspondence well attests, are intended to introduce the exact words of
the speaker. We are therefore, not to consider these words as
the outworking upon the part of the *apilum* of the god's mes-

sage. They are intended, rather, to be the exact words of the god's message.

Of particular interest is it to note that there is a certain resemblance between the content of this "prophecy" and that of some of the Old Testament prophecies. However, there are certain peculiarities of the Mari "prophecy" which need to be emphasized. In the first place the god is localized in a sense that is never true in the Old Testament. It is Adad, the lord of Kallasu, or Adad, the lord of Halab, who speaks. Furthermore, in calling to the king's attention what had been done for him, the god does not speak merely as Adad. It is not Adad as such who has elevated the king to his throne, but it is Adad the lord of Kallasu. Again, Adad speaks of having brought up the king upon his knees (sha i-na bi-ri-it pa-ha-al-li-ia u-ra-ab-bu-shu-ma), a rather strange anthropomorphism, indeed. The whole passage amounts to little more than a threat upon the part of the god to have the king deliver some animals. Whatever resemblances there may be to the prophecies of the Old Testament are therefore, at best, but accidental.

Apart from the material discovered at Mari there is very little from Mesopotamia that can even remotely compare with the phenomenon of prophecy in the Old Testament. There are extant a few oracles concerning Esarhaddon, which were derived from various diviners and which give general statements as to the wellfare of the king and his prosperity.

One of these oracles will serve as an example.[13] It reads: "Oracle from the lips of the woman Istar-latashiat of Arbela. King of Assyria, fear not! The enemy of the king of Assyria I deliver to slaughter."

These oracles are characterized by a polytheistic background. In one of them the king is told that sixty great gods are standing with the god Bel to protect him.[14] Sin is at his right, and Shamash at his left. He is not to trust in men, but in Ishtar, who tells him that sixty great gods are ranged for battle on his behalf.

Oracles such as these are also temporary and local. They are not concerned with great issues of right and wrong, but merely with assurances to the king of victory over his enemies in battle.

Very interesting is the account of an appearance of the god Ashur to Sennacherib in a dream in which it is related how Esarhaddon, on his way to Egypt, saw in the district of Harran a cedarwood temple.[15] Within was the god Sin, leaning on a staff and with two crowns on his head. Before him was the god Nusku. When Esarhaddon entered the temple, a crown was placed upon his head and it was said to him, "To countries you are to go, (and) in them you will conquer." Thereupon, he conquered Egypt.

Another text purports to be a message of the goddess Ninlil in which she promises sovereignty to Ashurbanipal over certain kings who will rise up against him,[16] "With blood," she says, "shall I make the land a shower of rain." The passage closes with the assurance that, as a mother bears her child, so Ninlil cares for Ashurbanipal.

In the account of his seventh campaign Ashurbanipal relates that he approached Ishtar in prayer and that she heard him.[17] During this same night a seer lay down and dreamed. Upon his awakening, Ishtar caused him to see a night vision, the content of which was given to Ashurbanipal. In the night vision Ashurbanipal appeared before Ishtar, who spoke with him as a mother, and assured him that wherever he went she would be with him. She then commanded him to stay where he was, at the dwelling of Nabu, and to live a life of ease while she went forward to carry out his desire.

There is one passage which approaches in form and content the prophecies of the Old Testament more closely than the others which have been mentioned.[18] It is a "prophecy" of the reign of Ashurbanipal. The text announces the appearance of the king by saying that "a prince will arise and exercise sovereignty for eighteen years." During this time the country will be in prosperity, but the ruler himself is to be slain during an uprising.

The text then goes on to announce the reigning of a prince for thirteen years, during which time Elam will rebel against Akkad, and there will be a period of calamity. The throne will be seized by an evil man, great scarcity will follow, and in the ravines of Tupliash the fallen troops of Akkad will fill the plain and hills.

A prince will arise, we are told, who will reign for three years, and during this time the rivers will fill with sand. At this point the text breaks. Later, however, another prince is said to arise, and prosperity will again be present. Then follows the prediction of a prince who will arise and reign eight years. After a break in the text there is the prediction of a prince who will reign for three years with the result that great desolation will come upon the land. At the same time this ruler will defeat the ruler of Amurru. The last prediction announces the appearance of a prince who will reign for eight years and who will restore prosperity to the land.

These prophecies, if such they may be called, center about prosperity or its lack. Under the reign of one king, prosperity will come, whereas under the reign of another it will give place to calamity. Accompanying the prosperity which is to be introduced, there will be a restoration of the temples of the gods. Righteousness, however, is not mentioned, and the formal similarity of these predictions to those of the Old Testament becomes obscured in the face of the great difference of content. All in all the "prophecies" of Mesopotamia, as far as content is concerned, are worlds apart from the Divine revelations granted to the prophets of Israel. Certain formal similarities are present, but that is all. If we are to seek the origin of the remarkable prophetic movement which appeared in Israel, it is not to Mesopotamia that we must look.

Egypt also had its share of diviners, and some of the oracles which have come from Egypt seem to approximate the Old Testament prophecies, as far as content is concerned, more closely than do those from Mesopotamia. We may begin our investigation with a consideration of the "Admonitions" of

the sage Ipu-wer.[19] Ipu-wer appeared before the reigning
Pharaoh, pointing out to him the woes that existed in the land,
and finally denouncing the Pharaoh as responsible for them.

Ipu-wer begins with a general description of the calamity
and chaos that are abroad in the land. "Robbery is everywhere . . . the Nile floods . . . Women cannot conceive . . . the
land spins around like a potter's wheel . . . laughter is gone . . .
grain has perished . . . fire has mounted up on high."

After this general description Ipur-wer introduces a series
of stanzas with the word "behold!" in which he continues the
description, but centers it more about the abject conditions of
the royal house. Then, after a damaged section of the text,
Ipu-wer bids the Pharaoh remember the days of old when
times were better. An ideal king would understand the true
nature of his subjects, and would smite down evil. Such a king
is not now present. Possibly he is sleeping. The requisites for
proper administration were with the king, but he only sets
confusion in the land. In this and similar language did Ipu-
wer condemn the king.

There is, of course, a resemblance between Ipu-wer's description and that of the prophet Isaiah, "Your land is desolate; your cities are burned with fire; as for your land, before
you strangers are devouring it, and it is desolate, as the over-
throwing of strangers" (Isaiah 1:7). The similarity in language cannot be explained as the result of borrowing, but is
the natural language to be used in describing a chaotic land.
Isaiah however, is doing far more than pointing out a rebellious condition in the land; he is describing rather a spiritual
apostasy from God. There is nothing similar in the language
of Ipu-wer.

There is one section of Ipu-wer's message which has been
considered by some to be a "messianic" prophecy. This section
reads: "it shall come that he brings coolness upon the heart.
Men shall say, 'He is the herdsman of all men. Evil is not in
his heart. Though his herds may be small, still he has spent
the day caring for them' . . . Would that he might perceive
their character from the (very) first generation! Then he
would smite down evil; he would stretch forth the arm against

it; he would destroy the seed thereof and their inheritance."[20]

This passage is quite difficult to interpret. Is Ipu-wer actually engaging in prediction and so prophesying the advent of
an ideal king or is he simply describing the ideal king in terms
taken from the past?

It is of interest to note that this ideal ruler is pictured as
a herdsman. Ezekiel had prophesied of the Messiah as follows:
"And I will set up one shepherd over them, and he shall feed
them, even my servant David; he shall feed them, and he shall
be their shepherd" (Ezekiel 34:23). It is to be expected that
such terms as shepherd and herdsman, taken from the daily
life of the people, might be used to describe the relationship
which would exist between a great deliverer and his people.
At most, however, the "herdsman" of the Egyptian text is a
man who will understand and protect his people. He will deal
justly with them. The Shepherd of Ezekiel, on the other hand,
is One who will reign for God, the true Shepherd, who will
establish a covenant of peace with His people. There is thus a
profound difference in content between the two passages. The
herdsman of Ipu-wer, if the passage is a real prediction, is
one who will reign justly, and will wisely administer the
affairs of his people; the "Shepherd" of Ezekiel is the true
Messiah who will bring a spiritual deliverance and peace to
His own. Between the two concepts there is a world of difference.

Very interesting and instructive is the prophecy of the downfall of the Old Kingdom and the restoration under Amen-em-het
I, uttered by one Nefer-Rohu.[21] According to the text Snefru
(of the Fourth Dynasty) sought to know from the official council of the capital if there was someone known to them who could
entertain him with fine words and well-chosen speeches. In
reply, the name of Nefer-Rohu, a priest of Bastet, is mentioned,
and the king commands that Nefer-Rohu be summoned.

When Nefer-Rohu appears the king tells him that he wants
to hear about the things that will take place in the future.
Nefer-Rohu brooded over what was to happen and then spoke.
The land is in a miserable condition, he asserted, and no one
is concerned with it. Then occurs a strange statement, since

it was concerning the future that the king desired to hear. "I shall speak of what is before my face; I cannot foretell what has not (yet) come."[22] Following this utterance, Nefer-Rohu continues his description of the desolations of the land.

Finally he announces that a king from the south will come, Ameni the triumphant by name. He is described as the son of a Nubian woman, and born in Upper Egypt. At his presence those who plot rebellion will subdue their speech. The Asiatics and other enemies will be put down. "And justice will come into its place, while wrongdoing is *driven* out."[23]

In this text it is stated that during the time of this king "the son of a man will make his name forever and ever." Barton however translates, "The people will rejoice in the time of the son of man," and suggests that the term "son of man" is the same used by Daniel in his seventh chapter.[24] However, in our opinion this identification cannot be maintained. The phrase translated "the son of a man" indicates a man of importance. In Daniel, however, the name does not necessarily indicate nobility or standing, but has reference to the humanity of the heavenly Figure in distinction from the beasts.

One must notice the utter lack of seriousness in this text. The king is seeking merely for entertainment, and so he desires to be informed concerning the future. Nefer-Rohu makes no pretense of being a prophet; in fact, he even states that he cannot foretell the future. Furthermore, the text states that it is dealing with the message of Nefer-Rohu, as he brooded over what would happen in the land. In other words the message is not a revealed one, nor does it purport to be. It is in a class with the many "predictions" of the ancient world, and far removed from the prophecies of the Old Testament.

It may also be well to notice the account which the Egyptian king Thut-mose III has given of the manner in which he was nominated to be king.[25] Before he became an official of the temple Amon-Re appeared to him and marvelled over him, so that Thut-mose III flew to heaven to see the god's mysterious form. At the house of Amon-Re he was equipped for the service of a king. Amon-Re also made other peoples subject to him and caused his reign to flourish. As a reward for

thus elevating him to the throne the king causes the worship
of Amon-Re to prosper, even asserting that he has made him
greater than other gods, and repaid him with greater good
than had been received from him.

Somewhat similar in nature to this statement of Thut-mose
III is the account of the elevation of an Ethiopian king to the
throne. According to the account the Ethiopians found them-
selves without a leader and so decided to consult Amon-Re of
Karnak, who is described as a resident of the Pure Mountain.
A purifying rite was then performed in his temple, and Amon-
Re indicated that the king's brother Aspalta was to be the
ruler.

In the above account the god indicated his choice of the
king. One short inscription tells how the ownership of a field
was determined by setting a choice before the god.[27] A priest,
Pa-ser, first states that the field belongs to Pai and the children of Hayn. No answer however is given to this statement.
Hence, the priest tries again, "It belongs to the priest Pa-ser,
the son of Mose." At this the god nods vigorously in the
presence of the witnesses, and so the ownership of the field is
determined.

A stele found between the paws of the Sphinx tells how
Thut-mose IV came to the Sphinx and rested in its shadow.[28]
In a dream the god (i. e., the Sphinx itself) spoke to him declaring that he would make him king. However, Thut-mose
is to remove the desert sands which are covering the Sphinx.

It will be well also to consider the important story of Wen-
Amon, an official of the temple of Amon at Karnak, who,
without adequate means, was sent to Byblos to obtain lumber
for the Divine bark.[29] At the court of Byblos one of the youths
was seized by a god and became possessed. It should be noted
that while the prince of Byblos was making offering to his
gods, one of the youths became possessed, apparently acting
like a person in convulsions. However, the possessed youth
did not deliver a message nor act in any way like the Old
Testament *nabhi*. It appears to have been an instance of

ecstasy, doubtless self-imposed, such as is found, for example, among the whirling dervishes.

This survey of alleged prophecies from the ancient Near East has been somewhat brief and does not claim to be exhaustive. It will serve at least to give the reader an idea of the kind of "prophecy" which was produced in the world outside of Israel. The mere comparison of these "prophecies" with those of the Old Testament will at once make it evident that they were separated by a wide gulf. They were different one from another as day is from night. And the reason for this difference is to be found in the fact that in Israel God spake through His servants the prophets.

NOTES

Chapter I

1. "Josiam virum iustissimum, sub quo in Templo Deuteronomii liber repertus est, ab Holda uxore Sellum instructum refert," *Adversus Jovinianum,* Book I, Migne: *Patrologia Latina,* vol. xxiii, col. 227. Here Jerome merely states that the book found in the Temple was Deuteronomy, and says nothing on the question of authorship. Procopius of Gaza (*Patrologia Graeca,* vol. lxxxvii, col. 916) also shared this view.

2. "Certe hodiernus dies illius temporis aestimandus est, quo historia ipsa contexta est, sive Ezram eiusdem instauratorem operis, non recuso. Nunc hoc quaeritur, an id quod dictum est, *usque in diem istum,* ad illam referatur, aetatem, qua libri editi sive conscripti sunt" (*De Perpetua Virginitate,* Book I, in *Patrologia Latina,* vol. xxiii, col. 199.) Whatever be the precise force of these words, they must be understood in the light of the clear testimony to the Mosaic authorship of Deuteronomy which Jerome makes in the following statements; "Sunt autem montes auri fertiles in deserto, procul undecim mansionibus a Choreb, iuxta quos Moses Deuteronomium scripsisse perhibetur" (*De Situ et Nominibus Locorum Hebraicorum, idem,* col. 932); "Dysmemoab, id est ad occidentem Moab, iuxta Jordanem contra Jerichum: ubi Balac rex Moab et maiores natu Madian, Israelem insidiis deceperunt, in quo loco et Moses scripsit Deuteronomium (*idem,* col. 937); "Lobon, solitudinis trans Jordanem, in quo Deuteronomium scribit Moyses, contra Jericho," (*idem,* col. 972); Deuteronomium, quoque secunda lex, et Evangelicae legis praefiguratio, nonne sic ea habet quae priora sunt, ut tamen nova sint omnia de veteribus? Hucusque Pentateuchus quobus quinque verbis (1 Cor. 14:19) loqui se velle Apostolus in Ecclesia gloriatur," (*Patrologia Latina,* vol. xxii, col. 545.)

3. Wilhelm Martin Lebrecht De Wette: *Dissertatio critica, qua Deuteronomium a prioribus Pentateuchi libris diversum, alius cuiusdam recentionis opus esse monstratur."* 1805. The same view is presented in the *Introduction,* cf. the English translation, *A Critical and Historical Introduction to the Canonical Scriptures of the Old Testament,* Two Volumes, Boston, 1859.

4. C. P. W. Gramberg: *Kritische Geschichte der Religionsideen des Alten Testaments,* pp. xxvi, 153ff., 305ff. I have not seen this work, but am dependent for this information upon Lewis Bayles Paton: "The Case For The Post-Exilic Origin Of Deuteronomy," in *Journal of Biblical Literature,* vol. xlvii, 1928, p. 322.

210 NOTES

5. "Uber den Ursprung des Deuteronomiums herrscht noch weniger Zweifel; in allen Kreisen, wo überhaupt auf Anerkennung wissenschaftlicher Resultate zu rechnen ist, wird anerkannt, dass es in der Zeit verfasst ist, in der es entdeckt und der Reformation des Königs Josias zu grunde gelegt wurde: diese letztere wurde etwa eine Generation vor der Zerstörung Jerusalems durch die Chaldäer durchgeführt" (Julius Wellhausen: *Prolegomena zur Geschichte Israels*, Berlin, 1905).

6. *Composition des Hexateuchs*, 1889, p. 193ff.

7. Emil Kautzsch: *An Outline of the History of the Literature of the Old Testament*, E. T. 1898.

8. Abraham Kuenen: *Historisch-Critisch Onderzoek naar het Ontstaan en de versameling van de Boeken des Ouden Verbonds*, Eerste Deel, 1887, pp. 106-136; 255-264. *The Origin and Composition of the Hexateuch*, E. T. 1886.

9. Jeremiah 2:26; 5:31; 6:13; 23:11.

10. The Levite mentioned in Deuteronomy 18:6-8 is not to be looked upon as a priest of the high places. In 2 Kings 23:9 we are expressly told that "the priests of the high places came not up to the altar of Jehovah in Jerusalem, but they did eat of the unleavened bread among their brethren." The reference is to the Levite who will dwell in the towns as a sojourner (i. e., since the Levites unlike the other tribes, had no hereditary possession), in distinction from the Levites who were engaged in the service of the sanctuary. The humanity of this law is difficult to reconcile with the character of the priests of Josiah's day. On the other hand, Deuteronomy 18:6-8 is told in terms of the future (note the phrase, "which the LORD will choose"), and this agrees well with Mosaic authorship. See Oswald T. Allis: *The Five Books of Moses*,[2] 1949, pp. 187-189.

11. R. H. Pfeiffer: *Introduction To The Old Testament*, 1941, pp. 179ff.

12. For a presentation of these arguments see Allis: *op. cit.*, pp. 178-184; Wilhelm Möller: *Are The Critics Right?* pp. 1-55.

13. C. Steuernagel: *Das Deuteronomium übersetzt und erklärt*, 1898. Cf. his *Einleitung in das Alte Testament*, 1912. *Die Entstehung des Deuteronomischen Gesetzes*,[2] 1901.

14. Such interchange is a characteristic found quite often in the Old Testament. Cf. also Alex. Sperber: *Zeitschrift für Assyriologie*, 1918, p. 23 ff. and Hospers: *De Numeruswisseling in het boek Deuteronomium*, 1942.

15. Alfred Bertholet: *Deuteronomium* in *Kurzer Hand-Commentar zum Alten Testament*, 1901.

16. Johannes Hempel: *Die Schichten des Deuteronomiums*, 1914.

17. In 1920-21 G. Ch. Aalders, writing in the *Gereformeerd Theologisch Tijdschrift*, defended the Mosaic authorship of Deuteronomy.

18. Gustav Hölscher: *Komposition und Ursprung des Deuteronomiums, in Zeitschrift für die alttestamentliche Wissenschaft*, 1922, Vol. 40, pp. 161-255. Hölscher had hinted at these views in his *Geschichte der israelitischen und jüdischen Religion*, Giessen, 1922, pp. 130-134.

19. "Das Urdeuteronomium deckt sich mit dem singularischen Grundbestande der Kap. 6-28, . . .", *op. cit.*, p. 225.

20. Theodor Oestreicher: *Das Deuteronomische Grundgesetz*, Gütersloh, 1923 (in *Beiträge zur Forderung christlicher Theologie*, 27 Band, 4 Heft, pp. 347-466).

21. Adam C. Welch: *The Code of Deuteronomy*, London, 1924; *The Framework to the Code*, London, 1932.

22. Edward Robertson; *The Old Testament Problem*, 1950, pp. 33-55.

23. Gerhard von Rad: *Das Gottesvolk im Deuteronomium*, Stuttgart, 1929. ". . . jedenfalls zeigt sich die Notwendigkeit, dass wir vor allem fernerliegenden Fragen und Kombinieren die Pflicht haben, das Dt. aus den Voraussetzungen heraus zu deuten, die uns in seinem eigenen Inhalt an die Hand gegeben sind" p. 2. Von Rad's *Deuteronomium-Studien* appeared in 1947, in which he seeks to show that in realtiy there is no Deuteronomic Code. He also compares Deuteronomy with the so-called Holiness Code and gives particular studies on various topics in Deuteronomy. A good introduction to the more recent literature on Deuteronomy may be found in W. Baumgartner: *Der Kampf um das Deuteronomium*, in *Theologische Rundschau*, 1929, pp. 7-25. Cf. also J. A. Bewer, L. B. Paton, G. Dahl: "The Problem of Deuteronomy. A Symposium," in *Journal of Biblical Literature*, Vol. 47, pp. 305-379.

24. The following considerations also support the Mosaic authorship of Deuteronomy:

a. The setting favors the latter part of Moses' life. The people are pictured as ready to cross the Jordan (e. g., 1:1). A definite date is given (1:3). The historical survey of the wilderness wanderings is well adapted to a nation which is about to enter the promised land (chapters 1-4). The people are constantly addressed as those who are on the point of entering the land (e. g., 18:9, "when thou art come unto the land which the Lord thy God is about to give thee").

b. The book displays an intimate acquaintance with the geographical conditions of Transjordania. This thought, particularly with respect to Moab, has been ably developed in an article by the Rev. G. T. Manley: "The Moabite Background of Deuteronomy"

in *The Evangelical Quarterly,* April 1949, pp. 81-92. The statements which are made concerning the eastern side of the Jordan
are so detailed that they may most naturally be explained as the
work of an eyewitness. On the other hand the descriptions of the
western side (Palestine) are throughout of a more general nature.
The reader will appreciate the force of this argument if he will
carefully consider such passages as the following:

Eastern 1 :1, 2, 4, 19; 2 :8, 10-13, 20-23, 36, 37; 3 :5, 8-17; 4 :43,
46-49; 10 :6, 7; 11 :30; 32 :49, 51.

Western 1 :24; 3 :20, 25, 27; 4 :1, 22, 26, 40; 6 :1, 3, 10, 11, 18;
7 :1, 5; 8 :7-9; 9 :1; 11 :10, 11, 14; 12 :10-29; 15 :4, 11; 17 :14; 18:
9; 19 :8; 21 :1; 26 :15; 27 :3, 12, 13; 30 :20.

c. Throughout the entire book the conquest is presented as in
the future. The people are pictured as not yet in the land. The
country to be taken is described as "Every place whereon the sole
of your foot shall tread shall be yours: from the wilderness and
Lebanon, from the river, the river Euphrates, even unto the western sea shall be your border" (Deuteronomy 11 :24). Imagine
someone living in the days of Manasseh writing such a description!
See Geerhardus Vos: *The Mosaic Origin of the Pentateuchal
Codes,* 1886, p. 187.

d. There are many statements in Deuteronomy which are without meaning if the book was composed during the reign of Manasseh or Josiah, but are most pertinent if the book came from the
hands of Moses. Thus, for example, there are frequent commands
in Deuteronomy to destroy the Canaanites. In 7 :22 the Israelites
are forbidden to ". . . consume them quickly, lest the beasts of the
field increase upon thee." What would be the purpose of such a
command at any time other than before the Canaanites had actually
been conquered? Such statements are quite frequent in Deuteronomy (cf. Möller: *op. cit.,* pp. 32-40).

e. Deuteronomy contains references to the Egyptian bondage
which are relevant to the situation of a people which has recently
come from that bondage but which are strangely out of place if
they were uttered at a later time (particularly as late as the seventh
century B. C.) Cf., e. g., 11 :10; 20 :1; 23 :4, 7; 24 :22.

25. Gaster's glowing account of Canaanite religion ("The Religion of the Canaanites" in *Forgotten Religions,* ed. Vergilius Ferm,
pp. 111-143) cannot be accepted. What he calls the ". . . bias and
censure of its enemies . . ." (p. 140) is nothing less than the judgment of God. He says that "Canaanite religion is assuredly one of
the many mansions in the Father's house" (p. 140). The Father,
on the other hand, says, "For an abomination of the Lord is everyone that doeth these things" (Deuteronomy 18 :12a).

26. Abraham Heschel: *Die Prophetie,* 1936, p. 112. "Gegenüber jeder Losbefragung, dem sogenannten *qesem,* der als heidnischer Brauch bezeichnet und verboten wird, wie auch gegenüber der technisch-magischen Weissagungskunst überhaupt hebt das Deuteronomium die prophetische Offenbarung hervor, die von jener wesensmässig unterschieden wird."

27. Johannes Pedersen: *Israel Its Life And Culture,* III-IV, 1940, p. 111.

28. *op. cit.,* p. 124ff. Cf. also Aubrey Johnson (*The Cultic Prophet In Ancient Israel,* 1944, p. 32) who translates the passage in the same way and also seeks to show that *qesem* was a legitimate branch of prophetic activity.

29. Pedersen: *op. cit.,* p. 125.

30. cf. chapters six and seven.

31. Cf. Jeremiah 27:9; 29:8; Ezekiel 13:6, 9, 23; 21:29; 22:28; Micah 3:7; Zechariah 10:2.

32. Cf. Adam C. Welch: *The Code of Deuteronomy,* pp. 107ff.

33. "It is not that the promised prophet is to be 'like' Moses in every respect, or in other words to be *equal* with him: he is to be like him, as v. 16-18 show, in the *fact* of being Jehovah's representative with the people, but not necessarily in being His representative in the same *degree* in which Moses was . . .," S. R. Driver: *Deuteronomy* (*The International Critical Commentary,* 1916, p. 228).

34. Numbers 12:1-8; Hebrews 3:1-6.

35. According to Ibn Ezra the prophet was Joshua; Abravanel, Baal Hatturim and Jalkut referred the passage to Jeremiah.

36. Origen: *Contra Celsum,* 1:9.

37. In writing this section I have been greatly helped by the exposition of Ernst W. Hengstenberg: *Christology of the Old Testament,* English Translation, Vol. I, 1878, pp. 104-115.

Chapter II

1. Bruno Baentsch: *Numeri,* in *Handkommentar zum Alten Testament,* 1903. "Wie schon die doppelte Motivierung in v. 1 f. zeigt, ist die Erzählung nicht einheitlich" (p. 511).

2. August Dillmann: *Die Bücher Numeri, Deuteronomium und Josua,* in *Kurzgefasstes exegetisches Handbuch zum Alten Testament,* 1886, p. 63.

3. Deuteronomy 7:3.

4. see Dillmann; *op. cit.,* p. 63.

5. G. Ch. Aalders: *Recent Trends in Old Testament Criticism,* 'E. G., do you think it possible for a humble servant of the Lord

like Moses to call himself 'very meek, *above all the men which were upon the face of the earth*' (Num. xii. 3)?"

6. The Vulgate *mitissimus*, is not as faithful to the original as is the Greek translation.

7. E. W. Hengstenberg: *Dissertations on the Genuineness of the Pentateuch*, English Translation, Vol. II, 1847, pp. 142, 143.

8. In speaking of Himself, Matthew 11:29, 30, Christ uses this same word, *praus*.

9. The LXX of vs. 4 may be translated; "And the Lord spoke suddenly to Moses and Miriam and Aaron . . . ."

10. According to Dillmann the three are commanded to go to the Tent of Meeting (cf. 11:26, 30), and not in it (*op. cit.*, p. 65). Baentsch (*op. cit.*, p. 512) thinks that in verse five the narrator has forgotten that the three are already outside the tent. This, however, is to misunderstand the passage. The correct interpretation appears to be as follows: In 12:4 the three are summoned to come out, evidently from the camp, where Moses at least, had been (cf. 11:30). They are to come unto (not into) the tent of meeting. The Lord then came down in a pillar of cloud and stood at the door of the tent, i. e., evidently the door of the court itself and not the actual door of the Tabernacle. Aaron and Miriam are then commanded to come out (i. e., from the court before the Tabernacle).

Ibn Ezra regarded the first command to come out as having reference to the tents of each individual. It is also possible that the command to go unto (*'el*) the Tent of Meeting was obeyed to the extent of entering the Tent. If this were the case, then the difficulty disappears. In any case we need not charge the author with an error. The language is difficult, but there is certainly no need for emending the text.

11. i. e., the LXX does not accurately represent the Hebrew, see Dillmann: *op. cit.*, p. 66.

12. as given in Baentsch, *op. cit.*, p. 513.

13. H. H. Rowley: *The Biblical Doctrine of Election*, 1950, p. 110.

14. Baentsch: *op. cit.*, p. 513 would make a slight emendation and read, visions and dreams. This is not necessary; in fact, it somewhat weakens the force of the statement.

15. Baentsch: *op. cit.*, p. 511.

16. cf. Exodus 14:31; Deuteronomy 34:5. See also the following note.

17. "Der Ausdruck ist von den menschlichen Verhältnissen entlehnt (Gen. 15, 2. 24, 2). Alle Diener Gottes (Profeten) erhalten vom Herrn Aufträge, die indessen immer nur einzelnes Betreffen; Mose's Auftrag umfasst das ganze Haus; er nimmt die Stelle

des Oberknechtes ein" (Knobel, as quoted in Dillmann, *op. cit.,* p. 66).

18. e. g., Baentsch: *op. cit.,* p. 513, who believes it may be rendered, "zu einem Vertrauensposten ausersehen." He admits however that Moses has always shown himself "als treuer Diener seines Herrn." Vos (*Biblical Theology,* 1948, p. 120), says: "Here he is called 'my Servant,' not in the menial sense of merely a servant, but in the high sense of a trusted servant, initiated into all that his master does."

19. C. F. Keil: *Biblical Commentary on the Old Testament. The Pentateuch,* English Translation, Vol. III, 1949, p. 80.

20. Keil: *op. cit.,* p. 80.

21. Since the revelation granted to the prophets was less clear than that given to Moses; indeed, since it contained elements of obscurity, we must take these facts into consideration when interpretating prophecy. We must therefore abandon once and for all the erroneous and non-Scriptural rule of "literal if possible." The prophetic language belonged to the Mosaic economy and hence, was typical. Only in the light of the New Testament fulfillment can it properly be interpreted.

22. Hebrews 3:1-6.

Chapter III

1. Wilhelm Gesenius: *Thesaurus Philologicus Criticus Linguae Hebraeae et Chaldaeae Veteris Testamenti,* Vol. II, 1840, p. 838.

2. Alfred Guillaume: *Prophecy And Divination Among The Hebrews And Other Semites,* 1938, p. 112.

3. Theophile J. Meek: *Hebrew Origins,* 1936, p. 147.

4. R. B. Y. Scott: *The Relevance of the Prophets,* 1944, p. 45.

5. Cf. Geerhardus Vos: *Biblical Theology,* 1948, pp. 209, 210.

6. Theodore Robinson: "Neuere Propheten-Forschung" in *Theologische Rundschau,* 3, 1931, p. 80.

7. Johannes Pedersen: *Israel Its Life And Culture,* III-IV, 1947, p. 111. Cf. Abraham Heschel: *Die Prophetie,* Krakow, 1936, p. 23ff.

8. William F. Albright: *From The Stone Age To Christianity,* 1940, pp. 231-233.

9. Eduard König: *Der Offenbarungsbegriff des Alten Testaments,* Erster Band, 1882, p. 71ff.

10. For the uses cf. Brown, Driver and Briggs: *A Hebrew And English Lexicon Of The Old Testament,* 1907, p. 612.

11. Alfred Haldar: *Associations Of Cult Prophets Among The Ancient Semites,* 1945, p. 109. Haldar derives the word from the Assyrian nabu.

12. I regard these passages in Exodus as completely historical and consequently cannot agree with Haldar, (*op. cit.,* p. 92) who regards Moses as a mythical founder of the priesthood and the watcher of temple flocks.

13. Gustav Hölscher: *Die Propheten,* 1914, p. 125.

14. cf. Hubert Junker: *Prophet und Seher in Israel,* 1927, p. 90.

15. cf. Pedersen: *op. cit.,* p. 111.

16. Aubrey Johnson: *The Cultic Prophet In Ancient Israel,* 1944, p. 11f.

17. Cf. H. H. Rowley: "The Nature Of Prophecy In The Light Of Recent Study," in *Harvard Theological Review,* January, 1945, p. 9. Cf. also Haldar: *op. cit.,* pp. 122, 124, 126.

18. cf. Haldar: *op. cit.,* p. 118.

19. cf. A. Lods: *Israel,* 1932, pp. 442-448.

20. König: *op. cit.,* Vol. I, p. 59.

21. This thought is not disproved by 2 Kings 17:13; cf. Rowley: *op. cit.,* p. 9.

22. König: *op. cit.,* Vol. II, p. 35f.

23. Cf. also 2 Chronicles 16:7 with 2 Chronicles 19:2.

24. Amos 7:12-14.

25. Heschel: *op. cit.,* p. 23.

26. H. H. Rowley: "Was Amos A Nabi?" in *Festschrift Otto Eissfeldt,* 1947, p. 195.

27. Paul Heinisch: *Theology Of The Old Testament,* English Edition, 1950, p. 117.

28. There are not therefore in the books of Samuel two conflicting accounts of the origin of this proverb.

Chapter IV

1. Theophile J. Meek: *Hebrew Origins,* 1936, p. 152.

2. Gustav Hölscher (*Die Propheten,* Leipzig, 1914, p. 143) points out that it was not prophecy as such, but Samuel who was used in opposition to the Philistines.

3. Amos 2:11, 12.

4. Walther Eichrodt: *Theologie des Alten Testaments,* Teil I, 1948, p. 7.

5. Deuteronomy 17:14-20.

Chapter V

1. as given in C. F. Keil: *Biblical Commentary On The Old Testament,* English Translation, The Pentateuch, Vol. III, Grand Rapids, 1949, p. 70.

2. Theophile J. Meek: *Hebrew Origins,* 1936, p. 147.

NOTES

3. Johannes Pedersen: *Israel Its Life And Culture*, III-IV, 1947, p. 108.
4. Gustav Hölscher: Die Propheten, 1914, p. 10.
5. Pedersen: *op. cit.*, p. 108.
6. There is no evidence that the wound was necessary so that a bandage might be worn in order to hide the "mark of a prophet." That the prophets had some kind of tattoo as a mark of their office is a supposition for which there is no warrant. Cf. A. Sanda: *Die Bücher der Könige*, Erster Halbband, 1911, pp. 485, 486; S. Landersdorfer: *Die Bücher der Könige*, 1927, p. 130.

Chapter VI

1. Sigmund Mowinckel: *Psalmenstudien III : Kultprophetie und prophetische Psalmen*, 1923.
2. Aubrey Johnson: *The Cultic Prophet In Ancient Israel*, 1944.
3. Johnson: *op. cit.*, pp. 16-17.
4. H. H. Rowley: "The Nature Of Prophecy In The Light Of Recent Study" in *Harvard Theological Review*, January 1945, vol. xxxviii, no. 1, p. 15.
5. Alfred Haldar: *Associations Of Cult Prophets Among The Ancient Semites*, Uppsala, 1945, p. 145.
6. Johnson: *op. cit.*, p. 17.
7. *op. cit.*, p. 17.
8. cf. Rowley: *op cit.*, p. 14.
9. Johnson: *op. cit.*, p. 25.
10. *op. cit.*, p. 26.
11. E. W. Hengstenberg: *Dissertations On The Genuineness Of The Pentateuch*, English Translation, Vol. I, 1847, p. 183.
12. Johnson: *op. cit.*, p. 27.
13. *op. cit.*, p. 52.
14. e. g., H. H. Rowley: *The Unity Of The Old Testament*, reprinted from the "Bulletin Of The John Rylands Library," Vol. 29, No. 2, Feb. 1946.
15. *op. cit.* Haldar's inaugural dissertation is a remarkable and valuable survey of the prophetic phenomena in the ancient Near East. His thesis is that in the ancient world there were two principal expressions of these phenomena. On the one hand there was the attempt to divine by "technical oracle methods" such as the observation of omens. Among the east Semites this was the function of the baru priest, whereas in the west, including Israel, it was carried on by the kohen. In the second place divination was carried on by means of oracles which were delivered by the priest when in a state of ecstasy. In the east this was the mahhu, and in the west the nabhi.

In actual practice, thinks Haldar, there was no clear cut line of demarcation between the two categories as respected their functions. Thus, the baru priest could take part in ecstatic rites, and the mahhu could also divine by means of the observation of omens. Likewise, the kohen could act as an ecstatic and utter "prophetic" oracles, and the nabhi could deliver "sacerdotal" oracles which he had obtained by the technical methods of divination. No clear distinction, then, can be made between "sacerdotal" and "prophetical" oracles. In Israel, therefore, the literary prophets are the true spiritual descendants of the cult prophets, and stress must be placed upon this continuity.

Designations such as "man of God" show that the cultic personnel was the special property of the god, and the media through whom the god spoke.

In the nature and organization of these cultic associations, Haldar points to certain alleged similarities. For one thing, he thinks that these associations have issued from a "mythical cult founder," who is everywhere depicted as the sacral king. In the case of Israel this "mythical" founder was Moses, whereas in the case of the baru priests it was the king Enmeduranki. Secondly, the organization of these associations is thought to be similar throughout the whole Semitic area.

The role played by the cultic functionaries is also said to be of a similar nature. Both types of functionary acted as physicians and judges, were consulted before military expeditions, accompanied the army into battle, etc. The cultic societies could oppose the king and could take opposite sides as to who should be the king's successor. The winning side then became the "legitimate" party, and interpreted traditions accordingly. In the prophetical books we have examples of the transmission of such traditions.

16. N. W. Porteous: "'The Basis Of The Ethical Teaching Of The Prophets" in *Studies In Old Testament Prophecy,* 1950, p. 144.

17. Morris Jastrow (*Hebrew And Babylonian Traditions,* 1914, p. 150) gives a restricted meaning to the term, such as the inspection of a liver, or the observation of a phenomenon in the heavens or of a birth sign to forecast the future.

18. Haldar: *op. cit.,* p. 34ff.

19. allapit kīma mahhe, sha lā idū ūbal.

20. ihzishu kashdu.

21. Haldar: *op. cit.,* p. 4.
pirishtu ilāni rabūti
mūdū mūdā likallim
lā mūdū ai ēnnu
ikkib ilānī rabūti.

22. Amos 7:10-14.

23. In this connection we may stress the hesitancy of some of the prophets to undertake their work. They were not eager aspirants for initiation into the same guild; they were men who were overcome by a sense of the majesty and holiness of God and the magnitude of the task unto which He had called them.

24. Haldar: *op. cit.*, p. 2. It should be noted that no abstract noun, such as baruti, is employed in the Old Testament to describe the prophetic body. The idea that the prophets as such were a particular association or organization is not present in the Old Testament.

25. Certain initiatory rites were required that the priest be pure (ellu). The *namburbu* rites were initiatory by which the priest gained cultic purity.

26. See Leviticus 8.

27. This is Haldar's phrase.

28. *op. cit.*, pp. 91-92. Cf. Ivan Engnell: *Studies In Divine Kingship In The Ancient Near East,* 1943.

29. Cyrus H. Gordon: *Ugaritic Handbook,* II, *Texts In Transliteration,* 1947, p. 147, text 62:55. Cf. also Homer's Iliad II:821 where Anchises had charge of flocks and herdsmen in the foothills. No doubt other parallels might be adduced, all of which would be interesting but none of which would support the view that Moses was the shepherd of divine flocks.

30. Edward J. Young: "The God Of Horeb," in *The Evangelical Quarterly,* January 1938, pp. 10-29.

31. If Moses was not an historical figure, how is he to be explained? How also is the great emphasis upon the events of the Exodus to be accounted for?

32. *she-al-na belohim,* which may be rendered, "ask the gods." There is no indication that the word here refers to the true God.

33. I Samuel 21:1.

34. This evidence includes the prophetic claims to be the recipients of Divine revelation.

35. Exodus 28:30; Leviticus 8:8; Numbers 27:21; Deuteronomy 33:8; 1 Samuel 28:6; Ezra 2:63; Nehemiah 7:65.

36. *op. cit.,* p. 101ff.

37. *op cit.,* p. 102.

38. If *boqer* is to be translated "Schauopfer," as Mowinckel does (*Psalmenstudien,* I, p. 146) it must have this sense in both its occurrences in the verse.

39. *'ark.*

40. In Ezekiel 21:21 which presents a clear case of divination, the verb used is *ra'ah.*

41. *op. cit.*, p. 102.
42. *op. cit.*, p. 102.
43. *op. cit.*, p. 104.
44. Ferdinand Hitzig: *Die Zwölf Kleinen Propheten*, 1881, p. 277.
45. 2 Kings 9:17.
46. *op. cit.*, p. 105.
47. *'ari* "belonging to" is found in Hurrian. Cf. *'ari* in Urgaritic.
48. There is no need to emend *'adhonai* to *'adhoni*.
49. *op. cit.*, p. 107.
50. *op. cit.*, p. 109.
51. *op. cit.*, p. 114.
52. *op. cit.*, p. 118.
53. *op. cit.*, p. 122.
54. The word *tertu* does not seem to have had the breadth of usage of the Hebrew word *torah*.

Chapter VII

1. A. B. Davidson: Old Testament Prophecy, 1903, p. 307.
2. cf. Klaus Harms: *Die falschen Propheten*, 1947, and Gerhard von Rad: "Die falschen Propheten" in *Zeitschrift für die alttestamentliche Wissenschaft*, li, 1933, pp. 109-120.
3. H. Th. Obbink: "The Forms Of Prophetism" in *Hebrew Union College Annual*, Vol. XIV, 1939, pp. 23-28.
4. Wm. F. Albright: *From The Stone Age To Christianity*, 1940, p. 233.
5. Sigmund Mowinckel: " 'The Spirit' and the 'Word' in the Pre-Exilic Reforming Prophets," in *Journal Of Biblical Literature*, Vol. liii, 1934, pp. 199-227.
6. *op. cit.*, p. 201.
7. *op. cit.*, p. 201.
8. H. H. Rowley: "The Nature Of Prophecy In The Light Of Recent Study" in *Harvard Theological Review*, Vol. xxxviii, no. 1, p. 20.
9. *op cit.*, p. 21.
10. Mowinckel: *op. cit.*, p. 212.
11. *op. cit.*, p. 208.
12. *op. cit.*, p. 201.
13. *op. cit.*, p. 229.
14. G. Ch. Aalders: *De Profeten Des Ouden Verbonds*, 1918, p. 229.
15. cf. also 2 Chronicles 18:1-34.

16. Alfred Haldar: *Associations Of Cult Prophets Among The Ancient Semites*, 1945, pp. 138-140.

17. The evidence for this has been presented by Albright: *op. cit.*, p. 229. The idolatrous character of Jeroboam's act thus appears to be on the same low level as the idolatry of the surrounding nations.

18. *Iliad*, Book I, Lines 106-108.

19. J. Gresham Machen: "Prophets False And True" in *God Transcendent*, 1949, p. 109.

20. Although God has included evil in His decree, yet He Himself is not the Author of sin. There is a mystery here which the finite mind of man cannot fathom. We must simply receive in faith what God has seen fit to reveal to us in His Holy Word.

21. Rowley: *op. cit.*, p. 18.

22. Jeremiah 17:9.

23. Georg Heinrich August Von Ewald: *Prophets Of The Old Testament*, English Translation, Vol. I, 1875, pp. 15-25.

Chapter VIII

1. A. B. Davidson in *Hastings Dictionary Of The Bible*, iv., p. 118b.

2. A. B. Davidson: *Old Testament Prophecy*, 1903, p. 245.

3. I do not think that this statement is too strong. If the prophet speaks only to his own generation, he obviously is not speaking of a Saviour Who will come long after that generation has passed from the scene.

4. Hermann Gunkel: *Genesis*, 1901; *Die Israelitische Literatur*, 1906; *Einleitung in die Psalmen*, 1926.

5. I. G. Matthews: *The Religious Pilgrimage Of Israel*, 1947, p. 132.

6. Hermann Gunkel: *Die Schriften des Alten Testaments*, 2 Abteilung, *Prophetismus und Gesetzgebung*, 2 Band, 1923, p. xxxvi.

7. *Studien zum Hoseabuche: zugleich ein Beitrag zur Klärung des Problems der alttestamentlichen Textkritik*, 1935.

8. H. Birkeland: *Zum hebräischen Traditionswesen; die Komposition der prophetischen Bücher des Alten Testaments*, 1938.

9. Ivan Engnell: *Gamla Testamentet*, I, 1945, p. 208f.

10. Sigmund Mowinckel: *Prophecy And Tradition*, 1946.

11. Geo. Widengren: *Literary And Psychological Aspects Of The Hebrew Prophets*, 1948.

12. Ivan Engnell: *The Call Of Isaiah*, 1949.

13. *op. cit.*, pp. 54-60.

14. cf. also Daniel 9:2.

Chapter IX

1. "The Prophetic Literature" in *The Old Testament and Modern Study*, ed. H. H. Rowley, 1951, p. 134.

2. Gustav Hölscher: *Die Propheten*, 1914, pp. 141-143.

3. Alfred Jepsen: *NABI*: *soziologische Studien zur alttestamentlichen Literatur und Religionsgeschichte*, 1934, pp. 144 ff.

4. Alfred Haldar: *Associations of Cult Prophets In The Ancient Near East*, Uppsala, 1945.

5. Hölscher: *op. cit.*

6. "Wer deshalb heute den seelischen Erlebnissen der Seher und Propheten psychologisch auf den Grund gehen will, wird sich von diesen religionsgeschichtlichen Begriffen möglichst unabhängig machen und versuchen, sie in Begriffen der heutigen Psychologie und Physiologie zu erfassen" (*op. cit.*, p. 2).

7. F. Giesebrecht: *Die Berufsbegabung der alttestamentlichen Propheten*, 1897. I have not seen this work.

8. A. W. Knobel: *Der Prophetismus der Hebräer*, i, 1837. I have not seen this work.

9. Bernhard Stade: *Biblische Theologie des Alten Testaments*, i, 1905.

10. *The Loeb Classical Library, Philo, IV, Quis Rerum Divinarum Heres*, LI, 1932, p. 409ff.

11. Hermann Gunkel: *Die Schriften des Alten Testaments*, II, ii, 1923, pp. xvii-xxxiv.

12. *Die Ekstase des alttestamentlichen Propheten*, 1917.

13. "Neuere Propheten Forschung" in *Theologische Rundschau*, iii, 1931, pp. 75-105.

14. *Prophetismen i Israel*, 1934. I have not seen this work.

15. *Prophet und Gott*, 1923.

16. *The Prophets And The Rise of Judaism*, 1937.

17. "Einige Grundfragen der alttestamentlichen Wissenschaft," in *Festschrift Alfred Bertholet*, 1950, pp. 325-337.

18. Abraham Heschel: *Die Prophetie*, 1936.

19. I. P. Seierstad: *Die Berufungserlebnisse der Propheten Amos, Jesaja und Jeremia*, 1946.

20. The text may be found in A. Goetze: "Hattusilis, der Bericht über seine Thronbesteigung nebst den Paralleltexten" in *Hethitische Texte in Umschrift*, Heft I, *Mitteilungen der Vorderasiatisch-Aegyptischen Gesellschaft*, 1925. It is also given in Sturtevant and Bechtel: *A Hittite Chrestomathy*, 1935.

21. literally, "but when my father Mursilis became a god"; ma-ah-ha-an-ma-za a-bu-ia I Mur-shi-li-ish dingir-lim-ish ki-sha-at.

22. The Westminster Shorter Catechism, Question 4.

23. Numbers 24.

24. Numbers 22:18, 38; 23:5, 12, 16.
25. Numbers 24:3ff.
26. *History of Balaam,* English translation, 1847, p. 449.
27. Numbers 24:4, *asher mahazeh shaddai yehezeh.*
28. Geo. Widengren: *Literary And Psychological Aspects Of The Hebrew Prophets,* 1948, p. 96.
29. *op. cit.,* p. 97.
30. *op. cit.,* p. 97.
31. *op. cit.,* p. 102.
32. The text is given in Widengren: *op. cit.,* p. 101. It describes a visionary appearance of Mohammed and is taken from the Kitab al Tanbih of Al-Malati.
33. II Enoch LVI:2, Widengren: *op. cit.,* p. 101.
34. *op. cit.,* p. 110.
35. *op. cit.,* p. 116ff.
36. The work has been translated into English under the title *Christology of the Old Testament and A Commentary On The Messianic Predictions,* and appeared in four volumes.

Appendix

1. A portion of the section on Mari in this Appendix was delivered in a paper before the Evangelical Theological Society in New York, December 1951.
2. Thus, the chief butler says *ba-h^a-lo-mi* (Genesis 40:9). The Mari text reads *i-na shu-ut-ti-ia a-na-ku* (line 5). Text no. 1 in Von Soden (see following note).
3. Wolfram von Soden: "Verkündigung des Gotteswillen durch prophetisches Wort in den altbabylonischen Briefen aus Mari," in *Die Welt Des Orients,* 1950, p. 401.
4. Von Soden: *op cit.,* text no. lines 43, 44.
5. Von Soden: *op. cit.,* p. 401.
6. Hence, I cannot agree with Von Soden's statement, "Eine Parallele besteht zweifellos darin, dass dem Stand des nabi in Mari der Stand des muhhum entspricht" (*op. cit.,* p. 402). The relationship between the deity and the addressee may be expressed as follows:

> Mari: Dagan ... muhhum ... official ... king
> Israel: God ... prophet ... people.

There is a vast difference. The position of the prophet in Israel as mediator between God and the nation finds no real parallel elsewhere.

7. von Soden: *op cit.,* p. 402. This fact is really acknowledged by von Soden who says, "Eschatologische Themen werden nicht berührt."

8. *idem.*
9. This text is given second by von Soden.
10. This text is the fourth given by von Soden.
11. 1950, "Une Tablette Inédite de Mari, Interessant pour l'Histoire Ancienne Du Prophetisme Semitique," pp. 103-110, with comments by G. Dossin and Ad. Lods.
12. Lods in *op. cit.,* note 11, p. 108.
13. A translation by Robert H. Pfeiffer is given in James Pritchard: *Ancient Near Eastern Texts Relating To The Old Testament,* 1950, p. 450.
14. Pritchard: *op. cit.* p. 450.
15. *op. cit.,* p. 450.
16. *op. cit.,* p. 450, 451.
17. *op. cit.,* p. 451.
18. *op. cit.,* pp. 451-452.
19. *op. cit.,* pp. 441-444.
20. The translation is by John A. Wilson in Pritchard *op. cit.,* p. 443.
21. *op. cit.,* pp. 444-446.
22. Translation by John A. Wilson, *op. cit.,* p. 445.
23. Translation by John A. Wilson, *op. cit.,* p. 446.
24. George A. Barton *Archaeology And The Bible,*[5] 1927, p. 481.
25. Pritchard: *op. cit.,* p. 446-447.
26. *op. cit.,* pp. 447, 448.
27. *op. cit.,* p. 448.
28. *op. cit.,* p. 449.
29. *op. cit.,* pp. 25-29, translated by John A. Wilson.

INDICES

Indices

A. Subjects

B. Authors

Scripture References